Public Radio

Public Radio

Behind the Voices

LISA A. PHILLIPS

Designed by Brent Wilcox
Set in 11.25 point New Caledonia

Library of Congress Cataloging-in-Publication Data
Phillips, Lisa A.
    Public radio : behind the voices / Lisa A. Phillips.
      p.   cm.
    Includes bibliographical references.
    ISBN-13: 978-1-59315-143-0 (hardcover : alk. paper)
    ISBN-10: 1-59315-143-8 (hardcover : alk. paper)
     1. Radio broadcasters—United States—Biography.   2. Radio journalists—
United States—Biography.   3. Public radio—United States.   I. Title.

    PN1991.4.P45 2006
    791.4402'8092273—dc22

                                                                    2005037104

CDS books are available at special discounts for bulk purchases in the U.S. by corporations, institutions, and other organizations. For more information, please contact the Special Markets Department at the Perseus Books Group, 11 Cambridge Center, Cambridge, MA 02142, or call (800) 255-1514 or (617) 252-5298, or e-mail special.markets@perseusbooks.com.

06 07 08 09/ 10 9 8 7 6 5 4 3 2

For Bill and Clara

Contents

PART I
News and Information

PART II
Talk and Entertainment

PART III
Music

Acknowledgments

When you write a book and have a baby at the same time, there's simply no getting by without the help of family and friends. I'm grateful to my parents, Arthur and Barbara Phillips, who provided support and love in countless and invaluable ways and believed in this project from the start. I thank Kira Copperman, Marc Phillips, Jeanne and Bill Mead Sr., Diana Mead, Melinda Mead, Lori Catallozzi, and their families, for their encouragement, assistance, and shelter during my travels for this book.

Colette Dowling, Gail Bradney, and Valerie Paradiz are dear friends and writing buddies whose insights and commitment to the creative process helped this reporter rediscover her voice. Gerard Ryan and Val gave me a hand with my daughter so I could write, as did Avis and Greg Gebert. Jane Alsdorf and the staff at Footprints Daycare provided a nurturing and fun place for my daughter to grow.

I am much indebted to the tireless Joellen Craft, who put in countless hours transcribing interviews and assisting in the research for this book. Joanna Richards and Jennarose Weiss-Berman also gave generously of their time to research and transcribe.

Carolyn Dille, Claudia Rowe, and Emily Bauman offered editorial comments and wisdom. Alisa Pearson and Lisa Coxson's support for my writing has sustained me since long before I started this project.

Heidi Washburn helped me find the courage to leave my day job and live a writer's life. Martha Frankel, Joan Schuman, Rob Miraldi, and Debra Spark gave advice at several crucial junctures. Special thanks go to the Jentel Foundation, where I spent a writing residency in the spring of 2003.

Joan Schweighardt's fierce belief in this project opened doors. Hope Matthiessen, my editor, helped me see the book in my initial idea and guided it with a steady hand throughout. Jennie Dunham, my agent, has been an important presence in my writing life since I was in graduate school. I also want to thank Erin Sprague, my project editor at Perseus, for her fine work with the finishing touches.

Andy Danyo, Laura Gross, Chad Campbell, Dan Jensen, Jennifer Houlihan, Connie Stelter, Debbie Adler, and Sarah Mobley helped me arrange interviews with the hosts and reporters featured in this book.

Behind every mellifluous voice on public radio are talented editors and producers who work very hard in relative obscurity. The staffs of public radio affiliates across the country not only produce essential local programming themselves, they also raise the millions of dollars it takes to pay the dues for National Public Radio, Public Radio International, American Public Media, and other national program distributors.

Finally, this book is dedicated to my husband, Bill Mead, and our daughter, Clara Douglass Mead. They made this journey sweet.

Introduction

A few months into my first on-air job in public radio, as news director of KTPR in Fort Dodge, Iowa, I took a train to New York for the holidays. The isolation of my new life in a small city where I knew no one had me starved for social interaction, so I spent a lot of time on that two-day train ride in 1992 hanging out in the dining car. Making conversation, I soon discovered, was not going to be a problem. As soon as I answered the classic opener, What do you do? I was peppered with questions. Do you know Scott Simon? Terry Gross?

Even though I had only just started to learn the ins and outs of public radio, I tried to answer them. I had not then had the chance to meet Scott Simon, though I had talked to Terry Gross, my idol, at a reception in St. Louis. "She was nice," I said. "And short. Very short." I shared what she'd told me about her start in radio. Her roommate in Buffalo, New York, in the 1970s was a host of *Woman Power*, the feminist show at WBFO, the local NPR affiliate. The roommate and her lover, who also worked on the show, came out as lesbians on the air. The lover decided that, now that she was out, she would move on to the station's lesbian-feminist show. Terry stepped in to take her place on *Woman Power*. From there, she hosted a daily interview program and then was hired to host *Fresh Air* in Philadelphia.

With these few details, I had my train companions enthralled. The irony of my dining car popularity was that my day-to-day existence then was pretty humble. My audience was the northwest quarter of Iowa, one of the least densely populated areas of the country. At times I was nearly certain that the number of people listening would fit into the one-room schoolhouse where the Webster County Historical Society gave tours. My day at the station started at 4:30 a.m. so I could warm up the transmitter in time to broadcast the deep-voiced "Good morning" of Bob Edwards, then the host of *Morning Edition*. In the fiercest snowstorms, I drove my station wagon through unplowed streets so I could get on the air to tell everyone else to stay off the roads. One winter there was a stretch of twenty-five below zero mornings. I stepped very carefully down the stairs outside my apartment. Because I'd read the cold exposure warnings from the National Weather Service the morning before, I knew that if I slipped and fell and knocked myself out I would be frozen dead in mere minutes. And, of course, no one would be there to turn on the transmitter.

It was tough. I had to be in bed by 8:00 p.m. if I wanted any chance of a full night's sleep, an impossible feat in northern Iowa summers, when it doesn't get dark until 9:30 or so, and not easy the rest of the year. I tried to adjust by going to bed earlier and asking family and friends not to call after 7:30, but they didn't always remember. A college buddy would phone, and before I knew it, it was almost 10:00 and I'd lost my chance to feel human the next day. I'd catch myself nodding off over the computer keyboard as I wrote my newscasts, or messing up on the air, announcing the time was 7:00 when it was actually only 6:00. I remember a phone call I got in the studio at 5:30 one morning. "Dear, you sound tired today," the woman said.

I was. I was exhausted and underpaid and lonely. But I loved that job anyway. I loved hearing the *Morning Edition* theme music. Sometimes I'd do a little dance to it to wake myself up. I loved hearing Bob Edwards breathe between sentences in my headphones. He had a very distinctive, weary sigh-breath, from smoking and years of getting up at 1:30 a.m. Most of all, I loved being a part of public radio, something so beloved and respected and fascinating.

KTPR as I knew it back in the early 1990s is gone. The station now mainly transmits the signal of WOI, a larger and far better funded station sixty miles away in Ames. Public radio, though, is stronger than ever. Nearly twenty-seven million Americans listen to more than nine hundred and fifty public radio stations, broadcasting from Presque Isle, Maine, to Barrow, Alaska. The number of nationally distributed programs from National Public Radio, Public Radio International, American Public Media, and other sources is in the hundreds. As ownership consolidation forces commercial radio to neglect local news and information, public radio affiliates are investing an increasing amount of time and energy in these areas.

As commercial radio becomes increasingly formulaic, public radio is creating a veritable listening renaissance. Commuters arrive at the office and talk about the news stories they've just heard on *Morning Edition. Car Talk*'s Tom and Ray Magliozzi are just as much household names as Bob and Ray ever were. An appearance on *World Cafe* can be one of the biggest breaks of a new rock group's career, transforming it from obscure to adored on the independent music scene. *This American Life*'s Ira Glass is the epitome of American cool, ferreting out the most riveting and unusual stories of our time and setting them to a background of dreamy-hip music. We are turning to radio for stories, for music, for community, for insight, for laughter, the kinds of things that brought families around the Philco in the days before television took center stage in the living room.

One of the results of this listening renaissance is that we have an intimate connection with public radio hosts, the people who bring this magic to us. They are with us when we get up in the morning, when we drive to work, when we cook dinner, garden, sit in the bathtub.

We know them mainly by their voices, not their faces. This voice-to-ear relationship is a startlingly radical one in an era where image is everything, swaying its hips to seduce us, vivid and lifelike on giant screen digital television.

Without image to overwhelm us, we behave differently. Alone in cars and kitchens, we fume at the latest news on gas prices, cry at Linda Wertheimer's story about women veterans learning how to live with amputated limbs, talk back to Daniel Shorr's commentary. "It's like Freudian analysis," one listener said. "They never answer back."

How we want them to. Their voices leave us hungry. Despite our deep connection to them, we don't know very much about them. They are veiled by the invisibility, the inherent modesty, of radio. We delight each time the veil is briefly lifted. Remember when Susan Stamberg talked about her son's first job out of college? An aspiring actor, he was pumping coffee at Starbucks, not the most glamorous of gigs, but she was grateful that he had benefits and health insurance. Then there was the time Scott Simon mourned the death of his cat. He played tape of the animal's Halloween-perfect yowls, causing the fur on my own cat's back to rise. Of course, public radio personalities can't indulge themselves this way too often, even if we want them to. They have a job to do, and that's to deliver information, ideas, sounds—not their personal stories.

My job, in writing this book, was to collect these personal stories. I've profiled more than forty of the most listened to voices in public radio. Interviewing my broadcasting heroes was a great privilege and, when I wasn't quaking from nerves, a tremendous pleasure and a lot of fun. I've shared a beer with Michael Feldman (a local Wisconsin brew, of course). I've listened to Scott Simon coo on the telephone to his wife and eaten pistachio nuts that Jacki Lyden had just brought back from Iraq. I've sat in Nina Totenberg's cubicle at NPR as she reminisced about the days she typed news stories practically shoulder to shoulder with Cokie Roberts and Linda Wertheimer, in a time when money and space were tight and ambition was limitless. I've listened to stories about childhood, hometown, family, work, friends, radio, love, death, and dreams.

My only regret is that I wasn't able to interview more of public radio's luminaries. Time and space considerations limited the scope of this book to the most popular programs and voices (with a few personal favorites thrown in). It was with great consternation that I left out a number of prominent figures. I should also note that, much to my disappointment, a few of the people discussed in these pages declined my interview requests, and their profiles were based on research and observation.

I wrote this book because I love public radio and I've always been curious about the lives behind the voices. I also hope that deepening the connection between these voices and their listeners is one way to help safeguard public broadcasting in a time when political scrutiny of the medium is increasing and threats to its funding abound.

What I've discovered along the way is that the lives of public radio personalities have many of the qualities of the radio they bring us. Their stories are fascinating and significant—stories that enlarge our sense of history and humanity. I think of Michele Norris's father, who took his family on a summer vacation through Canada and made a point of talking to African American draft dodgers there about why they didn't want to go to Vietnam. Though a postal carrier by profession, he gave Norris her first lesson in journalism. I think of Noah Adams gathering many hours of interviews with single mothers in the low-wage workforce in Maine, yet being reluctant to return to Washington because in his perfectionism he could never be sure if he'd done enough. I think of Marian McPartland shocking her bourgeois British family by leaving her classical music studies at the acclaimed Guildhall School of Music to go on tour with a vaudeville group. I think of Nick Spitzer's restless mother, driving him and his siblings around New York City every night before bedtime, playing the radio and showing them the sights, giving him as a young boy the wanderlust that would be at the heart of his approach to music on *American Routes*.

Public Radio: Behind the Voices offers a look behind radio's veil of invisibility, a chance to get to know the personalities we listen to each day and the stories of their lives. In the end, I hope, you'll feel closer to the voices that fill our cars, living rooms, and offices, and you'll listen even more intently.

Public Radio: Behind the Voices is for that ever-growing community of listeners, whose insatiable curiosity about public radio I discovered on that Amtrak train back in 1992. Happy travels.

PART I

News and Information

Founding Mother:
Susan Stamberg

Special Correspondent,
National Public Radio

When **Susan Stamberg** began hosting *All Things Considered* in 1972, she became the first woman to anchor a national nightly news program. In an era when women entering the workforce imitated the way men looked, wearing skirted versions of gray flannel suits and bow ties, Stamberg tried to sound like a man. She lowered her voice and spoke carefully and authoritatively. After about a week of this, Bill Siemering, NPR's first director of programming and a founding visionary force in the network, told her to relax and be herself.

And so Stamberg gradually took back her own voice: nasal, quizzical, unashamedly female. It was a voice with a hometown—New York—and an ethnicity—Jewish. It was a voice with a distinct sense of timing and an artfully exaggerated way of emphasizing words and phrases. She even broke some of broadcasting's golden rules. She said "um" if she had to take a moment to think of what to say next and "uh huh" during her guests' responses. While querying recalcitrant guests, she could sound as if she was trying to get her son to do his homework (Would you *please* finish those math problems?), the domesticated, Yiddishkeit nudge brought to bear on the power brokers of the world.

What Siemering didn't tell her for many years was that in those first few weeks she hosted *All Things Considered,* he fielded calls from public radio station managers across the country, complaining about her. They said a woman would not be taken seriously, Stamberg did not sound authoritative enough, and they'd lose listeners because of her. But he refused to take her off the air.

"He knew that it would throw me if I knew," Stamberg told me in her office at NPR, in between bites out of chicken curry in a Styrofoam take-out container. She sounded in person exactly the way she sounded on the air. "He had enormous confidence in me, and he felt the more people got used to hearing me, the criticism would go away. And in fact it did." Stamberg's smile filled her face, her eyes squinting. "Isn't that a *story?*"

It is hard to imagine what NPR would have been like if Siemering had bowed to the pressure and taken Stamberg, now known as NPR's "Founding Mother," off the air. Her voice, style, and gift for conversation became the centerpiece of the unorthodox, creative approach *All Things Considered* took in those first years to the art of making radio. The show gave listeners the daily news, but the program also sought stories that would, as NPR's first mission statement put it, "celebrate the human experience." The show made an effort to include the voices and thoughts of everyday Americans by reading letters from listeners and doing interviews with farmers, homemakers, and shopkeepers to find out what people were thinking about Watergate, race relations, the murder of John Lennon, and other events of the times. Inspired by *The Shadow, The Lone Ranger,* and other radio programs of yesteryear that used creaking doors and other sound effects to create absorbing radio drama, NPR staff members sought to "use the sounds of life to tell real stories," wrote Stamberg in 1982 in *Every Night at Five: Susan Stamberg's All Things Considered Book.*

The staff wanted nothing less than to reinvent radio, she reminisced, with "missionary zeal" and "some 'let's save the world through the air-waves' thrown in for good measure."

Stamberg, whose cohosts over the years included Mike Waters, Bob Edwards, Sanford Ungar (now the president of Goucher College), and Noah Adams, shared these passions, but more importantly she gave *All Things Considered* a *personality*: funny, bold, playful, at times even mischievous. She took a microphone and a pack of wintergreen Lifesavers into a closet with science reporter Ira Flatow to find out whether the candy really sparked in the dark when you chewed it. She gave listeners her recipe (actually, Craig Claiborne's, passed down through her mother-in-law) for Mama Stamberg's Cranberry Relish every year around holiday time and broadcast a piece in which she discovered a woman actually selling the stuff at a Wisconsin farmers' market. Stamberg loved humor and laughter, and her laugh was distinctive: large, unbridled, and generous.

Thirty-five years later, at age sixty-seven, Stamberg is a special correspondent and a substitute host at NPR. She has fourteen years of hosting *All Things Considered* and three of hosting *Weekend Edition Sunday* under her belt. She has won virtually every major award in broadcasting and been inducted in the Broadcasting Hall of Fame and the Radio Hall of Fame.

In part because of this legacy, no one would dare suggest today that a woman would drive listeners away. The day before our interview, she had to step into the on-air studio during *All Things Considered* to use one of the computers there. Michele Norris and Melissa Block (who had been a desk assistant on the show when Stamberg was host) were hosting that day. Stamberg sat at the computer between them and realized how much had changed from her generation, when one woman host was controversial, to theirs, when two at a time were accepted without question. "There I am, and I'm listening to the two of them, on either side and ah, oh! I just felt so *wonderful!*" Stamberg said. "I can't tell you how *thrilling* that was, to hear how it's all evolved in this time, and how wonderfully they were doing, and I loved this generational line we made sitting there together."

When Susan Stamberg was Susie Levitt, growing up in Manhattan, radio was the center of the household, the main source of entertainment and news. "I would be very happy to be sick and stay home, because my mother would bring the radio in *my* room, and plump up the pillows, and we'd listen to the soap operas," she said. "I *loved* that, the sound of the radio playing through the day, telling these *magic* stories."

Stamberg was an art major in the 1950s at the High School of Music and Art (now called LaGuardia High School), one of the schools that the movie and television series *Fame* was based on. There, she rubbed shoulders with Billy Dee Williams of *Star Wars* trilogy fame; Ed Kleban, who wrote the lyrics to *A Chorus Line;* and Peter Yarrow of Peter, Paul, and Mary. She was a features editor of the school newspaper, and she told her former NPR colleague Bob Edwards on *The Bob Edwards Show* that Yarrow had once chased her screaming up a stairwell because she'd rejected his submission, which was about French kissing. "He was furious because I felt it should not be published in the school newspaper!" she laughed.

Being surrounded by young performers and artists led her to dream that someday she'd have a salon, "like the intellectual women of France did, and the best people would come and we'd sit and have grand discussions," she said. She was already preparing to be the host. A friend of hers from high school now teases Stamberg that she started practicing for radio work when they were girls. "She said, 'When I would go to your house for sleepovers, you would keep me up all night asking questions!'" Stamberg said.

At Barnard College, Stamberg was an English literature major and wrote for the student newspaper. She set her sights on a career in publishing. She did not set foot in the studios of WKCR, the Columbia University radio station across the street where, a few years later, her future colleague Robert Siegel would begin his broadcasting career. "It never occurred to me to go over there," she said. "First of all, radio was the glamour medium of my childhood, so I thought, I couldn't do *that*. And it was the boys' campus and the station seemed to be a male province and it was the fifties. I'm not sure how welcome I would have been."

After college, she worked for *Daedalus*, the journal of the American Academy of Arts and Sciences and then, after moving to Washington, D.C., *The New Republic*. The work was largely secretarial and she was bored. When she heard about an opening for a producer at WAMU, a radio station just getting started at American University, she was intrigued. When she asked a friend what a producer did, she replied, "A producer is someone who doesn't take no for an answer."

"I thought, I can do that!" Stamberg said, and proceeded to prove herself by calling the station manager every day for months until he hired her. "They were just getting on the air, you know, he had a million things to do," she said. "Then it was the Cuban Missile Crisis—this was 1962. The last thing he wanted was to be bothered by me. But I wouldn't quit."

Stamberg became a producer for a weekly public affairs discussion program called *Viewpoint Washington*. She worked at WAMU until her husband, Louis Stamberg, who worked for the State Department's Agency for International Development, was transferred to India. From overseas, she filed reports on development issues for Voice of America and produced radio essays for WAMU. Working with sound, she discovered, was becoming integral to the way she experienced the world. Intrigued by a curious *glug-glug-glug* sound outside the window of her New Delhi apartment, she ran outside with a tape recorder. The impulse turned into a radio story about a man whose job was to go from house to house airing out the stuffing in pillows with a tool that looked like a rudimentary archery bow. "Everything was so different there," she said. "There were a million stories to tell."

She brought that feeling of possibility and her ear for interesting sounds back to Washington when her family's stint in India was over. She was hired at NPR a month before *All Things Considered* went on the air in 1971. Her son, Joshua, now a professional actor who's had parts in *Six Feet Under, Sex and the City,* and *Law & Order,* was only a year and a half old then. She worked part-time as a tape editor from 11 a.m. to 3 p.m., a schedule that included his nap so she wouldn't be apart from him for too many of his waking hours. She became a reporter and then, before *All Things Considered* was a year old, began cohosting the show. She tried to keep her part-time hours by prerecording her part of the host script, but that didn't work for long, and she soon went full-time.

Stamberg finally had her salon. She interviewed actor and activist Dick Gregory about his hunger strike against the war in Vietnam, writer Joan Didion about the idea of emptiness in her novels, and national security expert Dr. Peter Sharfman about what the effects of a nuclear war might be. She developed a distinctively spontaneous, fresh, and frank interview style. She was unafraid to tell an author she found her characters distasteful. She once asked sex therapist Eleanor Hamilton, in a conversation about teen sexuality, "So you would encourage teenagers to stimulate themselves to orgasm?"

Stamberg came to her interviews well prepared but never hesitated to bring lofty ideas and people down to earth with the kind of question that you'd want to ask, but wouldn't dare out of the fear of sounding naive. "Don't your arms ever get tired?" she once queried Jorge Mester, then the conductor of the Louisville Orchestra. His reply? "Only when it's not going well."

Stamberg has been in the anchor chair through Vietnam, Watergate, the end of the Cold War, and countless other world-shaping news stories, but she does not like politics. Or, for that matter, breaking news, urgent news that happens as the show is under way, interrupting everyone's best-laid plans for the program. "I can't *bear* it," she said. "It's *totally* daunting to me." She has managed, of course, to handle breaking news on the air with aplomb, her skittishness not at all apparent. But in the mid-1980s, as *All Things Considered* became less salon-like and more adept at reporting breaking news, the pressure of anchoring the show mounted. Stamberg had also been diagnosed with breast cancer and felt she should decrease the stress in her life. So she jumped at the opportunity to leave in 1986 and help start *Weekend Edition Sunday*, a show designed to have a less urgent pace and sound, with jaunty live piano interludes. "Part of why we brought a musician in there was so that we would take very deliberate breaks in which people could read their paper," she said.

In 1989, Stamberg left the anchor seat to become a special correspondent and a substitute host. She also wrote *Talk: NPR's Susan Stamberg Considers All Things*, a select assortment of her interviews and reports, chosen from the estimated twenty thousand she'd done since she started hosting in 1972. As a special correspondent, she is no longer a daily presence on the network, but she continues to bring vibrant conversations to the airwaves on a regular basis. She often explores simple themes from a wide range of perspectives. She's talked to stage and screenwriters about scenes they wished they'd written, to a writer about taboo fruits and vegetables throughout history in a series about food, and to a scholar about ideas of beauty and ugliness in fairy tales.

These days, there is something significantly nostalgic about Stamberg's sound. NPR now has a much smoother, far less spontaneous approach, developed along with the mainstream respectability the network has gained over the years. Stamberg has served as a sly reminder of the adventurous early years. She told *The Nation* in a 2005 article critical of NPR that the network is "not nearly as quirky as it used to be. And I miss it." And when McDonald's heiress Joan Kroc's historic $200 million donation to NPR was announced, she quipped, "I'm changing my name to McStamberg."

But Stamberg still has plenty of *nachas* for the network she has been with from its humble beginnings. Being NPR's "Founding Mother," she said, "means something to me every day. I get a tingle in my spine when I hear something extraordinary on the radio that maybe somebody I've never even met did. I can't tell you how proud that makes me."

A Shy Man from a Shy Place: Noah Adams

Senior Correspondent, National Public Radio

Noah Adams is a shy man who has spent his life doing things that are difficult for a shy man to do. He anchored *All Things Considered* in the years the program's audience grew from a few thousand to more than ten million. He sang the Eagles song "Take It to the Limit" in a karaoke-style recording studio and played the funny yet embarrassing result on the air. He got onstage to host *A Prairie Home Companion*–style variety show when Garrison Keillor closed down shop for a while. He has done tens of thousands of interviews, talking to strangers about community organizing and Balinese music, plane crashes and worker strikes, the death of a three-year-old boy crushed by a rock that rolled down from a strip mine.

Before meeting him, I had read about his shyness. One writer even described him as "withdrawing into an icy vacancy" when approached by outsiders. In person, though, he was not at all cold and not difficult to talk to. He is short and wiry, almost elfin, with narrow shoulders, slightly jutting front teeth, and small blue eyes that seem at once bewildered and canny. He is also soft-spoken, which on the air comes across as a kind of reserve, an acknowledgment that the questions he asks are much more about the people being interviewed than they are about how aggressive, smart, or sympathetic he sounds in the asking.

In person, though, his voice is what gave away his shyness; at times it faded to a near mumble. When I asked him about being shy, Adams told me that even after more than three decades of working in radio, he still finds it hard to make phone calls, meet new people, and ask them questions about money, politics, work, and family that no one with his Scots-Irish Appalachian background would ever dream of asking. "I find myself wondering how I'm able to do it," he said. "But the stories are important."

He was, in fact, still ruminating on a reporting trip to Maine he'd just returned from. He was there interviewing single mothers for a series on America's low-wage workforce. He'd interviewed several, but he was still thinking about the woman he *didn't* get to talk to, a mother who had a job but wasn't making enough money to move out of the shelter she and her children were living in. What struck Adams about her was that she had suggested they meet on the top floor of the farmer's market in Portland. He'd been intrigued by the potential of the setting, both because it was rich with the sounds of the market, "alive and sort of tingly" is how he put it, and because the place seemed meaningful to her. There, she would have a chance to do what she'd seen young professionals her age, with enough money and freedom and time, do: talk together over coffee. "It would have been a wonderful, wonderful conversation," Adams said. "She wouldn't have felt that she was really being in any way part of a story about poor people."

Adams waited for three hours. The woman didn't show up. She called later to explain vaguely that she was having just too hard of a day to make it. It was the last day of his trip, and he knew he had more than enough tape from the other women he'd interviewed to produce the piece. But he couldn't quite let go of this particular woman, of wondering whether he should delay his return to Washington and try to reschedule the interview. So he called his editor and asked her to tell him that it was okay to catch his flight and leave, and she did. "But without that conversation, I'd still be sitting there trying to figure out how to get this woman back to this place," he said.

Adams may be a shy man from a shy place, but he is also too driven to let himself feel a shy man's relief when a reporting trip full of conversations with strangers is over. Instead, it's all about what he might have done, could have done, to make the story better. When he was hosting *All Things Considered*, he had the same struggle every evening after work. "I don't think I ever left saying, 'That was a good show,'" he said. "I'd always find fault with it. Then you have to go back the next day and do another show."

Noah Donald Adams, sixty-three, was born in Ashland, Kentucky, a steel mill town on the Ohio River. His ancestors included pioneers who followed Daniel Boone, then later homesteaders and farmers drawn to the region by the land. The first time Adams applied for a radio job at a commercial station in Grayson, Kentucky, he was turned down because his Appalachian accent was too strong. He found work in nearby Ironton, Ohio, as a rock 'n' roll deejay, going by the name Don Adams. He worked as an announcer, a program director, a salesman, and a station manager at stations in Kentucky, West Virginia, Virginia, and Georgia. A job at WOMN, a station in Atlanta that targeted women, lasted a week after the station ran out of money to pay him.

After five years in commercial radio, he soured on the business and left. He worked construction jobs for a while. In 1971, he went back on the air as a part-time announcer at WBKY, the public radio station at the University of Kentucky in Lexington. He had the late night shift and hosted bluegrass and rock shows. He'd sign the station off the air at 2:00 a.m. and would be on his way to a construction site four hours later. Later, he got a full-time job, which included running the control board during *All Things Considered*, then a new national program. When he found out there was a job open for a production assistant at NPR, he applied.

He wrote in *Noah Adams on All Things Considered: A Radio Journal* that when he started at NPR in 1975, he planned to spend only a couple of years in Washington before moving on to find a job in a good public radio market like Ann Arbor, Michigan, or Chapel Hill, North Carolina—a kind of public radio Cinderella fantasy in reverse, as most reporters dream of being swept away by the "Mother Ship" of NPR. Instead, Adams was chosen to cohost, along with Jackie Judd, the weekend version of *All Things Considered* in 1978. He was asked to use "Noah Adams" on the air to avoid any associations with the Don Adams who'd starred in *Get Smart*. Four years later, he was cohosting the weekday *All Things Considered* with Susan Stamberg. The dream of working for a member station slipped off his radar screen. "I realized one day—after about ten years—that I'd forgotten to leave," he wrote.

Adams's tenure as one of the lead voices of *All Things Considered* ran nearly a quarter century. His hillbilly accent had long since given way to a mellifluous, gentle delivery that has been called one of the most "aurally beautiful" in broadcasting, a contrast to Stamberg's merry brashness and then to the often professorial tones of Robert Siegel and Linda Wertheimer. But Adams isn't as invested in the music of his voice as he is in the sincerity of it. "There's a terrible joke that says if you can fake sincerity, you've got it made," he said. "But you actually can't. If you're a sincere person, I think you're going to hear it. And if you're not, I think you're going to hear that. So when a lot of people try to figure out who works on radio and who doesn't, that's really what's going on there, it's sincerity."

The premium Adams places on sincerity made him a restless host. Never a political junkie, he was determined to stay connected to the world outside the Washington Beltway and avoid burnout. "When I would say, 'A bus went over a cliff today in Ecuador and 200 people were killed, including 160 children,' and it didn't have a visceral feeling, that was always a trigger point for me," he said. "If you couldn't feel it viscerally, and that happened quite often, then I'd know it was time to get someplace and see some people and talk to somebody about some story that is not Washington and New York and policy."

Adams traveled to Alaska to cover how the Exxon *Valdez* oil spill affected whales in the Prince William Sound, to Maine to report on the history of the state's lighthouses, and to Romania to cover the Christmas Eve uprising against the Ceaușescu government in Romania. He rode an Amtrak train from St. Paul to Seattle to tell the story of James J. Hill, the man who built the Great Northern Railroad. Again and again, he journeyed to Appalachia to cover issues of farming, industry, poverty, and rural life, using his familiarity with the region's insularity to gently penetrate it. He wasn't always successful. Once, while he was trying to tape a service at a Baptist church there, a church elder noticed and said, "I don't feel like saying what's in my heart this morning because there's a tape recorder going."

In 1988, Adams and his wife, Neenah Ellis, then a producer for *All Things Considered,* left NPR and moved to St. Paul, Minnesota, to create *Good Evening,* a radio variety show launched by Minnesota Public Radio after Garrison Keillor decided to end *A Prairie Home Companion.* As the host of the new show, Adams got mostly good reviews for his blend of humorous skits, music, interviews, and literary readings. Though the show aired on 167 stations and had a major national funder, *Good Evening* was still in competition with *A Prairie Home Companion,* available to stations in reruns. And it wasn't long before Keillor began to hint he wanted to restart the show. So when Adams was asked to come back to *All Things Considered* after a year away, he did. "It was a great experience, doing a live stage program," Adams said. "But I saw there was going to be a difficult time ahead."

One attachment Adams formed in St. Paul lingered. He'd become entranced by the Steinway grand piano on the stage at the World Theater, where *Good Evening* was staged. The instrument was well received by Billy Taylor, Marian McPartland, Liz Story, Harry Connick, and other pianists who came to perform on the show. Adams didn't know how to play the piano, but he would venture onstage during the week at night, when it was dark and no one was around, and touch the keys, sounding single notes, thinking, as he later wrote, "The piano was so good it sounded as if I could play it."

Six years later, at the age of 51, he charged $11,375 on a credit card for a new Steinway upright and began to learn how to play. He fantasized that he might have a latent talent that would emerge the first time he sat down at the keys, but the reality was far more trying. He tried to teach himself "Bingo" using a science fiction–style computer program that told him he "had not reached the level of cosmic brotherhood" when he flubbed too many notes. He had trouble fitting the time to practice into his busy schedule at NPR. At times, he let the Steinway sit silently for days, afraid to even look at it. He persevered, though, and after a year he was accomplished enough to play Robert Schumann's "Traumerei" for his wife as a Christmas present.

He described the year in *Piano Lessons: Music, Love and True Adventures,* published in 1996. He'd already written two books, *Noah Adams on All Things Considered: A Radio Journal* and *St. Croix Notes: River Mornings, Radio Nights,* a collection of his on-air essays from *Good Evening.* But *Piano Lessons* gave him a literary identity separate from that of a public radio host. Though he insisted his story was not the result of a "midlife crisis," it had wide appeal because it touched on the soul-searching many go through at midlife about unexplored potential and dreams. The memoir became a best-seller, and Adams is still playing. "The piano thing's been great," he said. "I still get mail about that book."

In 2001, his fourth book, *Far Appalachia: Following the New River North,* a chronicle of his journey by foot, bicycle, raft, and canoe through Appalachia, was published. The following year, Adams stopped hosting *All Things Considered* and became a senior correspondent (he prefers the term "reporter") and substitute host for NPR. "I begged to leave the show and become a reporter," he said. "It was a few months after 9/11, and I was tired."

He also has a thriving literary career. In 2003, he published *The Flyers: In Search of Wilbur and Orville Wright,* a travelogue of sorts that tells the story of the Wright brothers, their adventures, and the people in their lives. He said his writing life and radio life are, for the most part, separate identities, but the creative process is similar. "I think it's all one thing," he said. "It's going out and finding stories and writing about them."

Witness to History:
Daniel Schorr

Senior News Analyst,
National Public Radio

When **Dan Schorr** was twelve years old, a woman fell or jumped off the roof of his building, landing outside the ground floor window of his family's apartment.

Schorr didn't scream or cry. In his memoir, *Staying Tuned: A Life in Journalism*, he wrote, "I felt no particular sense of awe or emotion about the first dead body I had ever seen." He telephoned the police, and when they arrived, he questioned them about what happened. Then he called the local newspaper, the *Bronx Home News*, which paid five dollars for news tips.

It was the beginning of a lifetime of near-single-minded devotion to journalism. "It's all I ever wanted to be," he said during our interview in the elegantly comfortable living room of his home in northwest Washington, D.C. He gazed steadily through large, square-framed glasses, and I felt in his presence the way I felt listening to his commentaries: that he was a man of great seriousness and focus. I'd been a few minutes late to the interview, having gotten lost on the way from the Metro to his house. Because I was five months pregnant, I couldn't sprint the way I wanted to to make up the lost time. When I arrived, out of breath and apologetic, he merely nodded and ushered me inside. I was relieved nothing more was said. The most important thing was getting on with it.

Schorr is NPR's senior news analyst, providing several commentaries a week for *All Things Considered*. He goes on the air live shortly after nine every Saturday morning on *Weekend Edition* to talk about the week's news with Scott Simon. The segment has obtained such acclaim that President Bill Clinton agreed to change the time of his weekly presidential radio address so it wouldn't compete with Schorr's audience.

Schorr is eighty-nine. He has no plans to retire. When NPR gave him a lifetime achievement award in 1999, he responded that he wanted to change the wording to "lifetime achievement so far."

"I see living as synonymous with working," he told me. "Being able to work at NPR not only keeps me interested in the world, it keeps me alive."

Schorr was born in 1916, the son of Jewish immigrants from Telehan, a shtetl in the region of eastern Europe now known as Belarus. He grew up in the Bronx. His father, a man Schorr has described as "artistic, poetic," skittered from trade to trade, waiting tables, attempting to go into the dry goods business, then real estate, both in vain. He died of a kidney infection when Schorr was six. He has speculated in *Staying Tuned* that this loss helped form the "sense of detachment from tragedy and customary lack of emotional response" that he felt as a reporter, from his *Bronx Home News* scoop to his reports from the death camps at Auschwitz and the urban ghettos of America.

Schorr grew up surrounded by relatives who boarded with his family upon their arrival from Europe until they could afford to go out on their own. He struggled with feelings typical of immigrant children: he criticized his family for speaking Yiddish at home and knowing little about American culture.

He attended DeWitt Clinton High School, where he wrote for the school newspaper. He and a friend started their own news syndicate. They found early success selling a story about the retirement of a high school football coach. But the story turned out to be an untrue rumor, and the syndicate folded.

The rest of his career was far more reputable. He has been, it seems, there to cover practically every crucial turning point in post–World War II Europe. He was one of the first journalists to visit the hidden garret where Anne Frank and her family took refuge from the Nazis. He covered the postwar reconstruction, the Marshall Plan, and the creation of the NATO alliance, filing stories for the *Christian Science Monitor* and the *New York Times*.

Schorr was asked to join CBS news after Edward R. Murrow took notice of his coverage of a flood that broke the dikes of the Netherlands in 1953. He hesitated, thinking he was about to be given a full-time job at the *New York Times*. His editor there told him to take CBS's offer. Several years later, Schorr learned that the newspaper had at the time imposed a brief freeze on hiring Jews as correspondents, out of concern that too many Jews on their reporting staff would hurt their ability to cover the Middle East. By the time he found out about the freeze, though, Schorr was doing quite well at CBS. He opened the network's first bureau in Moscow, where, in the relative openness of the post-Stalin era, he scored the first-ever television interview with a Soviet leader, Nikita Khrushchev. The honeymoon ended quickly, though. Schorr was trailed and investigated by the KGB and ultimately thrown out of Moscow for defying Soviet censorship. He went on to Eastern Europe and Germany and covered the building of the Berlin Wall.

In 1966, he returned to America to report from Washington, D.C. He was fifty years old. He was also a bachelor, with what he described as a "long-standing aversion to commitment." Meeting Lisbeth Bamberger, who worked for the Office of Economic Opportunity, changed his tune. After knowing each other for little more than six months, the two married. Their son, Jonathan, was born in 1967, and the couple had a daughter, Lisa, two years later. Jonathan now works for an organization called KIPP (Knowledge Is Power Program), designing schools for the urban poor. Lisa is the executive director of a Boston-based organization that helps poor people get access to health care.

Dan Schorr was never adored by the Nixon administration. Even before Watergate, he was investigated by the FBI for his reports for CBS questioning the administration's professed commitment to Catholic schools. After the *Washington Post* broke the story that illegal secret Nixon campaign contributions had financed the break-in at Democratic headquarters in the Watergate office building, CBS assigned Schorr full-time to the story. He had the challenge of following developments—many of them leaked quotes from sources who would not give their names, much less go on camera—in a medium that relied on visuals. Still, Schorr's reporting distinguished CBS from the other networks. CBS devoted more time than its competitors to the story and broadcast an in-depth series on Watergate three weeks before the 1972 presidential elections.

Then Schorr became part of the story he was pursuing so ardently. When Presidential Counsel John Dean III finally testified before the U.S. Senate, he submitted the famous Nixon "enemies" list, a document of "top priority" names of the people considered political adversaries, written by Charles Colson, the White House special counsel who had once said that he would walk over his own grandmother for Nixon. The list was given to Schorr moments before he was to go live on television. With no time to preview the list, he began reading it on the air. "I heard myself reading, 'number seventeen, Schorr, Daniel, Columbia Broadcasting system, a real media enemy,'" he wrote in *Staying Tuned*. "I managed not to gasp, though the impulse was there."

Schorr called the experience "the most electrifying moment in my career." He worried that now that he was part of Watergate, he wouldn't be allowed to stay on the beat, but CBS let him continue.

He stayed with the story after President Nixon's resignation, covering what he called the "son of Watergate," the role of the CIA and the FBI in the scandal and possible criminal CIA activities at home and overseas.

This assignment led him straight into the center of controversy and the end of his career at CBS. In 1976, the House of Representatives voted to keep the Pike Papers, a House intelligence report investigating possible illegal CIA and FBI activities, from the public. Schorr had obtained an advance copy, but CBS refused to publish it. Schorr gave it to the *Village Voice*. After the *Voice*'s supplement, called "The Report on the CIA That President Ford Doesn't Want You to Read," was published, CBS suspended him. The House Ethics Committee threatened him with jail for contempt of Congress for refusing to say who gave him the report. "To betray a source would mean to dry up many future sources for many future reporters," he testified at a public hearing. The committee decided narrowly not to cite him for contempt, and CBS asked him to return to his job, but he resigned on the advice of his attorney, who felt that his future at the network may be shaky.

After teaching journalism for a year at the University of California at Berkeley and writing a syndicated newspaper column, he returned to television in 1979 to help Ted Turner start CNN. Skeptical about the maverick businessman's commitment to journalism, Schorr insisted that his contract with the network include a clause that "no demand will be made upon him that would compromise his professional ethics and responsibilities." He brought up the clause a year later, after being ordered to share the reporting responsibilities at the Democratic convention in 1985 with former Texas governor John Connally. Schorr saw Connally as a news source, not a journalist. The conflict led to Schorr's dismissal and the end of his television career.

He was sixty-nine, and he had no desire to stop working. He had come to be wary of television. He has criticized it for its "affinity for violence" and for forcing political leaders to act too fast and with too much superficial polish. "Television is more a medium of the senses than a medium of the mind," he told me. "It's not very good for conveying broad ideas, a sober view of the world."

But, once having left the medium, he worried about where his career would go. "Once when I went with my family to dinner, somebody was coming through the revolving door the other way and then went all the way around again in order to come out where I was, and he said to me, 'Excuse me, didn't you used to be Daniel Schorr?'" he said. "It drove home to me the effect of television—that if you're not on television, there's a question of whether you exist anymore."

Public radio listeners, though, have no doubt that Dan Schorr exists. He began doing commentaries for the network while he was still with CNN. After he left, his involvement with NPR gave him a place that embraced his fifty-odd years of experience. His speech is halting and pensive, with a deep voice that, though well articulated, sounds slightly muffled, as if it's coming from a tunnel. He insists on bringing historical perspective to bear on current political developments. These qualities make his commentaries occasions of particular gravitas on the NPR airwaves, whether he is remarking on the Monica Lewinsky scandal or the war in Iraq.

Schorr's sound is a bit looser when he's on live with Scott Simon on Saturday mornings. The two are very good friends, with a rapport Schorr calls "unique in all the professional relationships I've had in all these years.

"Scott has a marvelous quality of being deferential," Schorr said. "Murrow had that too. The more important he is, the more important he tries to make you feel you are. And if you're not sure how important you are, it's a very nice thing to have."

Simon will also do what few colleagues in Schorr's career have dared to do: tease him on the air. One winter Saturday morning on the day before the Super Bowl, with only fourteen seconds left to their segment, Simon asked Schorr, a complete sports ignoramus, who he thought would win.

Schorr dished it right back. "Gee, Scott, I don't know," he said. "Who's playing?"

For many on the NPR staff, Schorr is a symbol of the great early days of broadcast journalism, the last of Edward R. Murrow's legendary CBS news team still active in news. He gives them eyewitness insight into, as Schorr put it, "the history that they learned or didn't learn about in school" as they cover the news of the day. They stop by his office to ask him about his days in the army during World War II or what the building of the Berlin Wall was like. "When they call me Senior News Analyst, the word 'senior' has a very specific meaning," Schorr said. "I'm an old guy, who may not be very smart or may not be very pretty, may not even be very bright, but by God, I've lived through the things that most people have vaguely heard about."

The Voice in the Box:
Bob Edwards

Host, *The Bob Edwards Show*

Bob Edwards has landed well. For nearly a quarter century, he was the deep-voiced, laconic host of NPR's *Morning Edition*, seeing the program through its ragtag early days to become the most listened to morning radio show in the country. Just a few months before *Morning Edition*'s twenty-fifth anniversary, NPR executives removed him from the host's chair, for the enigmatic reason that the change was part of the "natural evolution" of the program. Tens of thousands of listeners complained, and Edwards made no secret of his sadness and confusion about the decision.

Then came XM Radio, a three-year-old company in the upstart world of satellite broadcasting, with a CEO who had always loved public radio and a tempting offer: a daily interview show bearing Edwards's name.

I spoke with Edwards in the offices of *The Bob Edwards Show* at XM's headquarters, located in the former *National Geographic* printing press building in the scrappy, not yet urbanly renewed Eckington neighborhood in Washington, D.C. XM is subscription radio, giving listeners a choice of 140 different types of commercial-free music and entertainment, ranging from neo-soul to classical vocal music to Opie and Anthony, the syndicated duo fired from Infinity Broadcasting after they aired audio of a couple having sex in New York's St. Patrick's Cathedral (without the antiobscenity regulations of the traditional broadcast spectrum, XM and its competitor, Sirius Radio, which has hired Howard Stern, don't have to worry about offensive material and swear words). The look at XM is slick and whimsical, with glass-walled on-air studios decorated to match the sound of each channel. A Wonder Woman doll sits on the console at the channel that plays seventies music. Crayon drawings hang on the walls of the children's music channel, and a jukebox blinks brightly in the corner of Hank's Place, a country music channel.

Bob Edwards, it should be said, is neither slick nor whimsical. He is given to stern expressions and ironic, curmudgeonly airs and stands a lanky six feet four inches tall. He wears blue jeans, a plaid shirt untucked over a slight potbelly, and has unfashionably cut gray blond hair and crooked teeth. But XM has made a place for him, and a grand one at that. At the end of a long hall of studios, past the bustling traffic and weather center, is the wing dedicated to *The Bob Edwards Show*. The entrance is flanked by two black-and-white photographs, blown up larger than life, of Edwards's broadcasting heroes and the subjects of his two books: legendary sports announcer Red Barber and journalist Edward R. Murrow, a key figure in the creation of broadcast journalism.

The photographs were a surprise from Hugh Panero, XM's CEO, on Edwards's first day of work in 2004. "The guy knows just the right touch," Edwards said, and smiled. He has a closed-mouth, flat smile, his lips curving up only slightly at the ends.

The photographs are only one of the many signs that Edwards is adored here. Panero is a long-time public radio fan who, upset over the way NPR treated Edwards, wasted no time snatching him up at XM. The company has invested several million in the new show and an advertising campaign that included a full-page ad in the *New York Times* asking, "What do you give a man who's interviewed dozens of world leaders, reported on every major news event of the last 30 years, won numerous awards for journalistic excellence and informed, entertained and enlightened millions of loyal public radio listeners? Simple. A microphone." Just weeks after *The Bob Edwards Show* went on the air, it was XM, not NPR, that trumpeted the news that Edwards would be inducted into the Radio Hall of Fame that year. And XM has even agreed to reunite Edwards with his beloved public radio audience. The company is teaming up with NPR's main rival, Public Radio International, to offer a weekend version of his show to public radio stations.

Panero said he considers *The Bob Edwards Show* "one of the crown jewels" of XM and listens faithfully every morning at eight on his way to work. If he arrives at the office before the show is over, he puts on the headphones to his portable XM receiver, called a "MyFi," to listen on his way up to the office so he doesn't miss a word. His staff leaves him alone until nine. "People just know if I have headphones on they should wait until I finish listening," Panero said. He often drops by Edwards's office or stops him in the cafeteria to talk about the day's show, though he places no editorial restraints on him, not even when Edwards urges XM listeners to donate money to their local public radio stations or when he travels to NPR affiliates to speak at fundraising events.

Edwards's staff of seven is similarly enamored of him. He hand-picked his producers and assistants, mainly from colleagues who'd worked with him at NPR. They regaled me with stories of his generosity to his family and his fans and showed off the birthday present they got him (he'd just turned fifty-eight), a globe with a top that opened to reveal a mini-bar with Edwards's favorite whiskeys, Kentucky Straight and Jack Daniels Single Barrel. Chad Campbell, a producer, told me that he decided to work at XM after he realized how much Edwards had changed. "I had been convinced the Bob I knew from *Morning Edition* was surly and unapproachable, but just hearing him on the phone, he sounded so happy and engaged," he said. "I wanted to work with Happy Bob."

And he is happy, Edwards told me, his feet up on his desk. He can interview anyone he wants, from Kentucky poet James Baker Hall to country singer John Prine to journalist Bill Moyers. Interviews can run as long as an hour, the entire length of the show, an eternity compared to the maximum eight-minute segment length on *Morning Edition*. He is reading more fiction and spending less time scrambling after breaking news. He is enjoying the underdog feeling of starting a new show in a new technology, the suspense of wondering where it will all go. "This could be really something exciting that people are going to embrace," Edwards said.

So, could he say what happened with NPR was all for the best? I asked him.

"Yeah, I suppose," he said, his voice lifting hopefully. But there was also a question mark in his tone, as if he was still trying to figure the whole thing out.

The sleek, digitized XM receivers that broadcast *The Bob Edwards Show* are a far cry from the "magic box" of Edwards's childhood, a 1939 Zenith console radio in the den of his family's home. From the time he was a toddler, he thought of radio as his "buddy." At night, it brought him to places far beyond his hometown of Louisville, Kentucky, picking up signals from AM stations all over the country, short-wave radio, ships at sea, even foreign broadcasts.

"I always imagined myself being in radio," he said. "My dream was to be the voice in the box."

As soon as he learned how to read, he would read the newspaper out loud, trying to get rid of his Kentucky accent so he could sound like the announcers he heard on the air. His ambitions were far beyond what his family expected of him. His father, the only one among his siblings to graduate from high school, worked a white-collar job as an accountant for the city of Louisville, and his mother was a home-maker and a bookkeeper. The family's background was solidly working class. All his aunts and uncles worked in plants. As for his own future, "it was like, go to the grocery store, get a job bagging groceries, maybe you'll be assistant produce manager someday," he said.

Attending St. Xavier High School, a Catholic all boys' school founded after the Civil War, changed Edwards's expectations of himself. The school produced more than a dozen National Merit scholars a year, along with championship sports teams and award-winning newspapers. As an alumnus, Edwards is still quite involved in the school, occasionally flying to Louisville for board meetings and other school events. "Whatever it does, it has to be the best," he said. "That was very stimulating for me as an insecure, working-class kid."

In 1968, while he was attending the University of Louisville, he started hanging out at WHEL, a tiny station across the Ohio River in New Albany, Indiana. Its signal was so weak it could barely be heard back in Louisville. He wanted to learn what he could about radio, and "they didn't throw me out," he said. He was invited to try announcing when the police came in and arrested the deejay on the air for failing to pay his child support.

WHEL was what was called a "beautiful music" (also known as "easy listening" or elevator music) station, a now bygone format of orchestral covers of soft pop. When Edwards started, the station aired newscasts from the ABC news network. Then, much to his de-light, ABC dropped the station. He started doing the news himself, rewriting stories from the local newspaper and scrounging up his own reports. The station's format, he laughed, has since switched to gospel, with new call letters "because you can't be having hell in your call letters."

After he graduated with a degree in business in 1969, he was drafted into the U.S. Army. He became a news producer and anchor for television and radio for the American Forces Korea Network in Seoul, a job that, to his relief, kept him out of Vietnam. He used the G.I. bill to go to graduate school at American University, which he chose because it was where Ed Bliss, who had written for Murrow and later Walter Cronkite at CBS, taught. "I thought, here's a guy who's been where I want to be, who has worked with the people I most admire, and he can teach me something," Edwards said. He became Bliss's teaching assistant, and Bliss continued to be his mentor and close friend until his death in 2003.

Edwards worked at the CBS affiliate in Washington, WTOP-AM, and the now-defunct Mutual Broadcasting System. He was hired at NPR in 1974 to be a newscaster on *All Things Considered* and soon became cohost of the program. It was a heady, experimental time at the network. The staff was young, too small, underpaid (Edwards started at $15,000), and determined to rejuvenate the power of the "magic box" through the creative use of sound and vivid writing. The social scene at NPR was similarly adventurous. Edwards was seen, as Susan Stamberg teased him when she was a guest on *The Bob Edwards Show*, as "a *god*, a *blond god*, tall and handsome."

"She's so full of shit," Edwards said fondly when I reminded him of this. But he did admit that NPR in the early days was quite a flirtatious place. "You didn't need office parties in those days," he said. "They had edit booths with no windows on the doors. We were very young because they couldn't afford to pay experienced people, so there were couplings all the time. You had to remember who was seeing whom— you couldn't talk about so and so if they were seeing so and so." Edwards was evasive when I asked about whom *he* dated at NPR, though he did confirm that he'd had a brief romance with Nina Totenberg. He met his wife, Sharon, while she was a receptionist at NPR, and became the stepfather to her son, Brean Campbell, now thirty.

Edwards initially saw NPR as a stepping-stone, hoping he'd eventually get hired at CBS to follow in the footsteps of Murrow and Cronkite. After a year at NPR, he applied for a job at CBS. The day he took his writing test there was the day Saigon fell, and he decided he didn't want to leave NPR after all. "I had kind of a conversion because I realized that *All Things Considered* would do a terrific job on that story, a big production reviewing the whole history of the Vietnam War, taking up most of the ninety minutes of the show, and I wasn't there to be part of it and I felt really bad," he said.

When *Morning Edition* was launched in 1979, Edwards agreed to host the program for the first thirty days. When the month was up, he stayed on, thrilled to be the voice of the show. The schedule, though, was grueling. He was in bed by 6:00 p.m., woke up at 1 a.m., and started work at 2:15, preparing for the show's broadcast at 5:00. The schedule meant that "the whole world was upside down," he said. He couldn't go out at night, and he had to back-time his days, planning everything around getting to bed on time. "It's a stupid, idiotic way to live," he said. "Everything is programmed."

A small consolation was being able to leave work in the early afternoon and spend time with his family. His and Sharon's oldest daughter, Susannah, was born in 1980, before *Morning Edition* was a year old. Eleanor followed five years later. Sharon homeschooled Eleanor, and Bob pitched in to teach writing, current events, and other insights from a life of watching history unfold daily.

As the host of *Morning Edition*, Edwards conducted about eight hundred interviews a year, with a stately presence and a deep voice slightly roughened by the Benson & Hedges menthol cigarettes he hustled outside to smoke on the street in front of NPR once an hour. His authoritative sound belied, in the early years, a deep insecurity about a skill fundamental to news announcing: the ability to deal with the unexpected. Most of the reports and interviews on *Morning*

Edition and the other NPR news programs are prerecorded. But when news broke, or new developments occurred, Edwards had to do live interviews, which he hated. The unpredictability made him anxious, and his staff was instructed to script as much as they could in advance, including his name.

Edwards's resistance to spontaneity started to change in 1981, when he began doing weekly Friday morning interviews, live, with legendary sports broadcaster Red Barber. As Edwards wrote in his 1993 book, *Fridays with Red: A Radio Friendship*, Barber resisted any kind of preplanning and would talk about the weather, his garden, and then whatever sports story he felt was most interesting that day. "There was no script," Edwards said. "I just had to be prepared for whatever the hell he was going to say." Barber would often turn the tables, asking "the colonel," as he called Edwards, a few questions, shaking him out of the detached posture of a news host to reveal his arch sense of humor. The two often discussed camellias, which grew abundantly in Barber's yard in Tallahassee, Florida. When Edwards's wife insisted that he tell Barber that they had a camellia in their yard, Edwards did, only to be asked what kind it was. Pink, Edwards told him. But Barber pressed on, wanting to know the flower's name. Edwards said, "Fred, or Frank—I don't know Red, it just bloomed and we haven't really got to know each other yet."

Yet it must be said that though Edwards loosened up in conversations with Barber and some other guests, often musicians and authors, he was never very lively. At times he could sound plodding, even unenthusiastic—like a guy who never quite got used to getting up at one in the morning. When I was the local host of *Morning Edition* at a small NPR affiliate in northern Iowa in the early 1990s, I would listen to Edwards closely through my headphones before and after my news and weather breaks. He would give these weary little sighs in between phrases, and I'd think, how tired we both were.

But there was something about his slower pace, even his moments of ennui, that was fundamental to his appeal. He was on at a time when it seemed every other broadcast outlet in the country was doing either bright and cheery Ken and Barbie or lewd and crude shock jock. Edwards was more somber, a little wry, more like most of us were at that hour of the day. He delivered the news without shoving sunshine down our throats. He had an intimate place in our lives. "They heard from me before they heard from the old man, or whoever they're sleeping with," Edwards said. "People told me, 'I wake up with you every day,' which always amused my wife, because she never woke up with me."

For these reasons and others, the announcement in March 2004 that Edwards would no longer be *Morning Edition*'s host was met with widespread protests from listeners. NPR received more than thirty-five thousand emails (fifty thousand, according to Edwards) about the change. A "Save Bob Edwards" Internet petition, which pledged that signers would not donate money to their member stations or NPR until Edwards was brought back, got 25,802 signatures. (Edwards actively discouraged listeners from holding back on donations.) Several station managers, many of whom were about to conduct their spring pledge drives, protested the change, though others said they accepted or welcomed it. Speculation about the reason for the move was rampant, with journalists and bloggers speculating that Edwards may have been too old or too outspoken; he was a national vice president for the American Federation of Television and Radio Artists union and has given public speeches against media ownership consolidation and what he called the media's failure to challenge the Bush administration on the war in Iraq.

During Edwards's tour for his newly published book, *Edward R. Murrow and the Birth of Broadcast Journalism*, listeners told him how much they would miss him. Several of them brought gifts for his new dog, Sam, a border collie he and his wife bought after he stopped hosting *Morning Edition*. They'd heard him tell Terry Gross on *Fresh Air* about how he'd never allowed a dog in the house before, concerned the barking would disrupt his sleep schedule. He broke the news that he'd been removed from *Morning Edition* to his wife by telling her that now she could get a dog. "The first day that was free of that program, we had a dog," he said.

In the meanwhile, new job offers were pouring in. He was invited to work at CNN and ABC, teach at several universities, and host programs at public radio affiliates. Then came the letter from XM's Hugh Panero, offering him a daily interview show.

"It said, '[NPR Senior Vice President for Programming] Jay Kernis may not want to hear you every day, but I do,'" Edwards said. "Is this guy good or what?"

The ending of the saga of Edwards's departure from NPR was a happy one, but, like most real-life happy endings, it's more complicated than that. Edwards is still haunted by what happened at NPR. He has the air of a man whose wife left him suddenly and without sufficient explanation, a man for whom a new love—XM, in Edwards's case—helps ease but does not erase the pain of the split. He is angry at what he calls NPR's "smears"—suggestions, made in the press or in emails forwarded to him from listeners and former colleagues, that he was uncooperative, unwilling to share the anchor chair or to do the kind of field reporting "they" wanted their anchors to do. "Lies, just lies!" he said. He's not happy either that NPR is treating *The Bob Edwards Show* as competition. Plans to have *Weekend Edition* host Scott Simon on the show to talk about his new novel were canceled after NPR enforced its policy of not having staff appear on programming that directly competes for its audience. When, at the end of our interview, I asked Edwards the question I always close interviews with: "Is there anything else I should know?" he said, "Yeah, there are things you should know, and there are things I should know, too. Like, what was the deal? If you ever find that out, let me know."*

And, oddly, he can't get enough sleep. His face still has the ashen complexion and weary lines it had when he was doing *Morning Edition*. After years of driving to work in the dead of night, he has no patience for rush hour, so he's awake by five and in the office by six. That's a far more natural clock than his old schedule, but something inside him is still turned around. He now tends to go to bed at 1 a.m., his old wake-up time. "I've got this feeling somewhere in the back of my head that it's okay to stay up," he said.

There are other things that he's still not quite accustomed to. He once had 13 million listeners a week. Now all he knows is that XM has 4.4 million subscribers, with no means yet to measure how many of them listen to his show. "When you have thirteen million listeners, it's a big deal," he said. "At the moment, we're not a big deal, so I'm getting used to not being a big deal." He also worries that though XM is projecting rapid audience growth, satellite radio could end up being just an interim technology, losing out in the tussle of traditional broadcasting, webcasting, podcasting, and cable in the early years of the twenty-first century.

---

*In an effort to answer to this plea beyond the reasons summarized earlier in this chapter, I contacted Andi Sporkin, NPR's vice president of communications. Her emailed reply follows: "Regarding Bob Edwards' situation at NPR, when the decision was made to make a change at *Morning Edition*, Bob was offered a prestigious senior correspondent position. Moving from show host to senior correspondent has happened several times at NPR. Why he chose to pass on that opportunity can only be answered by Bob, since he did not share it with us. As to reasons why the change was made, I suggest you use the extensive listener communications generated around the time of the change and available on the http://www.NPR.org site. This includes lengthy postings from Jay Kernis, our SVP for Programming and Jeffrey Dvorkin, our Ombudsman. They would be most relevant and factual because, as it's now a year and a half since Bob left NPR, there's simply nothing new to add."

But after mulling over all this for a bit, he brightens. Maybe XM and *The Bob Edwards Show* will be a big deal, he muses. His own history gives him reason for optimism. He points out that when he started at NPR in 1974, the network had been up and running for three years, the same amount of time XM has been around, and had only a handful of listeners. "It's the second time I'm with a start-up," Edwards said. "It has a lot of that excitement of thirty years ago."

The Fallopian Jungle:
Cokie Roberts,
Nina Totenberg, and
Linda Wertheimer

National Public Radio

When Cokie Roberts, Nina Totenberg, and Linda Wertheimer worked together at NPR in the late 1970s and 1980s, money and space at the network were tight, so the women shared the same small cubicle. They typed nearly elbow to elbow, racing to meet deadlines, working long hours, and breaking important news stories. They whispered, laughed, and confided in one another, forging a professional and personal connection so tight their colleagues had several nicknames for them, including "The Troika" and "The Three Musketeers." Their formidable and distinctly female power caused one daunted male staff member to dub them "The Fallopian Jungle."

The three had entered the workforce in the first years after the passage of the 1964 Civil Rights Act, which made it illegal for employers to discriminate against women. But plenty of newsrooms still did, and Roberts, Totenberg, and Wertheimer had their share of rejections, hands on their knees, and outright sexual harassment as they began their careers. Once the law gathered force, though, the women of their generation were the first with the opportunity to build a career with the law on their side. "We are of a generation that is by definition pioneers," Roberts said. "One of the things that a lot of younger women don't realize is that it made a difference to have the law changed. And that happened just as we were emerging from college."

NPR employed more women than the average newsroom then, mainly because the salaries were too low to attract many experienced men. Wertheimer was hired first, in 1971, when the network was just getting started. Totenberg followed in 1975. Three years later, the two lobbied to get Roberts hired. The three banded together to boost salaries and get promotions. Totenberg covered, as she still does today, the Supreme Court. Roberts and Wertheimer covered Capitol Hill and national politics. Sharing the same turf "could have resulted in a duel to the death or it could have resulted in what it did result in, which was co-operation," Wertheimer said. "We divided things up. We had no problem doing it, and the kind of competition we'd get into would be about how fast, how good, how detailed, how fresh our stories could be."

The three women formed the journalistic core of NPR, particularly in the network's early years, when it was often described as "quirky," a place where hosts hid in closets with microphones to see whether Life-savers sparked in the dark when you chewed them and a news report on a speech might very well include, quite purposefully, the annoying squeal of the prelecture microphone sound check. Roberts, Totenberg, and Wertheimer, meanwhile, were charging into the mainstream of Washington journalism, undaunted by the primarily male heritage of the D.C. press corps, feeding NPR breaking news on politics, government, and the Supreme Court. Many nights, the lead stories on *All Things Considered* would belong to at least one of the ladies of the troika.

The professional relationship the three women have has, over the years, been dwarfed by the depth of their friendship. Though Totenberg and Wertheimer now work in separate wings at NPR and Roberts does her weekly news analysis from her home office, the three remain very close. The three and their husbands have a standing Saturday night dinner and movie date. They usually eat at the same red-sauce Italian restaurant, the Pines of Rome in Bethesda, and try to compromise on the movie choice. Roberts and Totenberg don't like violence in movies, while Wertheimer's husband refuses to see movies with subtitles (though Steve Roberts likes them). The women are occasionally recognized. "Once someone said, 'Oh, look. There's Cokie Roberts and whatshername and whatshername," Totenberg said. "So Fred [Wertheimer] walked up and said, 'And I'm whatshername's husband!'"

The three have been there for each other through the illnesses and deaths of loved ones: Wertheimer's parents; Totenberg's first husband, former U.S. senator Floyd Haskell, who endured long hospitalizations from a head injury and then lung disease before his death in 1998; and Roberts's sister Barbara Boggs Sigmund, the mayor of Princeton, New Jersey, who died of melanoma in 1990. During these times, Roberts, Totenberg, and Wertheimer cooked for each other, handled media inquiries, and took precious vacation days to make sure whoever was in crisis would not have to be alone at a hospital bedside or in an empty house.

"I think all of us would tell you that the work is just about the easiest thing we do," Wertheimer said. "Work is not what gets you. It's when something goes wrong with somebody you care about. That's what gets you."

Cokie Roberts
Senior News Analyst, National Public Radio

Cokie Roberts has just arrived from what Washingtonians call "The Hill," short of course for Capitol Hill, where her father and then her mother were in Congress, and where she herself built her journalism career for NPR and ABC. When she went to hail a cab to get to her office for our telephone interview, a group of female tourists spotted her and shouted, "Cokie! We love you, Cokie!"

In this hub of national politics, amidst all the deal making and power brokering and cynicism and spin, what makes Cokie so revered? Perhaps it is all those years of seeing her on television every Sunday morning, surrounded by men, as confident a pundit as any of them, discussing the important political issues of the week. Perhaps it is that while she has this stature, she gracefully embraces many of the essential contradictions of the baby boomer professional woman. She has a vital career yet has always insisted that her identity is first and foremost as a mother. She was a member of the first generation of women to be granted legal equality in the workplace, yet at the height of her career insisted on her right to give up one of the highest profile jobs in television news. She is highly photogenic, even glamorous, with striking gray-green eyes and a trim figure that look great on television and the covers of her books, yet she has not forsaken her longtime connection to the invisible and far less lucrative medium of public radio, where she has a weekly engagement to talk about politics on *Morning Edition*.

What Cokie Roberts, sixty-two, told me is that one reason women cheer for her is that she has let them get to know her. She has written about her life in two best-selling books: *We Are Our Mothers' Daughters*, a collection of personal essays examining the nature of women's roles, and *From This Day Forward*, a reflection on marriage cowritten with her husband, journalist Steve Roberts (a third book, *Founding Mothers: The Women Who Raised Our Nation,* is about the women who influenced the Founding Fathers). She writes in an approachable, conversational style about studying at the Harvard libraries while she was a student at Wellesley in hopes of meeting Steve, the birth of her first child, and how putting her husband's career in front of hers in the early years of their marriage at first hurt and then helped her own professional life.

"There's a very strong sense among women that they want people like them in positions that they can see and relate to, and there are still a lot of women who feel that they don't recognize anyone on television or in politics," she said. "A part of that is their personal lives are not known. If somebody's just standing up and doing a fifteen-second straight reporting piece, how do you know what that woman's life is like? She probably is a lot like you."

Though Roberts, like many women, has juggled family life and career, overcome discrimination, and values the connections and support the women in her life provide, her life has also been characterized by the aura of specialness and exclusivity that comes from growing up in a high-profile political family. She was born Mary Martha Corinne Morrison Claiborne Boggs in 1943, the third and youngest child of a prominent New Orleans political family. Her older brother Thomas couldn't pronounce Corinne, so the nickname "Cokie" stuck. Her father, Hale Boggs, was a Democratic U.S. representative for Louisiana for twenty-eight years. The family spent part of the year in New Orleans and part in Washington. The family enjoyed close friendships with President Lyndon Johnson, former Speaker of the House Sam Rayburn, and a number of other prominent political families. Birthdays were celebrated on Capitol Hill, and Roberts was commissioned to stuff campaign envelopes from the time she was seven.

At Wellesley College in the early 1960s, Roberts stayed active in politics. She met Steve Roberts at a student political convention in Ohio. The two married four years later in the backyard of Roberts's childhood home in Bethesda, Maryland, in an interfaith service. Cokie is Catholic and Steve is Jewish, and the couple decided to honor both traditions in their marriage and family life.

Roberts's first stabs at the job market after college met with unusual success. She worked in Washington producing a television quiz show for teenagers and briefly hosted a new roundtable-style program for foreign journalists, *Meeting of the Minds,* the precursor to *Meet the Press.* She left the show after she got married to move to New

York with Steve, then a reporter for the *New York Times*, despite the fact that she was making more money than he was. In the tenor of the times, "it never occurred to me to try to keep my job," she wrote in *We Are Our Mothers' Daughters*.

In New York, her beginner's luck in journalism evaporated. At magazines, newspapers, and television stations all over the city, she was told again and again, "We don't hire women." That statement had become illegal in 1964 with the passage of the Civil Rights Act, but employers were slow to comply and enforcement of the provision was still rare.

She found work writing for a business newsletter and then at a local television station until her son, Lee, was born. Her husband's career with the *Times* took the family to Los Angeles, where she produced a local version of the high school quiz television show she'd worked on after graduating from college. She juggled work and family in an era before maternity leaves and flex time. Ten days after her daughter, Rebecca, was born, Roberts left the baby with her mother to attend a television taping. When her mother, shocked, said *she* had still been in the hospital when her children were ten days old, Roberts, as she described it in *Mothers' Daughters*, retorted, "Take her to the hospital if you want, I have to go to work."

In 1973, the *Times* moved Steve Roberts to a foreign post in Greece. She used the opportunity to develop her own reporting career, covering the war in Cyprus as a freelancer for magazines and CBS radio and television. When her husband got yet another reassignment, this time to Washington, D.C., to cover Congress, she balked. She liked the work she was doing in Greece and was daunted by the prospect of rebuilding her career yet again. "I actually came back here kicking and screaming because I thought that it would be going back to my childhood and the end of the fun," she said.

At first it seemed that way. The Robertses bought the home Cokie had grown up in in Bethesda from her mother. And, once again, she went job hunting. But things had changed. Her Cyprus coverage, which included a headline story on the *CBS Evening News,* had gotten her some acclaim in the industry. And, there were more women journalists working in Washington. An "Old Girls' Network" to rival that of the boys was starting to develop, particularly at NPR. Totenberg, who had heard about her through mutual friends, and Wertheimer, who remembered her from Wellesley, helped Roberts get hired at NPR in 1978 to cover Capitol Hill and national politics.

In 1988, Roberts joined ABC News to cover Congress and politics for *World News Tonight*, while continuing to work for NPR as a news analyst. She became the first regular female panelist to appear on *This Week with David Brinkley*. After Brinkley retired in 1996, Roberts became the coanchor of the show with Sam Donaldson. At NPR, she had developed a reputation as "the tactful one" in the trio, in contrast to Totenberg's fire and Wertheimer's rationality. Tact also characterized her approach to *This Week*. She always appeared eminently sensible and carefully moderate, often using current polls to talk about "what the American people want." She's even been criticized for being too middle of the road, more a talking head than a journalist; *The Nation's* Eric Alterman once called her a "windup Conventional Wisdom doll."

Though television has been a mainstay of her career, Roberts has said that she enjoys the medium of radio the most because listeners "aren't disturbed or distracted by the visual image." She stayed with NPR throughout her rise in television news, discussing politics every Monday on *Morning Edition*. Her voice, always a little raspy, sounds somewhat more phlegmatic during her 6:10 a.m. spot, as if she's just gotten up. And she may have. She's connected to NPR by ISDN, a live-sound quality telephone line installed in her home office. Few listeners knew she wasn't actually at the NPR studios until the morning a dog barked during her discussion of the latest bad economic news. A few days later, she explained the home setup and confessed to wearing her "very discreet nightie" during her Monday morning chats. As for the barking, it had come from her basset hound, Abner.

Inasmuch as Roberts's life has been characterized by good fortune, it has also been marked by devastating loss. When she was twenty-eight, busy with two preschool-age children and her television career in Los Angeles, her father, Hale Boggs, then the Democratic Majority Leader of the U.S. House of Representatives, disappeared aboard a twin engine plane while on his way to a political fund-raiser for a colleague in Alaska. After a four-month search, investigators concluded the plane had been weighed down with ice, crashed, and sunk to the bottom of Prince William Sound. Her mother, Lindy Boggs, was elected to the congressional seat left vacant and served until 1991. Roberts also lost her older sister Barbara Boggs Sigmund, the mayor of Princeton, New Jersey, to melanoma in 1990. "I had understood that you could fall out of the sky at any moment, as my father did, therefore you had to be very careful not to let things go by the way, make sure that you paid attention to the things that were important," she said. "But I think I learned that much more dramatically when my sister died. From that time on I have been determined not to let work get in the way of life."

This realization was one of the key factors in her decision to leave *This Week* in 2002, a year before her sixtieth birthday. Her announcement, which roughly coincided with a slew of "I quits" from Oprah Winfrey, Rosie O'Donnell, and then-Massachusetts governor Jane Swift, sparked off a wave of media attention, with articles in the *New York Times* and elsewhere pondering why women who'd succeeded in breaking through the glass ceiling were now leaving the building. "I think women are better than men at figuring out life stages, and I had reached a stage of life where I just didn't want to do this anymore," Roberts said. "I didn't want to be kept going that fast anymore."

As she was leaving *This Week*, she had to cope with her own bout of breast cancer. It was diagnosed early and since her treatment there have been no signs of recurrence. She continues to be a political commentator for ABC, and she does volunteer work for Save the Children and breast cancer–related charities. She serves on President Bush's Council on Service and Civic Participation, a role that's led to criticism that she has compromised her journalistic objectivity by becoming a part of what she covers. She defended herself by saying that she no longer covers the White House as a reporter, and encouraging volunteer work is something she "feels strongly" about. "I've been saying to young women for decades: Look, we pulled out of the volunteer force when we all went into the paid workforce, leaving communities high and dry that were used to having this cadre of women volunteers," she said. "You have to make it up at some point in your life. In the case of women like me who went right into the paid workforce, it was clearly going to be on the other end."

She has also continued to talk about politics on NPR every Monday morning. Her voice has become so familiar that people often say to her, "I love hearing you! I listen every morning," despite the fact that she is only on once a week. She's kept the gig for so long, she told me, because she feels that "same sense of connection" with her listeners. "If you want to reach people in government, people in the Fortune 500, people in academia, in the journalistic community, and then, remarkably unlike any other mainstream news organization, younger people, because it's on many college campuses, NPR is the place to do it," she said. "And you can do it with some depth and some humor."

Nina Totenberg
Legal Affairs Correspondent, National Public Radio

When she was a girl, Nina Totenberg's heroine was Nancy Drew, the fictional teenage sleuth who solved many a mystery and righted many a wrong with her sharp wits and intuition.

Totenberg grew up to become, though not quite a detective, a journalist who pieces together clues and hunches with a relentless persistence to get her story. As NPR's legal affairs correspondent, she has broken stories that forced the withdrawal of one U.S. Supreme Court nominee and turned the confirmation hearing of another into a political conflagration that opened the eyes of society to the problem of sexual harassment.

"You have to be willing to not give up, and to keep probing," she said. "And just be like a little dog with something in your teeth and you won't let go."

Totenberg, sixty-one, wears fashionable suits, a careful hairstyle, and a distinct air of readiness: to go to the Supreme Court, or Capitol Hill, or on camera for her regular gig at ABC as a panelist on *Inside Washington*. She impressed me as a woman with a sturdy and exacting pride, which is something very different than the boundless egoism that can also beset people of great accomplishment. She doesn't consider her big-as-Broadway singing voice, for example, a personal achievement, because it took no hard work for her to get it. She just opened her mouth when she was a little girl and there it was. "I have nothing to do with it," she said. "God gave me that voice." Her achievements in journalism are another story. Her best reports sprang from a moment of investigative instinct and then days of sheer toil when she would sit in her office until midnight to work the phones in three different time zones. She quickly corrected me when I referred to the Anita Hill sexual harassment story as a leak. "It wasn't a leak, I keep telling people," she said, as I stumbled to apologize. Leaks of course imply that the information was simply given to her, like her singing voice. Anita Hill was an *exclusive*, a scoop, something she'd dug up herself and gotten on the air before anybody else in broadcasting.

It was not surprising to learn, then, that Totenberg has a reputation at NPR for having very high standards. Staff members told me that she has a certain back-straightening effect on those she works with when she walks into the room. But they also acknowledge her humanity. There is an often-repeated story about a new intern who had all of her worldly possessions swiped from her car as she was moving into Washington. Totenberg paid to replace much of the woman's wardrobe.

Totenberg grew up witness to the passion and discipline of classical musicians. Her father, Roman Totenberg, is a virtuoso violinist who, at ninety-five, still performs occasionally and teaches at the Boston

University School of the Arts. Born in Poland, he was a pupil of the legendary Carl Flesch in Berlin and is one of the last living links to the pre–World War II European style of violin playing. He came to the United States in the mid-1930s on a concert tour and later returned to stay. Because he was Jewish, immigrating kept him from the grip of the Third Reich. He and his wife, Melanie Totenberg, who died in 1996, have three daughters. Nina is the oldest. Her sister Jill is a business executive in New York and her sister Amy is a prominent Atlanta attorney.

Totenberg attended Boston University in the 1960s, then dropped out to take a job on the women's pages of the old *Record American* (now the *Boston Herald*). Though sex discrimination had been outlawed by the passage of the 1964 Civil Rights Act, much of the journalism world didn't seem to be paying attention. When she called a Boston-area newspaper in 1965 about a job, a male editor told her "we don't hire women." She found work in Washington, D.C., at the *National Observer* and as the Washington editor of *New Times* magazine. In 1968, when she started covering Congress, she'd "walk through the lobby on the House side and Congressmen would give catcalls, like Saturday night on fraternity row," she told the *Boston Herald.*

Totenberg found the barriers to women were still up in 1975, though the excuses had changed. Though she continued to work, changing jobs wasn't easy. Instead of hearing "we don't hire women," she was told "we already have our women." She finally found an open door at NPR, a place that couldn't afford such excuses. The low salaries the network offered discouraged experienced men who could make more elsewhere and attracted talented women who still couldn't get hired elsewhere.

At NPR, Totenberg has always covered legal affairs, but when she started that included the Justice Department, the FBI, the CIA, and the House and Senate judiciary committees in addition to the U.S. Supreme Court. Now, the Supreme Court is the mainstay of her beat, though she continues to cover other subjects. It is rare for a reporter, at NPR or elsewhere, to cover a single beat for as long as Totenberg has, and her depth of knowledge about law, court proceedings, and legal history likely rivals that of many a legal scholar, though she has never been to law school.

Totenberg covers the court with something of a handicap: no recorders or cameras are allowed. That means no sound bites of passionate arguments from attorneys or probing questions from the justices. Totenberg compensates for the limitation with vividly written reports and a spirited delivery, her voice high-pitched, her lisp almost imperceptible, the effect brisk and authoritative. She essentially acts out the parts of the justices and the lawyers in a way that is both dramatic and fitting to the dignity of the court. There is no overt mimicry, yet her reportorial monologues successfully convey the range of emotions the justices display on the bench: surprise, amusement, defensiveness, anger, indignation. She told me that she wouldn't necessarily want to work with sound bites, even if she could. "I now have honed this way of doing it," she said. "If tape recorders were allowed, it would be much harder to deal with vast quantities of material and all the legal expressions, which make it a little bit impenetrable."

Totenberg's first big scoop came in 1987, when she reported that President Reagan's nominee to the Supreme Court, Douglas Ginsburg, had once used marijuana. With Reagan's war on drugs and "Just Say No" antidrug campaign in full swing, the story essentially forced Ginsburg to withdraw his nomination.

Then came Anita Hill.

It was 1991. Justice Thurgood Marshall, the first African American to sit on the U.S. Supreme Court, had announced his retirement. President George H. W. Bush nominated Clarence Thomas, a black conservative judge on the U.S. Court of Appeals for the District of Columbia. During the Senate judiciary committee hearings on his nomination, Totenberg saw manila envelopes "being delivered rather portentously" to committee members. Then she heard committee chair Joe Biden referring to "scurrilous allegations" against Thomas.

"And I thought, what scurrilous? There haven't been any scurrilous allegations in this hearing," Totenberg said. "At that point, it was all about ideology. And I thought, what is in that envelope?"

Totenberg discovered, through sources she told me she would never reveal, that the envelopes contained an affidavit by Anita Hill, a University of Oklahoma law professor, that alleged that Thomas had sexually harassed her while she was working for him at the U.S. Department of Education and the Equal Employment Opportunity Commission in the early 1980s.

Totenberg, once the object of sexual harassment herself, and *Newsday* reporter Timothy Phelps were the first to break the story. But Totenberg, as a woman, became a flash point for the political and emotional firestorm that exploded around the allegations. She was the first to interview Hill, who was initially reluctant to talk. She told Totenberg that she wouldn't talk about the allegations until Totenberg obtained the affidavit, which she then did.

Totenberg also had no qualms about pointing out, in a *Nightline* broadcast with committee members Republican Senator Alan Simpson of Wyoming and Democratic Senator Paul Simon of Illinois, that the Senate Judiciary Committee hadn't done its job by failing to investigate the charges. After the broadcast, Simpson followed her to a waiting ABC limousine and, holding the car door open to keep her from leaving, yelled at her for invading Anita Hill's privacy and ruining her life. "You're a fucking bully," she told him.

Remembering the incident during our interview, Totenberg at first spoke with some regret. "You never want to give your opponents ammunition," she said. "When you blow like that, you do." Then she paused. "In truth, in my inner self, I'm not the least bit sorry."

Later, she and Simpson made up nearly as famously as they'd fought. His daughter, Susan, introduced herself to Totenberg at a convention in New Orleans and offered to help her reconcile with her father. With Susan's support, Totenberg invited him to be her date at a White House radio and television correspondents' dinner.

"We were the bride and groom at that dinner, the cause célèbre, with our picture in the paper," she said. Ever since, the two have been good friends.

Among Totenberg's biggest champions during the Anita Hill story were the men in her life. Her father called her to say he was proud of her. Before the Hill story, her late husband, former Colorado senator Floyd Haskell, was "not a great husband for a journalist," always asking her why she wasn't home for dinner and whether her work "couldn't wait until tomorrow." But once she was on the trail of the scandal, he gave Totenberg his full support. "There was one time that he was selfless and that was Anita Hill," she said. "He was outraged by the fact that the Senate Judiciary Committee had not investigated this. He couldn't understand why the people he knew, Republicans, Democrats, liberal Democrats, didn't do this. And he just said to me, 'Go work. Do it. You don't have to go sailing, you don't have to do dinner, just do it. Go. Go, go.'"

Though she was only in her late forties when the story unfolded, she said it will likely forever define her journalistic legacy. "Well, I figure when I die, it doesn't matter that I've won every journalism award that there is to win for broadcasters, my obituary will say, 'National Public Radio correspondent Nina Totenberg, who broke the celebrated Anita Hill story,'" Totenberg said.

The story and the subsequent inconclusive Senate investigation into Phelps and Totenberg's sources turned her into a widely sought after journalist. Network television courted her. She did reporting work briefly for NBC and then joined ABC as a contributing correspondent for *Nightline* and a panelist on *Inside Washington*. Her punditry on *Inside Washington* has showcased her more fiery tendencies. When Senator Jesse Helms moved to cut AIDS funding in 1995, Totenberg quipped, "If there is retributive justice, he'll get AIDS from a transfusion, or one of his grandchildren will get it." She also came under fire in 2003 for saying that she hoped General William Boykin, a top intelligence official with the Defense Department who had been casting the war on terrorism in evangelical terms, was "not long for this world." She rushed to explain that she only meant she wished he'd be ousted from his job, but the remark still led NPR's ombudsman, Jeffrey Dvorkin, to suggest that NPR reporters may need to chose between "outside punditry and inside reporting." The suggestion never became policy, though, and Totenberg has stayed with *Inside Washington*. Other NPR correspondents, most prominently Juan Williams and Mara Liasson, also appear regularly as pundits on network television.

In 1994, Totenberg's husband, Floyd Haskell, was hospitalized after slipping on an icy sidewalk and hitting his head on the curb. He was not expected to live. At one point in the four years of hospitalizations that followed, Totenberg went to Oklahoma City to cover the bombing there, but when Haskell's health plunged, ABC chartered a plane to rush her to his side. "I cried all the way home because I thought he was going to die alone," she said. She arrived at the hospital to find that Haskell, though in critical condition, had held on and that Cokie Roberts was at his bedside keeping vigil until Totenberg's arrival.

Roberts and Linda Wertheimer used the power of the "Fallopian Jungle" to support Totenberg through Haskell's subsequent three brain operations and rehabilitation. They pestered the doctors with questions and didn't skimp on the follow-up. "Cokie went with me to the discharge appointment, when they told me what services he was entitled to," Totenberg remembered. "She took notes like Madame Defarge, and when they didn't deliver them, she'd say 'I have in my notes, you said you would have somebody coming to the house in the mornings for six weeks! And now it's four weeks and you're trying to cut it off!'"

Haskell's health never recovered. He died in 1998 of pneumonia in Totenberg's arms as she tried to get him back to Washington from Maine, where the couple was vacationing. Six years later, photographs of him still hang in her office, and she said she still feels his presence, in particular when she's in the Capitol Hill neighborhood where they used to live. When they married, almost twenty years before his death, she was, as she described it, "a very ambitious, insecure young woman" who told herself she could do anything. "But my inner self didn't believe it," she said. "He gave me the most enormous sense of being valued. He convinced the inner self. And by the time he died, you couldn't take that away from me. It was a gift that just doesn't go away."

Totenberg was remarried in 2000, to H. David Reines, a trauma surgeon and widower from Boston. Supreme Court Justice Ruth Bader Ginsburg, a long-time friend, officiated. Totenberg told me that Roberts and Wertheimer insisted on making her a chuppah, a traditional Jewish wedding canopy. "During the service, they were holding the chuppah, and it had begun to sag," she said, her eyes mirthful at the memory. "David is very tall, he's six four, so it drooped onto his head a little bit, and Ruth Ginsburg said in the ceremony, 'As we stand here, under the chuppah, the likes of which we will never see again'—!"

For the first two years of their relationship, Totenberg and Reines commuted between Washington and Boston. Then Reines moved to Washington to become the vice-chairman of surgery at Inova Fairfax Hospital. The two share a home in the Palisades area of northwest Washington. They spend as much time as possible together. She'll go to medical conferences with him and he'll go dress shopping with her—though, she added, he refuses to help her shop for shoes and pocketbooks because she's particularly picky about them and takes too long. "We do everything together, almost, that we can," Totenberg said. "I think both of us, having lost someone we love very much, know that sometimes there isn't a tomorrow, and so you just enjoy today together."

It has been three decades since Totenberg was hired at NPR, a place that, because it was too new to afford men, became an incubator for some of the best female journalism talent of our time. Totenberg has had many lucrative offers over the years to work full-time in television. She has turned them down because most of the better offers would have meant that she'd be stuck in a studio as an anchor, something that she knows, from the times she's been a substitute host at NPR, she doesn't like. "I don't like being stuck in the studio, not having any flexibility, being stuck doing the same thing every day, more or less," she said.

She also treasures NPR's commitment to news and its visibility, which has vastly increased since she started out with the network in those crowded cubicle days. "I have probably the best of all worlds here," she said. "No job is perfect. And no place is perfect. But for me, it works."

Linda Wertheimer
Senior National Correspondent, National Public Radio

When Linda Wertheimer was a young reporter covering Congress for NPR in the 1970s, she took her mother, who was visiting from New Mexico, to an interview with then–U.S. Senator Edmund Muskie. Wertheimer did what she would do in any political interview: she asked him tough questions. "I thought I had just been wonderful, and he left, and he was fine," Wertheimer, sixty-two, said. "It was just a normal reporter–senator interaction."

But her mother was horrified. "I did not bring you up to talk to people that way," she reprimanded, leaving her daughter speechless.

Indeed, girls growing up in Carlsbad, New Mexico, in the 1950s were not raised to challenge senators. They were raised to do as their mothers did: get married and have children, with perhaps a few years as a secretary or a schoolteacher, preferably in the same idyllic setting where they were born. Carlsbad, Wertheimer said, was a "perfect postwar spot for children," a mining and tourist town in the New Mexican desert, seventy miles from the Texas border. Veterans and their families flocked there from all over the country after World War II, causing the town to grow and thrive. Her father ran a grocery store and butcher shop, and the family enjoyed the healthy economy, good schools, and safe neighborhood streets teeming with children at play.

Wertheimer's mother modeled a proper and industrious life for Linda and her sister. She ran the Campfire Girls, made all her daughters' clothing, set high expectations for their schoolwork, and let them know when they weren't measuring up. Though she placed a high value on social graces, she was not afraid to challenge the status quo. When she learned from a black friend that administrators concealed the overcrowded conditions at Carlsbad's supposedly "separate but equal" school for blacks by sending busloads of children on a ride whenever school board members came to visit, Wertheimer's mother took the board on an unannounced visit. Their shock led them to integrate the schools even before the Supreme Court's *Brown v. Board of Education* ruling pushed the rest of the country to do the same. "My mother was entirely capable of being tough," Wertheimer said. "In some sense I guess she raised me to believe that there were lots of things that I could do and that if somebody got in my way I should get them out of my way."

But Wertheimer did not even begin to dream that the "things she could do" could include being a reporter until television reception came to Carlsbad in the mid–1950s. She watched, rapt, as Pauline Frederick, NBC's United Nations correspondent, reported on the Soviet invasion of Hungary. "I had never known that women did that kind of work, and that's when I decided that was the kind of work I wanted to do," Wertheimer said.

Wertheimer attended Wellesley College, graduating in 1965, the year after Cokie Roberts (though the two didn't know each other at school, Wertheimer remembered well who Cokie Boggs, from a famous political family, was). Wertheimer spent two years working for the BBC in London. When she returned to the United States, she applied for a job with NBC, but was told that "women are not credible on the air" and that she should become a researcher. She persevered, though, and became the first woman hired by WCBS radio in New York for a nonclerical position. In the photojournalism book *National Public Radio: The Cast of Characters,* Wertheimer said that she chose radio because she knew that a "flat-chested, brainy, dark" woman who rarely wore makeup would never make it in television.

She joined NPR at its inception in 1971. She directed the first broadcast of *All Things Considered* on May 3. Within months, she began reporting stories and was soon spending much of her time on Capitol Hill. By 1974, her main beat was Congress and politics, in time for the Watergate impeachment hearings. She was the first woman to anchor network coverage of election night in 1976. In 1979, she made history again as the host of the first-ever live broadcast of a debate from the Senate chamber during consideration of the Panama Canal treaty. She spent long months on the road, becoming one of the "boys on the bus" during four presidential and eight congressional campaigns.

Wertheimer was chosen to become a cohost of *All Things Considered* in 1989, joining Noah Adams and Robert Siegel in a new "rotating host" set-up. That meant that while two sat at the microphones, one could be on the road. Among the three, she had the reputation of being the "political" one, while Adams leaned toward stories of everyday Americans and Siegel, the network's cerebral "Renaissance man," took on the more intellectual fare.

Wertheimer took a studiousness and a strong historical memory from her years covering the Hill and national politics to the host's chair. While alienated voters were beginning to be drawn to the presidential campaign of Texas billionaire H. Ross Perot in 1992, Wertheimer got him on the air to ask him about an amendment offered in the House Ways and Means Committee in 1975 intended to help him and only him (though his name was not on the bill) get a $15 million tax break; she remembered the ploy because she was sitting in on the committee when the amendment was introduced. During the interview, he accused her of staging "a classic set-up," then asked,

"What is your show, anyhow?" When she told him she was with *All Things Considered,* he asked, "And is this a radio program? It's really a radio program? You're not just somebody calling in?"

"No, sir," she said, as polite as her southwestern, proper mama would have wanted her to be, but Perot had already done himself in.

Wertheimer's serious tone has also subjected her to some criticism and even teasing for sounding aloof. *A Prairie Home Companion* series of skits in 2001 featured Sue Scott playing an ultra-snobby "Linda Wertheimer," trying to get "John Knotwright," a correspondent in "Rillirillibad," to give his report. The two interrupt each other time and time again until Wertheimer chastises him, "Shut your mouth and listen and I'll ask you a question and when I do, you answer it."

Wertheimer is married to Fred Wertheimer, a long-time advocate of campaign finance reform. He headed Common Cause, a nonprofit government accountability watchdog organization, for many years, and he's now the president and founder of Democracy 21, which works to reduce the role of money in politics. His work has saddled her with a not-uncommon dilemma among Washington journalists: the suspicion that the politics or advocacy work of one spouse can taint the ability of the other spouse to be impartial. Wertheimer deals with the issue by staying away from campaign finance–related stories, but she doesn't let herself be daunted otherwise. "There are people who are so mad at Fred that they're spitting nails," she said. "But when they see me coming, they know that National Public Radio has millions of listeners, and not just millions of listeners but millions of listeners who are kind of the opinion forming class of people and people who vote, so they swallow hard and talk to me."

Wertheimer hosted *ATC,* as the show is known to NPR staffers, for thirteen years. Her tenure included the job of editing *Listening to America: Twenty-five Years in the Life of a Nation, as Heard on National Public Radio,* a collection of transcripts from the network put together for its silver anniversary. She was removed from the host chair in 2002 to become a senior national correspondent and substitute host.

The move was not her choice, and she told me that she thought NPR management "made a wrong decision, but they had the perfect right to make it." She said she still misses hosting. "It's like a pop quiz," she said. "You have to be a quick study and get up to speed on three or four different things every day, and it's very interesting to do that."

There are new pleasures in life away from the daily grind of hosting, though. She gets back much earlier in the evening to the 1915 Arts and Crafts–style home she and her husband remodeled in D.C.'s Cleveland Park neighborhood. That gives her more time to cook, one of her favorite hobbies (faithful listeners have probably guessed this much, from her occasional food stories—she's gone to the Zuni Cafe in San Francisco for a story on how to cook the perfect roast chicken, and to the Hershey chocolate factory in Pennsylvania to report on the creation of the white chocolate striped "Hug" to accompany the longtime favorite "Kiss" candies). And she has made a renewed commitment to the craft that made her name in radio in the first place: in-depth reporting, with a heavy dose of politics.

"I have enjoyed every minute of it," she said of her more than three decades at NPR. "It was a little hair-raising when I left *All Things Considered*, trying to figure out what the new life would be like, but even that has its advantages. You move on and do different things."

The Busiest Man in Public Radio: Steve Inskeep

Host, *Morning Edition*

I've been allowed to watch behind the scenes at a number of NPR news shows, and I have to tell you that, aside from the initial thrill of seeing the hosts in person, there usually isn't much to watch. On a typical day, a good 75 percent of the program has already been recorded, and, though the hosts must sit in the on-air studio in case of breaking news, there often isn't a hell of a lot for them to do. After the rush of putting the show together, the actual broadcast can feel like downtime. Hosts occasionally go on the air live to introduce news reports and interviews. Otherwise, they've been known to while away the time by reading the newspaper, playing solitaire, knitting, or Instant Messaging with their spouses.

But Steve Inskeep, a cohost of *Morning Edition*, isn't much for downtime. The morning I observed him was not a particularly peppy news day: the Bush administration was floating ideas for a new foreign guest worker program, several countries in Europe were starting to put more pressure on Iran to curtail its nuclear program, the governor of California wanted another round of special elections, and there were updates on Social Security reform and the insurgency in Iraq.

Only one live interview was planned, with a *Washington Post* reporter in Iran, and that wasn't until the second hour of the show.

Inskeep was busy anyway, revising the morning's script, a telephone receiver between his chin and a shrugged up shoulder as he talked to his editor out at the news desk, an insulated aluminum coffee cup beside him. He typed rapidly, his eyes peering down at the computer monitor, which was set under a glass pane in the studio table so as not to block hosts from seeing guests or cues from producers in the adjacent control room. When he wasn't typing, he flicked his pen quickly back and forth between his index and middle fingers. Inskeep has brown sideburns and wore a casual blazer, glasses, black penny loafers, and a blue oxford shirt without a tie, the kind of outfit favored by foreign correspondents on television.

When it was nearly time for Inskeep to announce the next report, he hung up the telephone and folded his hands together on the table, as if to rein himself in and focus. The on-air light went on. "It's looking more likely that California governor Arnold Schwarzenegger will call a special election this fall," he began calmly, nodding his head slightly at points of emphasis. He has one of the more classic broadcasting voices on NPR, without a trace of any kind of regional accent. Inskeep is from the Midwest, proof of the old broadcasting wisdom that great American voices often come from the country's midsection, where speech is plain and pure and whatever little local accents there might be are much more easily shed than Southern drawls or the sticky, tough-guy inflections of the Northeast.

It was 5:15 a.m. Inskeep had already been up for three hours. And he was surrounded by a staff with similar schedules. Some have been at the news desk all night. Jokes flew about using crack cocaine to stay awake and the lack of a social life outside work. One woman, dressed in Birkenstock sandals and a baseball cap, carried the largest go cup I'd ever seen, the words "Extreme Gulp" emblazoned on the side. It was as big around as a salad plate.

Two hours later, the first broadcast of *Morning Edition* was finished and the show was in its first "rollover," essentially a repeat, with any necessary updates done as needed along the way. The program will re-air three and a half times to cover the morning hours in several time zones. There were no updates to do right away, which made this an opportune time to kick back for a moment, but Inskeep was unhappy with the interview on social security reform that had aired in the second hour. He thought it wasn't as clear as it should have been, so he spent the next forty-five minutes in an editing booth with a producer, going through sections of the original interview that had been cut out, trying to find a passage or two that would make the conversation work better in the next rollover.

Inskeep has always been driven, from his twenties in New York City, where he piled freelance work for NPR on top of his jobs at public radio affiliates and occasional anchor work in commercial radio. I remember hearing another public radio freelancer at the time mutter enviously, "Steve Inskeep, the busiest man in radio." At thirty-seven, Inskeep has been with NPR ten years and has risen to a plum position (except, of course, for the hours), hosting the most listened to morning radio show in the country. He and cohost Renée Montagne, who is based at NPR's studios in Culver City, California, are central figures in NPR's effort to revitalize *Morning Edition* in the wake of the controversial removal of long-time host Bob Edwards, a change that generated tens of thousands of protest emails from listeners.

Transforming *Morning Edition* is a role Inskeep embraces enthusiastically, while giving diplomatic nods to the accomplishments of his predecessor. He told me that he and Montagne would be going out on reporting assignments more often, and everyone on staff was working on doing a better job of staying on top of breaking news, being more relevant to more listeners, and taking on controversial sources and ideas. "It's a huge challenge, an opportunity to very gradually remake an entire program," he said. "And I say very gradually because it was great before, everyone loved it before. But it can be different. It can get better."

Inskeep has covered the U.S. Senate and airplane crashes. He has gone to Ohio to knock on doors, David Broder–style, in search of voters with interesting things to say about the neck-and-neck 2004 presidential campaign. He has interviewed Cyndi Lauper and Macy Gray and reported on the booming rat population in Washington. He's been the recipient of a Pew Fellowship in International Journalism and a National Headliner award. He's been to war zones in some of the most dangerous places in the world: Colombia, Afghanistan, and Iraq. All this makes him seem like an uber newsman, tireless and fearless and perfectionistic, but he also has a little mischievous streak. He's serious about his work, but he doesn't always want to be serious about himself or the protocols of his profession. He said when he was growing up, he wanted to be Dennis Miller, doing the *Weekend Update* segment on *Saturday Night Live.* When he was a sports announcer at his college radio station, he got kicked off the air a few times for making wisecracks. He's also a huge fan of Jon Stewart and *The Daily Show.* "It's a fake newscast disguised as a real newscast, which is why it's funny," he said. "Part of the reason is because the real newscast is frequently an anchorman saying the most ridiculous things imaginable, except they don't get that they're ridiculous."

Inskeep said that Miller and Stewart inspire him to try to find "subtle ways to be a little subversive," to look behind the paradigm of what the news is supposed to be and sound like and seek something "more genuine and real." On the business segment of that morning's program, for example, he spoke with Ken Lloyd, an expert on how to handle difficult bosses and other bullies in the workplace. At the end of the interview, Inskeep asked him who *his* boss was. My wife, Lloyd sheepishly replied, and then went on to call her a great manager who is "communicative, responsive, and treats people with respect and trust."

"Are you kissing up?" Inskeep asked slyly.

"I kiss her and I kiss up," the guest said.

A moment like that might not be quite as subversive as Jon Stewart mocking the Bush administration's environmental policies, but it is a bit of a breakthrough in the typically somber tone of *Morning Edition*. Inskeep said it can be hard to slip a little levity into the show. His interviews go through as many as five editorial hands before broadcast. "Anything you do that you think is funny at least one of the five people might not, so that's a really high bar," he said.

One early sign of Inskeep's mischievousness—and his future in radio—emerged when he was a small boy, watching his older brother and father, the athletic director at the local high school, play hoops in the backyard of the family's home in Carmel, Indiana. Inskeep hopped up on a piece of playground equipment that overlooked the concrete court and started calling the play-by-play of the game. "It really annoyed the hell out of them!" he remembered. "But maybe that was my first broadcast."

As a teenager, he became the announcer for the Carmel High School football games and spun records for the school's radio station. He attended Morehead State University in Kentucky with a major in history and communications and worked as a sports announcer at WMKY, the university's NPR affiliate. He also covered high school sports games for a local commercial radio station for ten dollars a night, a gig that took him to crowded gymnasiums in little towns around eastern Kentucky. Though he guessed he probably had "like eight listeners" on the radio, doing the games gave Inskeep practice in one of the most crucial skills of radio reporting: putting what he saw into words to "cause someone to see it who can't see it," he said.

Until college, Inskeep hadn't been exposed to much of the world beyond his conservative Republican family and like-minded suburban community, where, he said, "it makes perfect sense that you would wonder what do you need the government to do here and why am I paying all these damn taxes?" At Morehead State, he went to school with the sons and daughters of eastern Kentucky coal miners. "I had a roommate whose father had died of black lung when my roommate was twelve, and whose mother lived in a trailer behind the Pentecostal church that she swept up to earn a little extra money," he said. "You get a different perspective on this country."

In his junior year, he went to New York City to study at Hunter College, "a kind of foreign exchange thing for someone from the Midwest," he said. He interned at WBAI, a left-wing community radio station that was ideologically about as far as he could get from his upbringing. His mentor was Amy Goodman, then the station's news director and these days the provocative host of the syndicated progressive news show *Democracy Now*. She sent him out to cover protests, evictions, even campaign events for the Ed Koch/David Dinkins mayoral race. Inskeep resisted letting the station's politics exert too much of an influence on his reporting. He remembered covering a press conference by a group contending that there were prisoners being held in U.S. jails solely for their political biases. Inskeep didn't see any evidence of this, and he told Goodman, who let him write the story as he saw it.

After graduating from college, Inskeep returned to New York. He freelanced for NPR and worked at WFUV and WBGO in Newark, New Jersey, where he was the local announcer for *Morning Edition* for four years. He started working full-time as a reporter for NPR in 1996, when he was twenty-eight. He was the host of the weekend version of *All Things Considered* from 2002 to 2004, when he got the *Morning Edition* job.

Inskeep told me that the controversy over Edwards's departure "hasn't really touched" him. He was reporting from Iraq when he was asked to become the host and didn't realize the depth of listener chagrin until he returned. But he said he feels listeners are judging the changes in *Morning Edition* on their own terms. "I really haven't heard from many people at all who have said, 'I hate what you're doing because you're not Bob,'" he said. "There have been people who have said, 'I miss Bob, but I like what you're doing.'"

Inskeep is married to his college sweetheart, Carolee, the author of *The Graveyard Shift: A Family Historian's Guide to New York City Cemeteries* and other reference books on genealogy. The two share a love of history and live in an 1889 home they renovated in Shaw, a historic, traditionally African American neighborhood of Washington, D.C., where Duke Ellington grew up and started his musical career. The couple have a daughter, Ava, born in January 2005. When Inskeep and I spoke, she was three and a half months old. He rhapsodized about her latest coos and smiles, how she'd reached out for a stuffed bunny for the first time the day before. "And what about the sleep, with your schedule?" I asked, remembering the middle-of-the-night cries of my own daughter at that age. That's worked out fine, he said. Ava was already sleeping up to seven hours at a stretch—and on her daddy's schedule. "She goes down at seven, around the same time I do!" he laughed.

Photographs of Ava and Carolee were tacked on the bulletin board in Inskeep's corner office on the second floor of NPR, along with a few postcards from listeners and guests. There was one from writer and public radio monologist David Sedaris, thanking Inskeep for a recent interview and remarking, "I think I sounded as if I were sucking on a bong, which I wasn't, *really*." Three neat stacks of mail and research materials sat on his desk, and a few books—*Inside Centcom, A Spy's Journey*, and one about biological weapons—were piled on an Oriental rug from a Middle Eastern reporting trip. The bookshelves and a long table against the back wall were empty, though, and the walls were bare, except for a couple of award plaques.

Even though Inskeep had been hosting *Morning Edition* for more than a year, his office looked as if he had just started to move in. When I first gave the room a glance earlier that morning, I actually thought for a moment that it was being left vacant, as a testament to the years Bob Edwards had worked there, an unspoken acknowledgment of the controversy that surrounded his departure. I couldn't help thinking about interviewing Edwards in that same office, a few months before his departure, a time when he thought he'd be hosting *Morning Edition* until he retired. Then, the office had the shrine-like, lived-in feeling of a man who'd been working there for more than a decade (though Edwards hosted *Morning Edition* for nearly twenty-five years, NPR moved into its current offices on Massachusetts Avenue in 1994). The shelves were packed with books from years of author interviews. The walls were covered with mementos, awards, and photographs of his family and the subjects of his two books: legendary sportscaster Red Barber and broadcast journalist Edward R. Murrow. There was a goosenecked, banker-style desk lamp that looked like Edwards had brought it from home. The office then felt like a legacy. Now the place looked like a beginning, unsettled, a history yet to be made.

Nocturnal Optimist:
Renée Montagne

Host, *Morning Edition*

There **was a** time when Renée Montagne was too restless to be happy hosting the news.

In 1987, after years of working as a freelance reporter in New York City and South Africa, she became the cohost of *All Things Considered*. She loved working with Robert Siegel and the show's staff, which then included Melissa Block, who now hosts the show, and Ira Glass, creator and host of *This American Life*. But Montagne didn't like being stuck in a studio all day doing interviews, most of them with guests connected to NPR through live-quality telephone lines or satellite connections.

"I was like, this is my life?" said Montagne. "I never meet anyone, I never see them, I never make eye contact."

Now, more than fifteen years later, she is back in the host's seat, this time on *Morning Edition*. Things are different this time around. The job is designed so she and cohost Steve Inskeep, another veteran reporter, can go out regularly on reporting assignments. And Montagne's feelings about doing studio interviews have shifted. She told me she feels more connected to her invisible guests, that interviewing them that way is often more interesting than seeing them face-to-face.

Interestingly, she is an invisible host, not only to her guests, but also to her colleagues at NPR. NPR's hub is in Washington, D.C., and she hosts from the network's studio in Culver City, California. She and Inskeep rarely see each other, though sometimes engineers in Washington put a photograph of her up in the on-air studio, as a tongue-in-cheek reminder of her presence.

"I feel like when I hear guests in my ears, it's like a phone call," she said. "You know how in a phone call, you can feel like they're right there? It's one of the reasons the technology of the videophone has never been pushed and never caught on. We don't want it!"

I understood what she meant, because I was talking to *her* on the phone. And at times the conversation felt surprisingly cozy, like I was talking to an old college friend. It was 12:30 p.m. Pacific time and she had just put in a twelve-hour day. She told me she was sitting in her living room with her door open, enjoying the beautiful spring breezes, feeling as if she'd just had a glass of wine, although, she hastened to add, she had not in fact just had a glass of wine. Montagne's manner is bubbly and effusive, making her sound far younger than her fifty-six years. She speaks fast, her stories full of little digressions and retakes. She'll interrupt one flow of thought with another in her eagerness to get all the details in and express what she wants to say more effectively. The experience of interviewing her was like reading the edited manuscript of a great short story, full of cross outs and notes scribbled in between the lines and down the margins.

Montagne's life story is one of adventurousness and determined optimism. All her life, she has taken things that for most people would be burdens and found ways to relish them. Like moving around so much as a child that she attended thirteen different schools before graduating. Like being on assignment in apartheid South Africa without a housing allowance. Like a workday that starts at 11 p.m.

Montagne's great-grandparents were pioneers who crossed through the prairies of the country's midsection in a covered wagon and began homesteading in Hay Springs, a tiny town in northwest Nebraska. Her mother grew up on a farm on that same homestead, inheriting her ancestors' spirit of adventure. She fantasized about becoming Amelia Earhart and learned how to pilot a plane while working on a military base in Colorado during World War II. Montagne's father was a major in the Marines. The two had three children, with Renée in the middle, and lived a peripatetic military family's existence, moving from base to base.

Montagne was always very close to her father, whom she called a "real feminist" who never questioned that she would have a career. "I would ask him a question about something, and we'd sit up until one in the morning talking about it," she said. "And he knew everything. I mean he knew—not everything, but he knew a lot about the world and knew things with great detail and he was pretty much always right, as best as I've been able to tell."

Her father retired from the Marines when Renée was eight, but he was a civil and aerospace engineer, and the family kept moving, mostly in Hawaii and Arizona, in pursuit of new contracts. Her mother liked to move, Montagne said, and even when her father's job didn't change, the family would move to a more comfortable house, or one that was closer to the beach, in search of something better than what they had before. Montagne said she liked the lifestyle, too. "I made friends easily, so I never felt weird when I moved into a new classroom," she said. "You know, hi! Here I am!"

She didn't listen to the radio much when she was a kid. She didn't even have a decent one, just a "little transistor radio you carry to the pool or the beach." She was good at writing, but she also excelled at science and math and had a vague idea that she might like to be a doctor.

While she was an undergraduate at the University of California–Berkeley in the early 1970s, she befriended two poets, both of whom would go on to successful writing careers: Ntozake Shange, author of the Broadway play *For Colored Girls Who Have Considered Suicide/When the Rainbow Is Enuf*, and Jessica Hagedorn, author of *Dogeaters* and novels, plays, and poetry about the Filipino American experience. The women had radio shows on KPOO, known as "Poor People's Radio," a noncommercial station in San Francisco, run mainly by volunteers. Montagne got a radio license so she could engineer Shange's show of arty music, called *The Original Aboriginal Dancing Girl*.

KPOO, Montagne said, was called a "third world" radio station, run by and for, in the language of the day, "people of color." "I was the odd man out, not being black or brown or Asian," she said. Station members suggested she start a news department, so she started calling herself the news director and hosted a show called "Women's Voices."

"Thank God none of it is on tape, none of it," she said. "But I sort of taught myself how to talk to people, and it was just a game. There were people there getting serious, going to journalism school. And I was just trying to do something fun and creative."

She started selling freelance pieces to the Pacific News Service, which distributed the work to radio affiliates across the country. On the urging of Hagedorn, who was working on a play at the Public Theater, Montagne moved to New York in 1980. There, she began filing news reports for NPR, which was then paying thirty dollars a story. "I still wouldn't have called myself a journalist," she said. "But within a month, I had more work than I could dig myself out of. I learned on the air."

As a freelancer, she worked without a producer, sound engineer, and the security of a full-time job. She never turned down work and rarely took time off, making a reputation for herself as an "I'll do anything" type. Her scrappiness, she found, helped her reporting stand out. On trips to South Africa in the mid-1980s to cover the growing antiapartheid movement, she didn't have a housing allowance, so she couldn't afford to live in the elite white neighborhoods of Johannesburg like the other foreign correspondents did. Instead, she lived in one of the "gray areas" of the era, mixed-race zones that defied apartheid's segregation laws and attracted many activists. The friends she made in her neighborhood gave her insight into how people's lives were changing as the movement gathered force. She shunned the groups of foreign correspondents who traveled together for protection. She drove her rented 1976 Volkswagen station wagon to the townships by herself, relying on locals she met along the way to help her find where she needed to go and with whom to talk. "It was intense and dangerous stuff," she said. "But I always had the theory that I was always better off to go alone. And that I would be protected, basically."

The independence and self-reliance she cultivated as a freelancer is still a part of her work ethic today. "I really got used to the idea that a story belonged to me, and I expect to have a hand in shaping it," she said. Many days, after she gets home from a twelve-hour workday, she'll call the office to get a producer to play back a piece she'd been working on to make sure she was happy with it.

After her two-year stint in Washington hosting *All Things Considered*, Montagne went on several more reporting trips to South Africa to cover Nelson Mandela's release from prison and the country's first postapartheid presidential and parliamentary elections. At home, she worked as a correspondent and substitute host. She and Steve Inskeep were picked to cohost *Morning Edition* in 2004, succeeding long-time host Bob Edwards. The odd *Morning Edition* work schedule has always been a source of fascination among listeners and the media; Edwards would often be asked to talk about how he'd rise at 1 a.m. and be at his desk by 2:15. Inskeep, based in Washington, keeps a similar schedule, but Montagne's life is even more nocturnal. She hosts the show from NPR's studios in Culver City, California, a set-up intended to provide the hosts with more opportunities to book interviews from different locations. She arrives at work at 11 p.m. to prepare for the show, which runs from 2 a.m. until 4 a.m. Pacific time. "I do the whole show in the dark," she said. "I'm really quite the vampire now." She sticks around to do any necessary updates on the show's "rollovers," as they're called, rebroadcasts that keep the show running through the morning hours in time zones across the United States.

She usually doesn't leave the office until 11 a.m. or later. After work, she takes long bicycle rides on the beach and gardens. She goes to bed at the bizarre hour of three in the afternoon. The schedule, she said, means she has no social life Sunday through Thursday. "I'm a little jet-lagged all the time," she said. "It's kind of a pleasant feeling, you know how when you're jet-lagged? You don't want to engage too much."

Home for Montagne is an eighty-year-old beach cottage, two blocks from the Pacific Ocean, in Santa Monica. The cottage shares a courtyard with four other similar homes. Her next-door neighbor is Patricia Neighmond, NPR's health policy correspondent, a good friend. Montagne is also close with the other residents there, and they cultivate a somewhat communal environment, keeping their doors open to each other and sharing a garden.

She is single and lives alone. She mused to me that she's so involved in her work that she "hasn't really noticed" that she's not married. "I've never experienced a sense of loneliness," she said. "People talk about that, being lonely, and I just don't even know what that means. I sort of love it, sitting here alone."

She speculated that the very job that keeps her away from the normal rhythms of society five days out of the week is what's kept her from feeling lonely. "It's being always out there in the thick of things, talking to people, finding out their stories," she said. "I like nothing more than doing that. So when I'm alone, physically alone, boy it's nice, a moment of calm."

Troubadour:
Scott Simon

Host, *Weekend Edition*

For the third time during my interview with Scott Simon, he is on the telephone with his wife. He is not being rude. A close friend's father has died, and they are discussing what to send to the family, whom to call, when the funeral is, and the impossibility of attending, as they are about to leave for London. He is treating the matter with the proper seriousness, but in his brief conversations with Caroline (pronounced the way of her native France, rhyming with "sheen"), there is the unmistakable sense of his pleasure in having yet another opportunity to communicate with her. He calls her angel, he calls her darling. He huddles with the telephone receiver, his back turned to me, though he has assured me I don't need to leave. Now he is saying goodbye again, using his pet name for her, the French word for "little pickle," their personal twist on *petit champignon*, a common French endearment that translates as "little mushroom."

"I love you, *cornichon*," he says. "Bye bye."

If Robert Siegel is public radio's Renaissance man, Scott Simon is its troubadour, its romantic. His voice has a sexy schmaltziness with a

generous emotional range, moving easily from straitlaced anchorman
to melancholy to good-old-boy sportiness to comic merriment in the
course of his program, *Weekend Edition Saturday*. He has roamed all
over the world, reporting stories with disarmingly vivid descriptions
and a rare sense of empathy from the Middle East, Africa, India,
Afghanistan, Sarajevo, and Kosovo. He's won every major award in
broadcasting, including a Peabody and an Emmy. He is spiritual, a
practicing Quaker since he was a teenager. He has volunteered for
Mother Teresa. He dresses in dapper clothes and is given to wearing
matching red pocket handkerchiefs and socks. He is passionate about
cats and ballet and Mexican cooking and sports. He used the word
"dulcet" four times in our interview.

He is also very handsome. I remember when a book of photographs
of NPR personalities was published in the early 1990s. At the pledge
drives I worked on at radio stations in Iowa and later Pittsburgh, female
volunteers would look through the book and linger admiringly on the
photograph of Simon. He's also long had a gay male following, accom-
panied by the occasional rumor that he is gay. When Simon told a gay
producer on *Weekend Edition* that he was getting married, the producer teased, "Oh my god, you're about to be outed as a heterosexual!"

Now Simon, known as "Scooter" or "Scotty" to NPR colleagues and
close friends, is fifty-three, with salt-and-pepper hair and a slightly
thickening middle, but he is still striking, with deep Celtic jowls and
moony, expressive brown eyes, framed with girlishly long lashes. Like
any good husband (and radio host, working in a medium where looks
are not supposed to matter), he is modest, though not displeased, about
the admiration. "I'm only conscious of it when people kid me," he said.

Simon was born in 1952 to, as he describes in his memoir, *Home and
Away: Memoir of a Fan,* "the funniest man and the most beautiful
woman in Chicago." His father, Ernie Simon, was a Jewish comedian.
His mother, Patricia Lyons, was an Irish Catholic actress whom Scott has
described as looking a little like Grace Kelly. The family moved to San

Francisco, then to Cleveland (where his father was for a short while a field announcer for the Cleveland Indians), and then back to Chicago. His father struggled with alcoholism and career setbacks, and his parents split up when Simon was six. They remained friends, though, and Simon has described his relationship with both of them as warm and loving. Simon and his mother would quip snatches of dialogue from *Our Town* at each other; she'd play the winsome Emily, he the Stage Manager. He and his father shared a love for good jokes and comic books and the Chicago White Sox. "My father had a great capacity to be a mimic, and have fun, and to make me laugh," Simon said. He also became very close to his stepfather, Ralph Newman, an internationally recognized bookseller, appraiser, Lincoln scholar, and former minor league baseball player. He made headlines in Chicago during the Watergate investigation, when he was fined for preparing a false affidavit that helped Nixon get an illegal tax break.

But it seems that the influence of Ernie Simon, who died when Scott was sixteen, is still the most prominent. On the day of our interview, Scott wore an old suit jacket of his father's, with a patch from his service in the British Army in North Africa. And Simon, like his dad, is a cutup. During that morning's broadcast of *Weekend Edition,* Simon sat in the studio and fake-talked along with a pretaped interview, his mouth opening and closing in an exaggerated fashion and his arms gesticulating widely, like a ventriloquist's dummy. He once gave a powerful Afghanistan warlord a reporter's notebook from the National Lesbian Gay Journalists Association with the slogan: "We're Here, We're Queer, We're on Deadline." The warlord, of course, couldn't read English and was delighted to have an American souvenir of any sort. "I can just imagine someone from the Royal Marines running into him and saying, 'This is not what I expected!'" Simon yelped in a mock British accent.

After his father's death, Simon got involved in the antiwar demonstrations at the 1968 Democratic convention in Chicago. He became a self-described "hippie" and "freak" who wrote for an underground newspaper and managed a city council campaign before he even graduated from high school (the candidate, a progressive Pentecostal minister, came in last in a field of four). He attended McGill University in Montreal and the University of Chicago but never finished his bachelor's degree. As a young journalist, he wrote for alternative newspapers in Chicago and worked as a reporter at public television station WTTW, where he reported on crime, sports, and local politics in the last years of the infamously ironfisted mayoral tenure of Richard J. Daley.

Simon began to freelance for NPR in 1976. He filed a number of significant pieces for the network on the death of Mayor Daley, and the following year he was asked to be a staff reporter. He became Chicago's first bureau chief for NPR in 1977 and made his mark as an innovative reporter with a story on an American Nazi Party rally in Chicago's Marquette Park. Instead of filing the standard demonstration piece, with quick, noisy sound bites of the chanting of protesters and counterprotesters, Simon revealed what went on at the fringes: the man who lived next to the park who "wanted to keep the park white" but planned to garden throughout the demonstration; a protester who'd slipped out of police custody to swim across the park's lagoon to cheers of both Nazi supporters and counterdemonstrators; the black news photographer who had to do his job surrounded by police protectors. In later stories, Simon developed a reputation for capturing the "elements of an event you're really not supposed to hear," as Susan Stamberg once described it, such as the sounds of an engineer testing the microphone before the beginning of a speech.

Weekend Edition Saturday was launched in 1986, conceived by Simon, then–executive producer Jay Kernis (now NPR's senior vice president for programming), and Robert Siegel, at the time NPR's news director and now the host of *All Things Considered*. Siegel said he wanted a program that would be driven by Simon's curiosity and colorful on-air presence, "a program that was going to be the best thing we've done yet, a program that was about Scott Simon almost in the way that *A Prairie Home Companion* was about Garrison Keillor."

The show was originally supposed to be broadcast out of Chicago, with a distinctly local flavor, in a pointed effort to prove that NPR's sensibilities could extend outside the Washington Beltway. Though technical difficulties kept the show based in D.C., the idea that Simon's personality and creativity would define the show remained. He has delivered an on-air obituary for his cat and given dramatic readings of children's books with author Daniel Pinkwater. He has sorrowfully related the words of a fifteen-year-old Albanian girl who, in the aftermath of the Serbian siege and the NATO bombings in Kosovo, told him, "We have had to put some things away in boxes in our minds, and we never want to open them up." He's developed an intimate camaraderie with several regular guests on the show, including sports commentator Ron Rapoport, who's always introduced with an over-the-top, high school marching band–style rendition of the *Weekend Edition* theme music; "doyenne of dirt" gardening expert Ketzel Levine; and *The Annoying Music Show* host Jim Nader, who plays the Jingle Cats meowing "Kitties We Have Heard on High" and William Shatner's self-mocking novelty songs. There's also, of course, Dan Schorr, who comes on live every Saturday morning to review the week's news with Simon. The two share a father-son rapport. Simon occasionally teases Schorr, nudging him out of his normally somber demeanor.

Simon left *Weekend Edition* in 1992 to host *Weekend Today* on NBC, which had been pitched to him as a televised version of what he'd been doing all along in public radio. But television wasn't a good fit. Simon looked uncomfortable on camera and asked long, complicated questions. After the show's debut, *Washington Post* television critic Tom Shales pronounced that it "reeks." Off camera, Simon tried to change things, pushing harder-hitting editorial content, yet ending up with ever-lighter fare, including an infamous segment with the program's "gadget guru," with a backdrop featuring a giant Lucite toilet. Simon was off the air two months before his first-year contract expired.

He was welcomed back heartily at NPR. Before he returned to the host chair on *Weekend Edition*, he was assigned to cover the war in Bosnia. There was something particularly impassioned about his reporting from Sarajevo, his stories intense creations of a man who'd been held back for a year from doing what he loved: in-depth, meaningful journalism. He filed a haunting and memorable story for *All Things Considered* that summer profiling Irena Millic, a girl of Bosnia-Muslim descent two weeks shy of her sixteenth birthday. He described her sardonic love of Phil Collins's song "Just Another Day in Paradise," her desire to see Los Angeles, her flirtations with French soldiers. He followed her around as she roamed through war-torn Sarajevo. Twice, sniper fire interrupted their interview. The second time, Irena refused to duck down, explaining that she didn't "give a damn shit about her life." Simon pleaded with her, then chastised her, for her nihilism: "I admire you," he said, "But that's the dumbest thing I've heard you say."

Simon's experience in Bosnia had a profound effect on him. Though a lifelong Quaker, he witnessed the limits of pacifism there. After the September 11 terrorist attacks nearly a decade later, his experience in the Balkans led him to publicly support the war on terrorism in Afghanistan. "In Sarajevo, Srebrenica and Kosovo, I confronted the logical flaw (or perhaps I should say the fatal flaw) of nonviolent resistance: All the best people can be killed by all the worst ones," he wrote in an op-ed piece for the *Wall Street Journal*. It is unusual in these times for a news host to make his opinions known, but NPR has always made a space for Simon's reflections, political or otherwise, in a short essay segment on *Weekend Edition*, where he has opined on matters as benign as love letters and as controversial as gay rights and the lyrics of Eminem.

Irena, who became his translator in Bosnia and has remained a close friend, is the inspiration for the protagonist of the same name in

Simon's novel *Pretty Birds,* published by Random House in 2005. It is Simon's third book; in addition to his memoir, he is also the author of *Jackie Robinson and the Integration of Baseball,* published in 2002. But *Pretty Birds* was Simon's first work of fiction. He insisted on taking full advantage of his first foray into the form, resisting the suggestion of one prospective publisher to put a journalist in the story.

"I said, 'Look, I know what you're thinking of here, an American or English journalist, probably a man, early thirties, meets a dulcet Sarajevan beauty.' And she said, 'Yeah, yeah, that's exactly what we had in mind!'" he said.

But he wanted to explore the characters of the novel in ways that he could not as a reporter, so he refused to edge the story closer to real life. "I always know that no matter how intimate a [radio] piece sounds, or how deeply we think we've gone into somebody's soul, or circumstance, that we can only go so far, that there's a part that they keep in reserve, that's private, that we don't touch, no matter how well we know them, no matter how close we get," he said. "And that's the part I wanted to approach in this book."

Simon did not meet the woman who would become his wife, Caroline Richard, until he was forty-eight. Richard, who is sixteen years his junior, had been an intern on *Weekend Edition,* but it was during the summer he was in Sarajevo, so their paths didn't cross. They met seven years later, at a party thrown by NPR reporter Jacki Lyden, a close friend of Simon's. On his way out of the taxi in front of Lyden's apartment, he hit his head on the door and spent the party with a cold compress on his head. Simon and Richard hit it off regardless. They were married that September, less than five months later. Richard wore a chartreuse dress, a tribute to her "little pickle" nickname. "I'm afraid the joke really has stuck," he said. "She now has *cornichon* stationery, a nice dulcet green, with *cornichon* embossed on the top in gold letters.

Simon told me that before meeting Caroline he was sometimes asked, as long-time bachelors are, why he never married. He used to blame it on his job, with the travel and the weekend schedule and the energy he invested into it. Now, he sees his past differently. "I really believe that I didn't get married until I did because I hadn't met Caroline," he said.

In 2004, the couple adopted a baby girl, Elise Sylvie Simon, from China. I had spoken with Simon as he was in the planning stages of the adoption and asked him how he felt about impending fatherhood, given the struggles he witnessed in the lives of his father and stepfather. "I think it can make a child wiser, to know that your father might be a wise person, but wise people can sometimes give unwise advise, or wise people are human and they get short-tempered and they get petulant and they get put out and they get scared and they will make mistakes because of these things," he said.

But before these challenges, he found laughter, and a love more abiding than romance. In a *Weekend Edition* essay that aired shortly after he and his wife brought Elise home, he played a sound bite of the child's Jerry Lewis–like giggle. "My wife and I were happy before we met our child," he intoned. "But now we feel we're just beginning to grasp the hugeness of happiness that's possible. Children wire you into the world through veins and chambers of your heart that seem to sprout as you hold them."

Sunday Morning Devotion: Liane Hansen

Host, *Weekend Edition Sunday*

Weekend Edition Sunday was created to be like the Sunday newspaper: less hard news, more think pieces, more arts and entertainment, something to be enjoyed in a leisurely manner. Liane Hansen has an ideal presence for the concept. She speaks with an inviting warmth, creating a space of calm, a Sabbath feeling. In person, her manner is kind and forthright. She wears neutral beiges and blacks. Her shoulders are broad, her cheeks slightly ruddy, her face long and thoughtful.

There is another side to Hansen, though, as listeners are well aware. Every Sunday morning, Will Shortz, the puzzle editor of the *New York Times,* gives the weekly puzzle to a listener. Hansen, fifty-four, plays along. She starts out soothingly as ever, making sure the listener is ready to play, but once the puzzle starts, she shifts from self-possessed host to bubbly co-contestant as she and the listener respond to the clues. The puzzler I observed being recorded (the segment is taped in advance) was called BRRR, in honor of the freezing January weather. Every answer was a two-word phrase or name in which the first word starts with "br" and the second words starts with "r."

Shortz gave the first clue. "In a contest that has no actual prize, this is what you're said to win."

The contestant, a retiree on the telephone from Middletown, New Jersey, was silent. Hansen cackled briefly and murmured, "B. R. Brrr," as if testing different phrases in her mind. Then she started to sputter. "Oh, op-bragging rights!" she shouted, a different woman entirely from the one who, earlier that day, had been discussing intelligence problems in the war in Iraq with journalist Kenneth Pollack.

"Yes, bragging rights," Shortz said. "Good job!"

Hansen beamed. The puzzle continued on, the contestant getting a few answers right away, Hansen taking over when his silence dragged on too long, preventing too much dead air. At the end, she complimented him: "Puzzles are your thing, huh?"

"Thank you for the help," he said, a little sheepishly. She told him he won a *Weekend Edition* lapel pin, a Merriam-Webster's collegiate dictionary and thesaurus, a Scrabble set, and a couple of word game books Shortz edited. It was a version of the prize every puzzle player wins, no matter how well or how poorly contestants perform. For all its erudite clues, the puzzle typically ends up feeling like a version of kids' softball where no one's supposed to be keeping score and everyone's a winner. Hansen, of course, is the enthusiastic mom volunteer coach who can't help but pick up the bat every inning or so to keep the bases moving.

Hansen's first passion was the theater. After studying for two years at the University of Hartford, her parents ran out of money to pay for college, so she ended up back home in Worcester, Massachusetts, acting in a children's theater company and the Entr'Actors Guild. She worked as a secretary for the theater department at Holy Cross College, where she also scored quite a few stage roles. "It was an all boys' school, so it was easy to get parts," she laughed during our interview in her office, an obstacle course of mail bins full of books and CDs.

She followed a boyfriend to the State University of New York–Binghamton, where she joined a community theater group and held down a day job as the secretary for the local public television station, WSKG, which had just started a sister radio station. The woman who'd been hired to host the morning radio show, *For Your Information*, backed out of the job at the last minute. In what Hansen describes as a "kind of Shirley MacLaine, Carol Haney story" (à la *The Pajama Game*), the general manager thought Hansen had a good voice and asked her to try the job, even though she didn't even know how to thread a tape machine.

The job marked the beginning of her career in radio and the end of her acting career, which, she said, earned her a total of twenty-six dollars (for playing the role of April the stewardess in *Company* at Caesars Monticello dinner theater in Framingham, Massachusetts). She left Binghamton to work for *Fresh Air* as a substitute host and contributor.

Hansen became a production assistant for *All Things Considered* in 1979. It was there that she met Neal Conan, a producer on the show and now the host of *Talk of the Nation*. She hosted *Weekend All Things Considered* for two years, then she and Conan married. Their daughter, Casey, was born in New York in 1981, and in 1983, when Conan was tapped to become NPR's London bureau chief, they moved to England, where their son, Connor, was born. Hansen was a stay-at-home mother, working part-time as an archivist and what was called a "dog's body"—known in the States as a gofer—for the acclaimed Maybox Theatres. "I did everything from tallying up sales of candy bars to literally baby-sitting Princess Margaret's coat, serving coffee to Richard Attenborough, and rounding up Americans to come to the London premier of *Pump Boys and Dinettes*," she said.

When she returned to the United States in 1987, she went back on the air, substituting for various NPR hosts until she was offered a permanent job hosting the classical music program *Performance Today*. In 1989, she became the host of *Weekend Edition Sunday*.

Along with the puzzle segment, the show's distinguishing features include a montage of "Voices in the News" from the previous week and regular "performance chats," a combined mini-concert/interview format similar to the kind of interviews Hansen did while she was hosting *Performance Today*. She also has a fondness for debut fiction; she gave novelists Edwidge Danticat and Jhumpa Lahiri, both of whom went on to great critical acclaim, their first radio interviews.

After more than a quarter century in radio, she still misses the stage. "If I got the offer to go back, I would do it, because I loved it," she said. "But in many respects what I do here is a performance as well, so that part of me gets satisfied." Acting is one of the many possibilities she dreams about pursuing during a leave of absence or, eventually, retirement. She'd also like to finish her bachelor's degree, perhaps in anthropology or theology.

"It's not the piece of paper that means something to me anymore, but I would love to be able to just learn," she said. "Everything I've learned has been by experience, which is not a bad thing. I know a lot. But to concentrate, to sit and concentrate, I would love to do that."

She would also love to spend more time with her husband. The two work opposing schedules, with Hansen at work Wednesday through Sunday and Conan on the air Monday through Friday. They can go for months without a day off together, and in the evenings they're often tempted to talk shop. "We need what we call 'decompression time,' where we each talk about what happened at work that day," she said. "But we try not to always talk about work."

Listening to Liane Hansen on Sunday mornings is a ritual for millions of listeners, as fundamental as sleeping late and drinking a second cup of coffee. For Hansen, though, this ritual starts at two in the morning, so she can get to the studio to prepare for the show, and doesn't end until two that afternoon, when she returns home after *Weekend Edition Sunday* has aired in three time zones. Then, Hansen has another, private ritual. She takes a long nap. Then she goes to six o'clock mass at Saint Elizabeth Catholic Church near her home in Chevy Chase, Maryland.

Hansen is an observant Catholic. She was raised in the religion while growing up in the 1950s and 1960s in Worcester, Massachusetts. When she was nineteen, she left the faith, swept up in the rebellious spirit of the times. She stayed away for thirty years.

Her return to Catholicism wasn't motivated by "a death or a foxhole" or anything similarly dramatic. She said she first began to reconsider her spirituality while attending her niece's graduation from a Catholic elementary school in the Worcester church she'd grown up in. The priest's homily touched something in her, a sense that there was something missing. "I felt like there was a hole and I didn't know where it was," she said. "I was always looking to fill it."

But at first the pull to go back to church perplexed Hansen. She is, after all, a woman used to asking questions. However motherly or exuberant she may be during the Sunday morning puzzle segment and some of the lighter arts interviews, she can be as hard-driving and skeptical as any of her colleagues with more serious subjects. She was not about to set aside these qualities, or her differences with church politics, at the church door. She confided her concerns with a priest she trusted. "The first thing I said to him was, I don't understand this," she said. "And second, I have a lot of problems with the institution, a lot of problems. And he said to me, 'Well, you know, Christ himself didn't have the best choice of apostles.'"

He directed her to read Thomas Merton, the Trappist monk who wrote *The Seven Storey Mountain,* a memoir of his conversion to Catholicism and his journey toward commitment to the monastic life. She also explored the writings of Joan Chittister and Kathleen Norris. She continued to go to mass, and she began a prayer life of her own, setting aside a time for contemplation every morning. She has not stopped having differences with the church, but they have not prevented her from connecting deeply with Catholicism, in particular the Benedictine community and its teachings on communal life, prayer, and making "the humdrum holy." She is now an oblate, the term for a lay person dedicated to the monastic life, with Saint Vincent Arch-abbey, a Benedictine monastery outside of Pittsburgh.

It was challenging for Hansen to explain her transformation to the people close to her, in particular her family. She fielded questions from her two children, then teenagers, about why she was going to mass all of a sudden. Though she has never pushed her family to join her in her beliefs, she did ask her husband to remarry her in the church. She and Conan had wed twenty years before, but because Hansen's brief first marriage had ended in divorce, their union was not valid in the eyes of the church until she got an annulment and married him again. Conan, who was also raised Catholic and moved away from the religion as an adult, at first refused. "I think he thought that he would have to make promises that he couldn't respect, but then he found out it didn't involve that at all," she said. The two were married in a private ceremony in the rectory overlooking the Secret Service office. "Afterwards Neal went to work and I took the cat to the vet and that was it."

The fact that Hansen's most important workday is Sunday has over the years taken on a certain significance. She has long received fan mail from clergy members, telling her they listen on their way to ser-vices or mass. One monk wrote that her show was "a fitting prelude to the Eucharist." Since her return to Catholicism, she has at times trou-bled over her obligation to "deliver the bad news" on Sundays, while the priest and monks she admired were in church delivering the good. But she strives to cultivate what she calls "a humanity" to the program. "It's a way of connecting with the world on a Sunday morning that's not a food fight, it's not somebody yelling at you, it's not somebody bend-ing facts to suit a point of view," she said. "It's a welcoming place."

Renaissance Man:
Robert Siegel
Host, *All Things Considered*

Robert Siegel is in NPR's studio 2A, conducting an interview about physics and the nature of existence. His guest is Professor George Ellis, a South African physicist who has just won the Templeton Prize, a $1.4 million award given for "progress toward research or discoveries about spiritual realities." Siegel is alone in the studio, clutching a can of seltzer water, listening intently to Ellis through a satellite link from NPR's New York bureau.

"I understand what benefit people in religion receive from scientists taking these questions up rather rigorously," Siegel said. "What benefit have you received as a scientist from the religious discourse about either the nature of the universe or the origin of ethics?"

Ellis's answer is heady and complex. He muses on the current trend of embracing what he calls a reductionist view of existence. "They say the higher levels of the structure, which includes the way our mind operates, have no real causal efficacy of their own. They are epiphenomena—"

"You mean we could reduce them—at some date, we could reduce them to physiochemical reactions of some sort?" Siegel asks.

"That is correct. And in a sense, I have gone into this question because of the religious issue, but then it stands on its own right as a very, very interesting scientific question. And I think that this reductionist view is completely wrong, and I've been writing a bit about that, the different reasons why it is, in fact, wrong."

"And the word 'soul' enters this discussion at some point, 'mind.'"

"Well, 'mind' and 'brain' certainly; 'soul' I'm very cautious about using," Ellis said. "But what I'm concerned with is—the one I'm really concerned about is free will, the ability that we have to make choices which have real meaning, so that we are responsible for our own actions in some moral sense. And that, to me, is the single, really, core issue in the current science and religion dialogue."

Ellis's research is risky material for broadcast, not easily reduced to a sound bite on the evening news. The interview will share the news docket that afternoon with segments on a massive car bomb in Baghdad, preparations for the trial of Saddam Hussein, and the Whitney Biennial. This kind of lineup is what gives the show its name—the ability to consider all things, from the urgent to the obscure.

Though Siegel lets slip (in a bit that will be edited out for broadcast) that he's only spent five minutes preparing for the interview, his questions are erudite, his voice carrying a slight suggestion of bewilderment, as if he's acknowledging to his guest and his audience that, yes, this subject is a lofty one, but together we can manage to break it down into something that makes sense.

Siegel, fifty-eight, is called NPR's "Renaissance man," able to take on any matter the show's producers toss his way. At times he conducts interviews more like a professor who himself could lecture on the subject than a news man confronting a dozen different topics each day. He looks the part as well, with a neatly trimmed dark beard; square, top-rimmed eyeglasses; and two-toned oxford shoes in brown and beige. The distinct sound of his voice complements the image. The pace is thoughtful and deliberate, the tone nasal, the effect profoundly authoritative. When he was a guest on the comedy quiz show,

Wait Wait . . . Don't Tell Me!, he gave an incorrect answer to a sports question, yet he sounded as sure as he did delivering the day's news, prompting host Peter Sagal to tease, "I've now figured out, one of the secrets of your success is that you speak with incredible confidence and gravitas even though you're wrong."

Proper speech—what was once known as "elocution"—preoccupied Siegel's parents, who were both raised in Yiddish-speaking immigrant families in New York City. As a child, Siegel was coached "not to sound as if I was halfway off the boat or like the kids from Long Island we'd go to summer camp with."

"Speech was extremely important to them," Siegel said. "It was the defining difference between the uneducated and the educated." His mother, the daughter of immigrants from Vilnius (then called Vilna), Lithuania, attended Hunter College in the 1930s and emerged "with a kind of spoken English that was almost theatrical by later standards," Siegel said. His father, the child of Polish and Latvian immigrants, was a public school teacher and, in his younger years, a labor socialist sympathizer. He spent long evenings at the kitchen table with a Wollensak tape recorder, reciting syllables into a microphone and playing them back again and again. He was intent on getting a chairmanship in the New York City schools, a process that entailed taking a number of qualifying exams. He'd passed them all—except a somewhat suspect speech test given by an examiner "who blocked people of dubious politics or habits by finding them to have unacceptable habits of speech—to sound too much like they're from New York, essentially," Siegel said. Eventually, with the help of the Wollensak, his father shed his Lower East Side accent and passed the speech test.

Siegel's cultivated speech opened doors for him in radio news, but his parents were wary of the career choice. Though they were both avid readers of the *New York Times*—what Siegel's father called "the quality paper"—and at least three other daily newspapers, a career in journalism, particularly broadcast journalism, was "quite outside their experience and comprehension," Siegel said. "They were both clear as to what sort of thing I should do with my adult life. It ranged from medicine to medicine, with a possible leeway for law if need be."

But rebellion was the order of the day when Siegel was first drawn to the airwaves. As a student at Columbia University, he joined the staff of WKCR, the student station. Near the end of his senior year in 1968, the campus was sent into tumult—and the national media spotlight—when students staged sit-ins at several university buildings, including the president's office. The protests culminated in what was at the time the biggest police action ever in New York City. WKCR covered it all, live, and Siegel found himself in the middle of history, in front of a microphone.

"I never knew what I would have done if I hadn't been on the radio," he said. "I wouldn't have sat in a building because I wasn't an activist of any kind. I wouldn't have counterprotested because most of my friends were inside the buildings. So here I had this role to play at a time when things were crazy and people wanted to know what was going on."

His vantage point on the protests also led him to realize that the news source lauded throughout his childhood, the *New York Times*, wasn't getting the story right. The day after the campus was swept with police brutality, the lead story focused instead on the damage students had done to the university president's office.

"The paper never came to grips with what was happening, with what the police had done," Siegel said. The incident shook his notion that newspaper reporting was the only true way to be a journalist. "We had been right where the *New York Times* had been wrong, and we were just twenty years old," he said. "So I thought, maybe there was something really valuable in radio news."

Siegel's first job was as the morning news reporter and talk show host at WGLI Radio in Long Island. From 1971 to 1976, he worked as a reporter, host, and director of news and public affairs for WRVR in New York City. There, he met future NPR colleagues Neal Conan and Jay Kernis.

He came to NPR as an associate producer in 1976. He and his wife, Jane, have a daughter, Erica, who is now pursuing a Ph.D. in Russian literature at Siegel's alma mater, Columbia. Leah Siegel, now a singer/songwriter who performs in clubs around lower Manhattan and Brooklyn, would be born two years later. Siegel assumed his stint at NPR would be short; the salary was low, and he thought he'd be able to better support his family once he got a job at "a real network." But it wasn't long before he got caught up in the mission of the fledgling news organization. "It turned out to be a place where you had the ability to try to put on the program you would really like to hear yourself as opposed to the program that some consultant had figured you probably should put on and what some caricature of a listener was supposed to absorb," he said.

Siegel was made public affairs editor in 1977 and senior editor in 1978. In 1979, Siegel opened NPR's London bureau and worked there as senior editor until 1983. He then returned to Washington to become NPR's news director in the midst of a financial crisis so severe that almost a third of NPR's staff was laid off and multimillion dollar operating deficits nearly drove the network off the air. Once NPR was back on its feet, Siegel took the lead in expanding news coverage to six days a week with the conceptualization of *Weekend Edition*. The program was originally proposed as a low-cost "best of" show recycling *Morning Edition* features from the previous week. Siegel said he found the idea "deadly." Instead, he proposed a Saturday morning program hosted by Scott Simon, then the Chicago bureau chief. The program would make Simon, a gifted reporter with a flair for sensitive conversation, radio essays, and comedy, central "almost in the way that *Prairie Home Companion* was about Garrison Keillor," Siegel said.

Weekend Edition Saturday took a year of planning, cajoling, and meetings to launch. Siegel called the program the "one really great

thing" he did as news director, but said working in management ultimately "didn't satisfy my short attention span, impatience, and all the
things hosting a radio program do satisfy." So when the opportunity
came in 1987 to host *All Things Considered,* he took it. "To me, the
idea of being able to come into work and by the end of the day put
something on the air is tremendously gratifying," he said. "Mentally, I
think I'm built for a short turnaround."

After eighteen years of hosting *All Things Considered,* he is reluctant to imagine a future anywhere else. "I feel so ambivalent about the
state of broadcast journalism, I don't know what I would do if I
weren't doing this," he said.

Beyond the Bright Lights:
Michele Norris

Host, *All Things Considered*

When she was a girl, Michele Norris spent weeks every summer traveling North America with her family, being initiated into the ways of the reporter.

But she didn't know it then. What she did know was that her father, a postal worker, had some pretty unusual travel habits. He'd always had wanderlust. It had brought him in his young adulthood from his hometown of Birmingham, Alabama, where he'd attended all-black schools in the segregated thirties and forties, to Minneapolis, where he hoped to find a more integrated environment in which to start a family. Not content to stay on the well-trod tourist path in the cities they visited, he'd make his family ride the municipal buses for hours, getting off to explore whenever they saw something he found interesting, whether it be an ocean view or a steel factory. He'd ask around to find out where the locals ate, which, on a trip to San Francisco, led them to the little-known back entrance of a popular Chinese restaurant—into the section frequented by Chinese nationals. "It was garbage day, so everything was out on the street," Norris remembered. "It smelled terrible. I was horrified. But we went and ate and had something that was unlike anything you would get if you just went in the front door where the tourists did."

Her father also sought out people to talk to with an equally unfettered curiosity. On a trip to Winnipeg, he stopped to pick up draft dodgers. "They were these young black men with backpacks," Norris said. "He'd buy them a meal. The deal was, I'll take you out with my family and you tell me why you left. At the time, I was like, he's a stranger. He looks like he needs a bath, dad! When you're young, you just don't get it at all, but now I understand what he was doing. In many ways he was a journalist."

His influence on Norris was apparent early. When she was five, she wrote illustrated stories about her south Minneapolis neighbors and went door-to-door selling them for five cents each. Cute, you might think, except that the stories tended more toward the exposé than the fairy tale. "So it was kind of like extortion!" Norris laughed.

"We had a man on our block who liked the bottle," she said. "This was a time when cars were really big and garages really small. He couldn't quite navigate his big car, and there was always someone over there fixing the garage. So I did this whole story about his car hitting the garage! My mother was mortified."

Though Norris wrote for her high school newspaper, she initially thought she was headed for a career in electrical engineering. She took college classes on the weekend through a program to encourage minority students to go into the sciences. Once enrolled full-time at the University of Wisconsin, her interest in engineering waned. She switched her major to journalism and transferred back home to the University of Minnesota.

She attended her college graduation in 1985, wearing a cap and gown, but left school with an empty diploma folder because some of her transfer credits hadn't gone through. She accepted a job with the *Los Angeles Times* and didn't go back to school to make up the missing credits. "I had to choose between a B.A. and a J-O-B," she explained. "The latter won." She didn't get her degree until May 2005, when she went back to her alma mater to deliver the commencement address and was surprised with a diploma.

Norris went on to work for the *Chicago Tribune* and the *Washington Post*. She became a correspondent for ABC News in 1993, where she covered education, poverty, and urban issues for *World News Tonight*. She'd had no prior television experience before coming to the network, but she was a good fit for the screen. She is stunning, with perfectly coifed short hair and a slender figure. She has a television reporter's poise and stylish wardrobe of jewel-toned suits and dresses, but there is also a genuine warmth and sense of caring in her presence, qualities not often associated with broadcast journalism.

Norris, forty-four, came to NPR in 2002. Public radio has a history of losing star reporters (think Martha Raddatz, John Hockenberry, Robert Krulwich, Deborah Amos) to the higher salaries and glamour of television. Norris, the mother of two young children, said she was attracted in the reverse direction by the more stable schedule and fewer travel demands of the *All Things Considered* anchor job.

But the more profound differences between her old life in television and her new one in radio hit home the day she interviewed black actor and comedian Bernie Mac. She was to meet him in the television room of his plush Los Angeles home. He'd recently taped a segment of Oprah, and it was to air that afternoon. He invited Norris to watch it with him before their interview started. She didn't mind. In fact she planned to roll tape, in hopes of capturing his reactions to the program.

When Mac made his appearance, he was dressed for television. Watching it, that is. The man known to make appearances in vividly colored sharkskin suits and $500 dollar ties was wearing silk basketball shorts with the number 23—Michael Jordan's—on them, a white muscle shirt, and house slippers.

"Like those slippers your dad wore," Norris said. "With black knee socks that have the ribbing on them. And a do rag. Not like a Tommy Hilfiger kind of do rag. An old-fashioned control-top panty hose tied at the top kind of do rag. And at that moment I thought, this is radio."

Their interview, broadcast in December 2002, achieved a kind of dressed-down feeling as well. Norris played an excerpt from *The Bernie Mac Show* in which Mac joked merrily with a group of stay-at-home moms about wanting to bust their teenage children in the head "until the white meat shows." Then she talked with Mac about his concerns about hitting the big time with the series. Mac spoke openly about how he'd watched Hollywood "kill comics" like Richard Pryor.

"Doing *[The Bernie Mac Show]*, I said to myself that I would not allow America or Hollywood to take my voice from me," he told Norris.

"Did they try?"

"No."

"Really?" she pressed.

"No."

"Because I was trying to imagine that meeting when they first looked at the script and they said, wait a minute, wait a minute, you're going to say 'I'm going to bust them in the head until the white meat shows'? And then you're going to have a trio of women at the counter saying the same thing?"

"My grandfather used to say that to me. It was cold, but it was funny."

"You got the point across," Norris laughed.

"Yeah."

The Mac interview is an example of what Norris described "a level of intimacy that probably isn't possible in the bright lights of television." The segment was from one of the first series Norris did for NPR, on comedy and race in America. She wanted to do the series because she'd always thought the most honest conversations about race in America take place in comedy dialogues, "where they can say things you don't say in conversation without people getting very uncomfortable," she said.

Norris has pushed NPR to increase its coverage of race issues, and she's contributed some notable features on the topic, including an in-depth, first-person report on the fate of an all-black Birmingham high school her father and uncles attended before the landmark *Brown v. Board of Education* ruling ending segregation. She's also pushed the network to seek diversity in the white male–dominated realm of experts and pundits. "When we want to go find a cardiologist, let's just make sure that every so often that cardiologist is also a woman, or a doctor who also happens to be Asian," she said.

NPR has in turn encouraged Norris to sound like herself, in contrast to her years on television, where she'd been coached away from using slang expressions like "she got game" and speaking in her naturally low—and, one might read, black—register. "It was always, there's so much smoke in your voice, can you lift it up a little?" she said. On *All Things Considered*, her deep voice has quickly become familiar, and she's been known to relax into "the black side" of what she calls her "bicultural vernacular." In a post–Thanksgiving Day interview with New Orleans chef Leah Chase about what to do with turkey leftovers, Norris slipped into the cadence of her Birmingham relatives. "That sounds like good eating," she cooed over Chase's description of turkey hash with poached eggs on top.

At NPR, Norris said, "It's we want you to be yourself, period. So when you listen to Susan [Stamberg] and you run into her in the hallway here, the person you've heard on the radio all these years is the same person you encounter on the elevator or in the cafeteria ordering a tuna sandwich. I hope to be able to achieve the same comfort zone, talking the dozens or whatever you want to call that patois or cadence, at certain moments."

But Norris's blackness has escaped some listeners, something she discovered when a producer surprised her by taking a digital photo of her on his cell phone. When she asked him what he was doing, he said he wanted to prove she was black to a cab driver he knew who'd been hassling him about NPR's lack of diversity—while his radio was playing *All Things Considered*, with Norris hosting! The producer tried to convince him Norris was black, but he didn't believe it.

Norris is married to D.C. attorney Broderick Johnson. In 2004, Johnson was a senior adviser to the presidential campaign of Democratic U.S. Senator John Kerry. NPR management decided that Norris should not do any political interviews during the race to avoid any appearance of partisanship. There are signs the arrangement wasn't easy for Norris, who frequently covers politics. On the web site for NPR's ombudsman, Jeffrey Dvorkin, Norris is quoted as saying, "I wonder if we should have been more open with listeners and with my coworkers at NPR about why this happened." What Norris faced is not an uncommon Washington dilemma. Linda Wertheimer, a former host of *All Things Considered* and a national correspondent for NPR, doesn't do campaign finance–related interviews, as her husband, Fred Wertheimer, is a leading activist for campaign finance reform.

Norris and Johnson have two children: Aja Johnson, six, and Norris Chase Johnson, five. Michele is also stepmother to Johnson's twenty-year-old son, Broddy, a college student in California. They are observant Catholics, and Norris also maintains her own private ritual of devotions in the early morning, before she turns on her home computer and checks the daily papers and her email. These devotions are influenced by both Catholicism and her substantial collection of inspirational books, including *Black Pearls for Parents,* a book of quotations from famous African Americans, and *Simple Abundance,* a collection of essays to encourage women to appreciate life. "I guess it's prayer, but it's not the kind of prayer you do before you sit down and have a meal," she said. "Faith is part of the architecture that holds my life, my family, and in some cases my sanity together."

Her days are hectic, more so, she said, than when she was a television correspondent. Then, she could focus on one story at a time. As a host, she'll be interviewing a military strategist one moment, a BBC reporter in a hostile crowd in Basra the next. "Then, a producer appears at my door and tells me that I have fifteen minutes before a two-way with the lead conductor of the Vegetable Orchestra in Austria!" she said. "All of their instruments are made out of hollowed-out vegetables. Carrots and leeks and the like. And I have to read what I can find on this group, and the producer tells me there's going to be a language impediment and I have to find it in myself to put together a witty and thoughtful conversation on a subject I frankly never gave any thought to at all."

Add to her day the challenge of motherhood, and she calls the routine "like juggling chain saws." But she also believes that balancing work and family has made her a better journalist. "You see the world in a different way," she said. "I think there's some benefit to that, to go through the little battles that children go through and experience epiphanies they experience."

Discovering the Phone
Family: Melissa Block

Host, *All Things Considered*

For Melissa Block, the challenge of new motherhood and starting to host *All Things Considered* came in quick succession.

Two weeks after her daughter Chloe was born in 2002, Block was invited to take the host job. In the tumult of caring for a newborn, she was overwhelmed by the offer. "It was all I could do to get a shower in in the morning and figure out what this little being needs, and I thought, how could I possibly add on to that?" she said.

But by early 2003, once her maternity leave ended, she was sitting in the anchor's seat, in the tense atmosphere of a newsroom during the buildup to the war on Iraq. The job was new to her, but few at NPR were more familiar with the program than Block. She'd worked for the network for eighteen years, many of them at the *All Things Considered* desk.

She was first offered a job booking interviews for Noah Adams, then the program's host, in 1985. She was a Harvard French history and literature major who had recently returned from a year in Geneva on a Fulbright scholarship to study literary theory. Her only experience in journalism was a brief internship at *Washingtonian* magazine.

She admits that back then, the network was "only mildly familiar" to her, but she was intrigued by the opportunity. So every evening, she shushed her roommates and listened attentively to *All Things Considered*. She knew the position was for her when she heard a segment by Alex Chadwick on the discovery of his "phone family."

"They took Alex's phone number and called it using other area codes to see what they'd get, then recorded the conversations," Block remembered. "It was whimsical, fanciful, and wonderful. I remember thinking, this is a place I really want to work!"

The *All Things Considered* Block worked on in her twenties was much less structured than it is today. The program began at 5 p.m. and was ninety minutes long. The program was divided into half-hour blocks, with fewer strictures on how to fill that time. Pieces could take up the entire block, while today the maximum length of a segment is twelve minutes, which Block notes is "still huge" compared to the average piece on network television news.

She said she gets nostalgic at times for the more open format. "I knew there are reasons for what we do now and stations want to be able to cut in and talk about traffic, weather, and local news. But from a producer's perspective, a host's perspective, there's beauty in having twenty-five minutes to do with it whatever you want. So I miss those days. It just felt more organic."

She is not nostalgic, though, for other aspects of her early years at NPR, when budgets were small and staff was scarce. "A lot of my time when I was booking things for *All Things Considered* was spent setting up other reporters. We'd talk with the *New York Times* reporter in Moscow because we didn't have anyone in Moscow, and Lord knows we didn't have anyone in China, Japan, India, South Africa."

In the more than two decades since Block started, she has steadily risen through the ranks, from working the newsroom phones to producing some of Noah Adams's most creative features of the late 1980s. She rode an Amtrak train with him from Minneapolis to Seattle for a report on James J. Hill, the man who built the Great Northern Railway; traveled through Appalachia to cover the United Coal Workers' strike against the Pittston Coal Group; and helped create a soundscape of foghorns and ocean waves to tell the story of the historic lighthouses of the Maine Coast. Block shared Adams's affinity for the stories of small-town America, having grown up in the rural upstate New York community of Chatham, where her parents owned a crafts store. "When I go to a small town to do a story, I don't approach it like, 'God, how could anyone live here?' but rather, 'I understand how this works,'" she said.

Adams has described Block as "intense," organizing fast-paced, efficient schedules for their journeys. She in turn studied Adams's reporting technique: his ability to engage interview subjects with his low-key, soft-spoken questions and his gift for finding what radio producers call "nat sound," the on-the-scene ambient sounds meant to transport the listener to the setting of a radio feature.

"He's incredibly perceptive in noticing things that would go right by me," she said. "We were doing a story about a ghost town up in Idaho, an old mining town that had pretty much been abandoned. It's a pretty quiet place. Noah noticed a little drip of water, an icicle that was melting, and said, 'Let's get that sound.'"

After a three-year stint as *All Things Considered*'s senior producer, Block decided it was time to try her own hand at reporting and moved to New York City for what she thought was a one-year sabbatical in 1994. She spent eight years there, making her mark covering a number of high-profile trials, including the 1998 bombing of two U.S. embassies in Africa and the Amadou Diallo and Abner Louima police brutality cases. "I loved the trials," she said. "For the Kenyan embassy bombing trial, I thought I'd just go now and then, but I stayed for most of it. No one was paying much attention to Al Quaida then—that was the year preceding 9/11—but we decided to pay attention and we did a lot of stories very few people were doing. It's a testament to NPR's commitment to things to let me stay there, even on the days that not much was happening. I loved the sense of knowing enough about a story that you can really cover it extensively, not just parachuting in out of the blue having to catch up and figure out who the players are."

During her New York years, Block did some reporting from Macedonia and Kosovo during the crisis of 1999. She also sought out the sort of offbeat stories that attracted her to NPR in the first place, with profiles on a group of Manhattanites obsessed with removing plastic bags from trees, a subway buff who claimed to hear music in the rails, and a man who's been running the Central Park carousel since he was a kid. "He had a fabulous New York accent and a very matter-of-fact way of talking, and his stories were so fascinating," she said. "When he was first working there he could never figure out how to hop off the carousel when it was moving, so he'd go smashing into the walls!"

While in New York, she started dating Stefan Fatsis, a *Wall Street Journal* reporter, author of *Word Freak*, a book about the world of competitive Scrabble playing, and *All Things Considered*'s commentator on the business of sports. On a vacation in Paris, after a seven-course gourmet lunch, Fatsis proposed to her by setting up two Scrabble racks with the mixed up letters to WILL YOU and MARRY ME, a scheme inventive enough to score the couple a write-up in the *New York Times*'s Sunday Styles weddings section. Don't expect to hear the couple together on the air, though. To ensure impartiality, one of Block's cohosts, Robert Siegel or Michele Norris, always interviews Fatsis during his regular Friday time slot.

Block is forty-four, but has a voice that sounds somewhat more youthful, her questions coming across as both earnest and sharply intelligent. While long-time NPR hosts have established distinct personalities—Scott Simon's merry humor, Noah Adams's quiet curiosity—Block said figuring out what her own voice is has been the trickiest part of the job.

"I learned a lot from all the other hosts," she said. "Ideally on any given day I'd like to fold a lot of it in together. What I hopefully bring is any person's curiosity about things and some degree of humor."

Just how much her role at NPR had changed hit home for the first time the day she and Noah Adams crossed the Potomac River to Fort Meyer, Virginia, for a story about the Wright Brothers and the events that led to the first plane crash fatality, five years after their historic first flight at Kitty Hawk. Adams and Block had been on location together before on plenty of reporting excursions, but this time was different. Block was the host, not the producer, and Adams, who'd just published *The Flyers,* his account of the lives of Wilbur and Orville Wright, was her guest.

"I remember just feeling sort of nervous all of a sudden," Block remembered. "I was interviewing Noah! It struck me as a funny little course of history over the last twenty years—that here we were."

A Close Second to
Waterskiing: Kai Ryssdal

Host, *Marketplace* and *Marketplace Money*

In 1997, **Kai** Ryssdal was shelving books at a Borders bookstore in Palo Alto, California, for $7.25 an hour. He was thirty-four, and he wasn't sure what he was going to do with the rest of his life.

Then he came across a book on internships in the "Career and Counseling" section of the store. Inside, he found the address of KQED, a public radio station in California offering a newsroom internship.

It wasn't long before he was learning how to use a tape recorder and edit tape with a grease pencil and razor blade. He was undaunted by the fact that most of the other interns hadn't yet reached their twentieth birthdays.

Four years later, he became the host of *Marketplace Morning Report*, a ten-minute business news program produced by American Public Media (APM). Four years after that, Ryssdal was picked to host *Marketplace*, APM's half-hour daily evening business show, with 4.7 million regular listeners. He also hosts *Marketplace Money*, a weekly show on personal finance issues.

Not bad for an erstwhile big-box bookstore clerk.

"I've been incredibly fortunate," Ryssdal, forty-two, said. "My timing has been spectacularly lucky, and it's all just fallen in place for me."

It must be said that the pre–public radio Ryssdal wasn't just your run-of-the-mill thirty-something Generation X slacker. Before he landed at Borders, he'd had a very respectable career. A couple of them, actually.

After he graduated from Emory University in Atlanta with a bachelor's degree in history and political science, he joined the navy and moved to Pensacola, Florida, for officer's training. He became a pilot and flew planes from the aircraft carrier USS *Theodore Roosevelt*. He was following in the footsteps of his grandfather, who'd been in the navy, and his father, who was in the air force, but he said he never felt pressure from his family to enlist. "I think it's fair to say my parents were fairly surprised when I came home one day my junior year of college and said, yeah, guess what, I'm going into the navy," he told me over the telephone from his office in Los Angeles.

He had grown up mainly in Westchester County, New York. When he was in elementary school, his family lived for a while in Denmark and England, where his father, a native of Norway, had a job with an airline. His father followed the news "religiously" and liked to discuss current events with the family. Though these aspects of Ryssdal's upbringing, in retrospect, seem to be harbingers of his eventual turn toward journalism, he was drawn to military service first, he said, by a sense of "belonging and participating in something more substantive than just yourself."

Ryssdal never saw combat. He was scheduled to rotate out of his squadron the week the Persian Gulf War started in 1990. He became a briefing officer for the Pentagon Joint Chiefs of Staff and earned a master's degree in national securities studies from Georgetown University.

He has not flown a plane since. "It was very exciting, invigorating," he said. "But flying for me was never this thing that I am. A lot of the guys I was with, flying was *it*. That was how they defined themselves. And for me it was just this cool thing to do when I was twenty-five."

At twenty-nine, he took the foreign service exam and went to work for the U.S. State Department. He met the woman who would become his wife at foreign service orientation. The two sought a post where they could be together and ended up in Beijing, where he was a second secretary to the vice-consul. "It was an extraordinary experience," he said. "We were there for two years, and from the very first day until the last, there was not a single day that I didn't see something on the street and go, 'Wow! Look at that!' It's an amazing, incredible place."

Ryssdal left the foreign service when his wife was admitted into the MBA program at Stanford University. "I figured, I'll get a job selling widgets at a firm in Silicon Valley," he said. "But it didn't take me very long to realize that I had very little interest in doing that."

And that's how he ended up at Borders, and then at KQED. He became a reporter there, and then a substitute host for *The California Report,* which was broadcast statewide. In May 2001, a producer from *Marketplace* heard him on the air and asked him to interview for the host position at *Marketplace Morning Report*. She called as Ryssdal and his wife were awaiting the birth of their first child, then two days overdue, and Ryssdal told her he couldn't do it. "And I talked it over with my wife later that night and she said, *Marketplace* only really calls you one time, maybe you should give them a call back," he said. He zipped down to Los Angeles and back before his son was born.

He got the job. It required a grueling schedule. He had to be at work by 1 a.m. to prepare for the first hourly broadcast at 3:50. He stuck it out until 2005, when he was picked to host *Marketplace*. "Getting up in the middle of the night was fine for a while, but it's nice not to be doing it anymore," he said, though he added that he missed having more daytime hours to spend with his growing family. His three sons are now seven, five, and two. Kai's wife works at an Internet company in Pasadena, and the family lives in Glendale.

That one drawback aside, hosting *Marketplace* is "the second best job I ever had," he said. "The first best was when I was in flight training. I was twenty-five, living in Pensacola, and when I wasn't flying airplanes, I was waterskiing. This job is a very close second to waterskiing for a living."

Ryssdal's rapid career rise in public radio was likely helped by the fact that he has, in the parlance of the industry, "great pipes," a naturally deep and authoritative voice. His manner fits perfectly into the hosting tradition of his predecessors, David Brown and David Brancaccio (currently the host of PBS's *Now*). They all have a firmly masculine sound, along with a breezy, somewhat jocular delivery. Ryssdal admitted he gets fan mail from women who think he sounds hot. "It's always flattering, of course," he said, lowering his voice to a mock-sexy depth.

I tend to find more mirth than sensuality in Ryssdal's sound. Not only are his scripts written with plenty of tongue-in-cheek touches, the tone of his voice always gives me the impression he was joking around with a colleague the moment before the microphone went on. When I told him this, he said, "If we took ourselves too seriously, we wouldn't be able to take what is really sometimes serious, intricate, complicated news and make it understandable."

He told me that making sense of the seemingly opaque world of business and the economy was one of the primary goals of the show. The program's interpretation of "business news" can range from the latest figures on housing prices to the relationship between bagels and the savings rate to how Starbucks is changing France's café culture. The staff does not include economists or MBAs. "These are regular people who try to sort through the complicated and sometimes arcane world of business economy and try to make sense of it," he said. "And that's what makes it work. I figure if I can explain it to myself well enough, I can go on the radio and help other people understand it."

The Outsider Inside: Juan Williams

Senior Correspondent, *Morning Edition*

When **Juan Williams** was growing up in Brooklyn in the 1960s, he often got home from school before his mother, a Panamanian immigrant who worked sewing dresses in Manhattan's garment district. So he would sit on the stoop of his apartment building in Crown Heights, waiting and looking around.

"I think it really developed in me this sense of watching the world go by," he said. "Which is a tremendous asset for a journalist. I always felt a little bit like the outsider, so I have a lot of these qualities of the observer."

Those qualities have taken Williams, fifty-one, from immigrant kid outsider to being a veteran reporter and analyst who interviews the ultimate insiders of Washington on the pressing political issues of the day. He's spoken with Dick Cheney, Condoleezza Rice, Alberto Gonzales, and Senator Hillary Rodham Clinton and analyzed the politics of Supreme Court nominees, the U.S. strategy in Iraq, and the rift in the AFL-CIO. He also huddles in the inner circle of journalist-pundits. He is a contributing political analyst for the Fox News Channel and a regular panelist on *Fox News Sunday*. He's authored four books about the quest of black Americans to move inside the mainstream of American political and cultural life: *Thurgood Marshall: American Revolutionary; Eyes on the Prize: America's Civil Rights Years, 1954–1965; This Far by Faith: Stories from the African American Religious Experience;* and *My Soul Looks Back in Wonder: Voices of the Civil Rights Experience.*

"It's only now that I feel, wait a sec, I'm a player in the world, too," he told me in an interview in his office at NPR. He has a neatly trimmed mustache and, even though his office on this early spring day is warm, wears a suit and tie, looking at the ready for a V.I.P interview or a television appearance at Fox. He credits much of his transformation into a "player" to his mother, who took her three children to America when Williams was a toddler. His father, a former boxing trainer and accountant, stayed behind for five years to pay off the plane fare and make money to send to his family.

While Williams's sister, then fourteen, and brother, then ten, threw themselves into their new school and surroundings, Williams felt "kind of left behind" as the youngest. His mother started to bring home newspapers she found on the subway. An early reader, Williams delved into the sports pages, comparing how different reporters covered the same baseball game. Then he grew curious about the other sections. "The newspapers became a window onto the world for me, because it was a place I could control and slowly study and come to grips with," he said. "It became a friend for me. I knew the writers and I knew the columnists and I loved that stuff."

His mother, who died in 2005, was a "very demanding, but also very loving" parent who pushed all of her children to succeed. "I think she was even more determined than my father, who trained boxers," he said. "But I never felt pushed by my dad so much as I would at times feel with my mother, who could be cutting with comments or harsh in her judgments. You win or you lose, none of this pat on the back."

He watched his older siblings succeed. His sister, Elena, graduated first in her high school class, went to college at Swarthmore, went to law school at Harvard, and is now an attorney in Switzerland. His brother, Roger, attended Haverford College, became a leader in affordable housing issues, and is now a Senior Fellow at the Annie E. Casey Foundation. Williams was bookish like they were, but he also liked to hang out and play basketball, which alarmed them when they came home to visit from college. "It got to the point where my mother was checking my arms for tracks," he said. "On the court, people had respect and knew me and I was one of the guys. But a lot of these guys were much older and into drugs and into women in a way I wasn't prepared for, so I think my brother and sister and everybody was concerned I was going down the wrong path."

He was accepted with a scholarship to Oakwood Friends School, a Quaker boarding school in Poughkeepsie, only an hour and a half train ride from home but culturally worlds away. "I remember the first day," he said. "I was a big city urban kid, and I was wearing purple Converse sneakers, and I had a big afro, a big powder puff afro. And I've seen a picture of that day, and I look like a dandelion because I'm real skinny, just totally weird looking, and I felt totally at sea."

He pushed himself to fit in in this new atmosphere of privilege and affluence. "Today, there are a lot of arguments in the society about assimilation and the value of assimilation and all the rest," he said. "For me, the goal was to assimilate, it was to fit into the society. I wanted better things, I never wanted to be poor, I wanted to succeed in life and feel a part of the community."

After graduating from Oakwood, he attended Haverford College, his brother's alma mater and also a Quaker-founded school (Williams is Episcopalian). He majored in philosophy, despite his mother's objections. "She asked me, 'Well, what kind of a job does a philosopher get?'" He wasn't worried. He'd edited his high school newspaper, he had summer jobs at major newspapers throughout college, and he knew what he wanted to do. "Philosophy and journalism go together like hand in glove," he said. "[Philosophy] is the key to who I am, to the deductive way I think about my interviews, the way I ask questions, the way I relate to exploring knowledge."

Williams worked at the *Washington Post* for twenty-one years as an editorial writer, columnist, and White House reporter. He's also published articles in *Newsweek*, *The Atlantic Monthly*, *Ebony*, *Gentlemen's Quarterly*, and *The New Republic*. He won an Emmy for TV documentary writing and received widespread critical acclaim for documentaries about blacks in politics, singer Marian Anderson, and A. Philip Randolph, the founder of the first black labor union to win a collective bargaining agreement.

Williams juggled his busy work schedule with raising three children. Antonio, now twenty-five, is a speechwriter for the Department of Veterans Affairs; Regan, twenty-three, is a law school student at Georgetown University; and Raphael, sixteen, is in high school. His wife, Delise Williams, is a social worker in Montgomery County, Maryland. His wife, he said, was the primary caretaker for the children, especially during the years he was covering the White House, which involved a considerable amount of travel. "The big lesson for me then was I always thought everybody, the kids and the wife and everybody would be waiting for me to get back home," he said. "There comes a day when you realize, you get home and you're the only one there, everybody's gone off and they're doing their own things, they have their own lives. It's just kind of accepted that dad goes away a lot so people do their own things."

After Williams published his first book, *Thurgood Marshall: American Revolutionary*, in 1999, he found himself at a career impasse. He'd just signed a contract with the *Washington Post* and *Newsweek* to write several long narrative pieces, a prospect he found intriguing at first. "But what happened was, I felt like I was lost," he said. "I was just coming off a book, I really wasn't back in the newsroom, I didn't feel like I belonged, I just felt like maybe I had too much space around me psychologically." Then came the call from Bruce Drake, then the managing editor of NPR, asking him to guest host *Talk of the Nation*, the network's daily call-in show. What was meant to be a three-day job turned into an offer to host the show full-time.

Though he'd had television experience as a panelist on *Washington Week in Review* and as a regular cohost of CNN's *Crossfire*, hosting

Talk of the Nation gave him a connection to his audience in a way he'd never experienced before. "I got to know the listeners and they got to know me," he said. For a show on getting into college, he reminisced about the day his daughter ran after the mail truck because she was so eager to learn about whether she'd gotten into her first-choice school— an anecdote that inspired both listener delight and reprimands that he was putting so much pressure on her to succeed that she was "going crazy, chasing after mail trucks and violating federal law," he said. Even worse was the time he spoke about his wife's appetite for romance novels. "People were like, oh, so what kind of husband are you, you don't have much romance, your wife has these needs and you can't even fulfill them, you should be embarrassed!" he laughed. But he was proud of the familiar way listeners responded to him, particularly in the polarized atmosphere of the political call-in shows dominating commercial talk radio. "For me, that was the height of the show, that I was a real person with kids and a wife and a dog and sports teams I liked and all the rest," he said. "But not a personality who put himself before the news or before ideas, or who would tell someone to shut up, or would turn away from people who had different opinions."

But Williams eventually felt limited by the pressure of having to prepare for a show every day and the largely in-studio nature of the job, which kept him from what journalists refer to as "the field"—the world outside his office. He became a senior correspondent and political analyst in 2001. "I have the capacity in this job to move around, to travel," he said. "This is a far more stimulating and less restrictive role for me to play in terms of my life and abilities as a reporter."

As the former cohost of CNN's *Crossfire* opposite Bob Novak and a panelist on *Fox News Sunday* with Chris Wallace and Brit Hume, Williams has parried with the most outspoken conservative pundits in broadcast journalism today. He insists that his politics are not predictably "liberal" or "black liberal." He's written in defense of Clarence Thomas when he was nominated for the Supreme Court and applauded President Bush's track record for appointing minorities to high-level positions, calling him "miles in front of any president, Democrat or Republican, in his treatment of black people." But Williams said that on Fox, "I am not as conservative as many of my colleagues so I become like a lightning rod or a foil for the argument, because I'm just challenging some of their preconceptions."

Williams is fond of Finley Peter Dunne's famous adage, "The job of the newspaper is to comfort the afflicted and afflict the comfortable," and he has steadfastly argued against right-wing criticism that the press is too liberal. But he has also faced some fire for being too soft when interviewing high-level officials. NPR's ombudsman, Jeffrey Dvorkin, pointed out that Williams failed to ask Assistant Secretary of Defense Paul Wolfowitz, in the days after Saddam Hussein's regime was overturned, about whether Iraq ever had weapons of mass destruction—the administration's professed reason for overturning the regime in the first place. A conversation with Secretary of State Condoleezza Rice in 2005 focused on classical music, hip hop, and her close friendship with President Bush instead of U.S. relations with Iraq, Iran, and other global trouble spots, causing a letter writer to the *Boston Globe* to complain that the interview was "evidence that the rumors of a GOP putsch at National Public Radio are true."

To be fair, William has pressed Rice on foreign policy issues, but this particular interview was intended to be, as host Renée Montagne put it in her introduction, an "informal" conversation. Although Williams says there are times when "you have to ask a tough question," he doesn't want to play into the current trend in journalism of making interviews "about the interviewer" and how aggressively he corners his sources. "I'd like to make news, that's the goal, but the highest goal for me is that you come away with a sense of what this person is about, what they're up to," he said. "Something that would help you, not only for the minute, have a sense of her personality and her larger worldview that would allow you to understand that person as they make decisions in the future."

Following the Origami
Chain: Jacki Lyden

Special Correspondent and Host,
National Public Radio

I **got to Jacki** Lyden's Brooklyn apartment shortly after she did. She was returning from a few days of work at NPR in Washington. Before that, she'd been in Iraq, researching a new book. We shared a dish of lemon-salt pistachio nuts she'd brought back from there, their taste slightly stale and dusty. I imagined the crowded market they came from, the dry desert heat, the postwar chaos that had been particularly awful that spring of 2004, in contrast with the calm of her spacious apartment. Light streamed in from the large, greenhouse-style windows overlooking Vanderbilt Street, and a Ricki Lee Jones CD played on the stereo. Lyden hungrily chewed the pistachios, at ease in her surroundings, enjoying the hum of the city below us.

Lyden has worked for NPR since 1979 as a reporter, host, and special correspondent. She is also the best-selling author of *Daughter of the Queen of Sheba*, a memoir of her life with her mother, who suffers from manic depression. Much of her adult life has been lived like the past few days. One of her main beats is the Middle East, and she travels to the region often. Even when she's in America, she's frequently

in motion. There are speaking engagements around the country related to NPR and *Sheba*, which is in its ninth paperback printing, and
she shuttles between two homes. She keeps an apartment in Washington, where NPR and her then-fiancé Will O'Leary, a photographer
for the *Washington Post,* are based (the two were married in October,
2004). The Brooklyn apartment gives her a place to write in and a toe-
hold in the city she calls her "personal capital."

Lyden has a portable, get-up-and-go-at-a-moment's notice glamour. Her jagged bobbed hair is a movie star shade of auburn, her pale
cheeks are dimpled, her face heart-shaped, her mouth a neat lip-
sticked bow. She is petite and youthfully slim (she declined to give her
age). She has written that she used to feel uncomfortable being in one
city for more than two weeks. She doesn't even have one profession
anymore, as she splits her time between radio and writing. I had wondered whether in person she would seem flighty or restless or divided.
She may be any or all of these things, but in the afternoon I spent with
her she showed no sign of it. Instead I felt in the presence of a woman
who made her home in ideas and stories and the creative work of
communicating them, a woman who needed the expansiveness of
writing books yet still fervently believed in radio, the medium she'd
fallen in love with in her twenties. She was eager to talk to me about
it. She mused about the way television allows for a certain passivity,
but with radio, "you can influence a listener," she said. "I'm not necessarily meaning politically, in terms of a political spectrum, but in
terms of, shouldn't you think about this? Can't I get you to think?
Can't I challenge you?"

Lyden is from rural Wisconsin and grew up mainly in Oconomowoc.
Her parents divorced after her father lost his hearing in a roofing ac-
cident, and her mother remarried an osteopathic doctor. Her childhood was punctuated with her mother's flights into mania, during
which she would dress up extravagantly and believe herself to be a
millionaire business owner, Marie Antoinette, or some other woman

of power. Lyden read voraciously and dreamed of what lay beyond Oconomowoc. "The outside world," she wrote in *Daughter of the Queen of Sheba*, "had multiple pages that stretched across the equator like an origami chain, each page connected to the next. I wanted to read them."

She went to Valparaiso University in Indiana, majoring in comparative literature and the humanities. She spent part of her undergraduate years studying in Cambridge, England. Lyden's voice, both on the air and off, has a cultivated, almost Shakespearean sound, without a hint of what she calls the "chubby o's" of her native Wisconsin. She told me she didn't consciously adopt a new voice, but that the change likely took place during her time abroad, where she and her classmates would pick up British phrases they heard in town. "Something happened to my vowel sounds, and when I listen to my mother and my sister and my niece, who never left Wisconsin, I sometimes think, oh my Lord, did I used to sound like that?" she said. "How could I not have? But there are no recordings of me so I'll never know."

After graduation in 1975, she got a job doing promotions for a traveling rodeo, hoping to write about the experience. She spent a summer on the road with the show and then moved to Chicago. She worked a number of odd jobs, including teaching journalism, even though she'd done little in the field herself. When a student approached her for a recommendation for a job writing the morning traffic reports at Chicago radio station WIND, Lyden told the student she wouldn't be able to get up that early in the morning. Lyden telephoned the station herself about the job. The news director asked her whether she'd ever driven a taxi, and she boldly assured him she had.

He told her later, "We knew you were lying but you sounded really cute and we wanted to meet you." She got hired to do the traffic reports, then switched to news. Her next job was at WKQX, where she was the producer for Art Roberts, a Chicago deejay who'd had a Wolfman Jack–like status in Chicago in the 1960s. He was the first person to tell her not just what to do on the air, but how to feel. "He would say, you're alone in that studio. It's Saturday night. You're talking to that one guy out there, he can't get a date, he's gonna go out to the bar and he's gonna see if someone's going to give him the time of day. But right now, there's only him and you. Or you're talking to that new mother, and she's rocking that baby and she's wondering what that baby's gonna turn out to be. And there's only the radio, and you and her," Lyden said. "I've never forgotten that."

She made her on-air debut on WKQX in 1979, hosting a two-hour public affairs show called *Backtalk*. "I was the producer, the writer, the director, the host, the everything," she said. "I worked seven days a week, and we actually got it into something that wasn't a complete laugh." Around that time, a friend told her about NPR, which she'd never heard of. Curious, she tuned in to WBEZ, Chicago's NPR affiliate, and caught Scott Simon, in one of several early reports that would mark him as a wry and iconoclastic journalist, asking a laid-off steelworker whether, if he could make just as much money making pink plastic flamingos as he did making steel, would he be just as happy making pink plastic flamingos?

"I thought, oh, that is for me! I love that," Lyden said. She went over to NPR's Chicago bureau, which had just opened an office that week. She knocked on the door, and Simon waved her in, offering to make her tea. "And the rest is history," she said.

Lyden described the early years of the Chicago bureau as a time of great "creative play," inspired by the legacy of Ben Hecht, Mike Royko, and other upstart Chicago journalists. There was less deadline pressure in those days, and the bureau's mandate was to provide in-depth, quality stories twice a week instead rushing to get out daily reports. "We had a load of adventures," she said. "We just were asked to use our imaginations, and we were people who had them to use, and we loved what we were doing." The bureau covered the failures of the rust belt and the family farm, the fall of Chicago's political machine, gang warfare, and race relations. She interviewed chiropractors and fly fishermen, politicians and traveling salesmen, and quickly became known as a vivacious reporter who could "get anyone to talk." She traveled to assignments in New York, California, Mississippi, and around the Midwest. Lyden, Simon, and legendary producer Jonathan "Smokey" Baer had lively discussions of story ideas, argued passionately, and, when the stress overwhelmed them, took the phone off the hook and went to a ball game. "Try getting away with that today!" she laughed.

She remains very close to Simon, whom she calls "like family." She is often asked whether they were ever romantically involved. "No, never," she said. "We were comrades. It would have been incestuous." *Morning Edition* host Renée Montagne, who started working for NPR around the same time Lyden did, is another dear friend. "You do grow up together when you do something that's unique in the culture," she said. "You understand what it means to sit behind that microphone and revere it . . . and understand what it takes to do it well, and that is really hard do."

In *Daughter of the Queen of Sheba,* Lyden describes the day she came home from school to find her mother dressed in a toga of silky yellow sheets, hieroglyphics drawn on her arms in dark eyeliner. She regally proclaimed that she was the Queen of Sheba and was bequeathing Mesopotamia to twelve-year-old Jacki. The moment, however delusional, was prophetic. In the summer of 1990, Iraqi leader Saddam Hussein invaded Kuwait, and Lyden, then based in London, rushed over to cover the imminent Gulf War in the land once known as Mesopotamia. "I really wanted to go, and absolutely was seduced from the first minute," she said. She has since reported from all over the Middle East. She's covered Afghanistan after the fall of the Taliban; the Iraqi insurgency against the American occupation; mourning rituals in Israel, the West Bank, and Gaza; and artists and musicians in Iran. She's been back to Iraq several times. Her book in progress, *Vox Babylonia,* is about the life of her Gulf War translator, Esho Joseph, who once worked in Saddam Hussein's inner circle. "Trying to reach these cultures in various ways just means everything," she told me. "It's not about the romance. It's about trying to understand, trying to articulate it through human life, so that it doesn't become a headline you can dismiss."

Just as her mother had prophesied Lyden's connection to the Middle East, Lyden's experiences in the region turned her thoughts back to her mother. Before leaving to cover the Gulf War, Lyden had started keeping a diary about her mother, with the thought that it might become a book. She thought of the project while interviewing a Palestinian who was getting kicked out of Kuwait, the country that had been his home for much of his life. "Now I'll lose my family history," he told Lyden. "I'll lose my country."

"That was an epiphany moment for me," she said. "I thought, if I don't go home, get to that book, I'm going to totally lose this whole Sheba reality. And I don't want to."

She took time off from NPR to write *Daughter of the Queen of Sheba*. She cast aside the necessarily spare language of radio, writing with poetic force, vivid imagery, and a virtuosic grasp of language. "It was this huge liberation," she said. But as she wrote she continued to cope with her mother's mania. Her mother was thrilled to see the Houghton Mifflin press release announcing the book contract for *Sheba,* then six days later called the publisher and threatened to sue if her daughter wrote another word about her. Lyden consoled her by telling her how the book might help others facing similar situations, and how she wanted to portray not only the difficulties of their life, but also the power and beauty of it. "I would say, 'Mom, you know, I wish you didn't have to go through this, but sometimes you're your best self when this happens to you," Lyden told me. "I wouldn't wish this illness on anyone, but let's not deny that it is often the companion illness of intense creativity, a fast mind, and that some of our greatest poets and inventors have been plagued with this."

The book, published in 1997, became a best-seller and made Lyden one of the "it" authors of the new wave of literary memoirists, joining the ranks of Kathryn Harrison, Lauren Slater, and Frank Mc-Court. The mental health community hailed the book for its realistic portrayal of mania and its impact on families. Lyden and her mother appeared on Oprah. *Sheba* has since gone through nine paperback printings. Filming for a Paramount Pictures film based on the book is slated to begin in 2006. Lyden, who worked closely with screenwriter Karen Croner on the script adaptation, said the movie will focus in part on the creative energy and adventurousness of her time at NPR's Chicago bureau. "How many movies have public radio as the matrix of their creative material?" she asked.

Though becoming a writer has meant that Lyden is on the air less (she now has a contract with NPR to work six months out of the year), she is not planning to leave radio, which she said connects her to new ideas, people, and places in a way no other pursuit can. "It's been my university forever," she said. "That's the best reason to stay—you can keep learning forever."

The Nicest Man in Public Radio: Carl Kasell

Newscaster, National Public Radio
Judge and Scorekeeper,
Wait Wait . . . Don't Tell Me!

Carl Kasell walks into a narrow booth next to NPR's studio 2A. He sits down, glances at his script, and looks up through the glass soundproof pane separating him from the control room. Claudette Lindsay, the director of the newscast that morning, raises her hand up, palm facing Kasell. "Open mike," she says. The on-air light goes on above the booth. She points sharply at him. "From National Public Radio news in Washington, I'm Carl Kasell," he intones and begins to read the day's news: the capture of a man wanted in connection with a series of shootings on an Ohio interstate; the search for bodies in a car bombing in Baghdad; Secretary of State Colin Powell's visit to Afghanistan. Kasell's voice is deep and authoritative and has a mythic steadiness, as if the sky could fall and he would still manage to get on the air to tell us about it, without a trace of panic.

Newscasters have the least glamorous on-air jobs at NPR. They sort through wire copy and spot reports from correspondents to put together the newscasts that air every half hour. While Kasell's colleagues in other jobs at NPR have interviewed presidents and movie stars and roamed the planet reporting on wars, floods, revolutions, and global warming, he has no complaints about life as a newscaster on a 2:30–11:30 a.m. schedule. "I'm happy right here," he told me, his North Carolina drawl more evident in person than it is on the air. "I was never trained as a journalist. It was all self-taught. I read books, and I listened, and I learned. There are a lot of things I don't know, but I know enough to do the newscast."

Despite his self-effacing manner, Kasell stands out as an elder statesman of the newsroom. He is seventy-one, trim, and has a long face. His thinning gray hair is cut close to his skull, making his large, fanned-out ears even more prominent. Nearly everyone I mentioned him to called him "the nicest man in public radio." In the world of *Morning Edition,* where sleep deprivation and tight deadlines can test tempers, Kasell is an old-school Southern gentleman with a sweetly avuncular manner. Even if he's five minutes away from going on the air for a newscast, he makes you feel as if he has all the time in the world to talk to you.

Kasell grew up in Goldsboro, North Carolina, the son of a manual laborer who worked at a sawmill, a box construction factory, and with the military at Seymour Johnson Air Force Base. Neither of his parents graduated from high school; his father only got as far as the fourth grade. They raised their family in the lean years of the post-Depression and World War II era and were determined to see all four children get their diplomas. They did, and went on to good careers. One sister became a bank vice president, the other an office manager. His brother is a medical researcher who developed a catheter widely used to treat heart arrhythmia. "I'm still trying to explain what I do," Kasell laughed.

As a child, he listened to the radio all the time, mesmerized by *The Shadow, The Lone Ranger,* and quiz shows. He dreamed of hosting one himself, and he loved to play deejay with his grandmother's old wind-up Victrola. In high school, his voice changed early, sliding down to the familiar baritone we know today and winning him a role on a radio program of high school news on WGBR, a local commercial station. In 1950, at age sixteen, the station hired him as an announcer, thus beginning his broadcast career.

Kasell also was involved in theater. He had the lead role in *Father of the Bride* and other plays, working on occasion with Andy Griffith, who was a drama coach at the school back before he made it to the big time. A more influential figure in Kasell's life was Clifton Britton, the head of the high school drama department, who helped him score a professional acting job after high school: the role of the Indian Chief in *The Lost Colony,* an outdoor historical drama still staged today on the Outer Banks, a vacation area on the North Carolina shore. "That was my first and only acting contract," he said. "I still have it at home somewhere. Thirty-five dollars a week, and I think about twenty-five of that went to my room and board."

Kasell also credits Britton with urging him to go into broadcasting. "Without his guidance and encouragement, I would probably be working today at our neighborhood Safeway in Goldsboro," he said. In college at the University of North Carolina, he majored in English and focused his attention on radio. In 1952, the college radio station, WUNC, now an NPR affiliate, was launched, and Kasell became part of the original staff, rubbing shoulders with fellow student and future broadcasting legend Charles Kuralt, who was the editor of the campus newspaper, the *Daily Tar Heel.* Kasell also worked part-time at WCHL, a local commercial radio station.

After college, in 1956, Kasell was drafted into the army. There, he met the woman who would become his wife, Clara (Chiara in her native Italy). She came to Goldsboro to get married to him in 1959. He was working as a morning deejay at his hometown radio station, WGBR-AM, playing country and pop music. In 1965, Clara convinced him that he could further his career if they went to a big city. They moved with their young son, Joe, to the Washington, D.C., area after Kasell got a job as the morning deejay at WPIK in Alexandria, Virginia, just outside the city. Two years later, he took a part-time weekend job at WAVA in Arlington, an all-news station. The station eventually gave him a full-time position. Before he took the job, he hadn't thought he wanted a career in news. "I wanted to entertain, be a performer," he said. But the salaries in news were higher, and he soon got swept up in the excitement of the events of the era: the Martin Luther King Jr. and Bobby Kennedy assassinations, the demonstrations against the Vietnam War.

He began working part-time at NPR in 1977, then went full-time two years later, when *Morning Edition* was launched. He and Ellen McDonnell (now the executive producer and then a news writer) are the two founding staff members still working on the show. The grueling schedule creates a high burnout rate, but Kasell doesn't mind the early morning, calling it "the best time to work." Every radio job he'd had since high school required him to work in the morning, though none quite as early as his 2:30 a.m. start time at NPR. So as not to miss out on evening family time with his wife and teenage son, Kasell developed a schedule he called "naps and snacks." He'd get home in the early afternoon and take a three-hour nap, then go to bed again at 9 p.m. for another four hours. It's a system he's kept ever since.

In 1997, Kasell's wife died of cancer. Even after a year of grieving, he rarely thought about meeting someone new. But at the London wedding of Barry Gordemer, his close friend and the director of *Morning Edition*, Kasell was seated next to Mary Ann Foster, a Washington psychotherapist. Back in Washington, the two began to date. With Foster, Kasell said, he discovered that "life can still be beautiful." They were married in 2003. The two live in Chevy Chase, Maryland. Kasell's son, Joe, and his wife, Lynn, live nearby in Ashburn, Virginia, with their two daughters. Kasell and Foster often spend weekends at a country home in Warm Springs, a tiny mountain town in the western part of Virginia, where they enjoy hiking with their two dogs. At the local cafe, the waitresses no longer fuss about Kasell's celebrity. "I'm blending in now, so it's just 'Hi, Carl,'" he said.

With all the pleasure Kasell has taken in his work at NPR, he never forgot about the impulse that drew him to radio in the first place—the desire to perform, to entertain. His *Morning Edition* buddy Barry Gordemer moonlights as a professional magician and taught Kasell a few tricks. The two do an act they call "Magic Edition," performing at NPR Christmas parties, public radio conventions, and fund-raisers for affiliate stations. In 1995, Kasell cracked a few jokes while hosting a panel of NPR personalities in Boston. His sense of humor got the attention of NPR's cultural programming division, which was just beginning to work up the concept for *Wait Wait . . . Don't Tell Me!*, NPR's news quiz show.

Kasell worked with *Wait Wait*'s producers on developing the show. At the time, he was still reading the newscasts on *Morning Edition* and hosting *Early Morning Edition*, which aired from 5–6 a.m. in the days when *Morning Edition* didn't start until 6. The show only lasted about six months before management decided to incorporate it into an earlier start time for *Morning Edition*. In 1998, Kasell started his role as the judge and scorekeeper of *Wait Wait*. The show, remembered host Peter Sagal, started out awkwardly, with too many scripted jokes. "We hadn't figured out how to use Carl," Sagal said. "We kept trying to make him sound zany." The approach now is to "let Carl be Carl." He's developed a persona that's a slightly ironic version of the straight man newscaster he is during the week on *Morning Edition*, a welcome contrast to the boisterous one-upsmanship Sagal and the show's rotating cast of panelists (Paula Poundstone and Roy Blount Jr. are among the regulars) engage in. "I'm there to bring a little class and dignity to this bunch of people," Kasell said.

But Kasell does have a zany side. The grand prize for winning contestants on *Wait Wait* is getting Kasell to record the message on their answering machine. In one message, he says, newscaster-style, "At this hour in Casper, Wyoming, Ann and Scott aren't answering their phone. Experts disagree over whether they're simply gone or are at home screening their calls because they're too cheap to buy caller ID." On another, he cuts loose and sings "What's New, Pussycat?" On a third, he pretends to be imprisoned in a rabbit cage in the contestant's basement. "In the name of all that is dear to you, send help!" he pleads, until a young girl's voice says, "Mom, Carl's doing it again!" and he whispers, "Sorry, I have to go. Leave a message."

Wait Wait has given Kasell a chance to get back to what he "always wanted to do in this business." When the show tours, he has an opportunity to meet listeners who compliment what he does both on *Wait Wait* and as a newscaster. "That's a great feeling," he told me. Even at seventy-one, he sees no reason to retire from either job. "Retire?" he shrugged. "Retire from what? This isn't work. This is fun."

PART II

Talk and Entertainment

Master Listener:
Ira Glass
Host, *This American Life*

Ira Glass is speaking to full house crowd of sixteen hundred at the State Theater in Ithaca, New York. In the dark.

"Well, the first thing you have to remember is that it's radio, that not seeing has a power in itself," he tells us.

He keeps talking. The lights don't come on.

He is testing us, I'm thinking, in a very Ira Glass way. It's true that radio, the invisible medium, is what's brought us here, and darkness is a way of reminding us of that. But we've also come here to see the face be-hind the voice. So he's defying expectations, building suspense, and I'm feeling the way I've felt countless times while listening to *This American Life,* his program of first-person narratives, interviews, documentaries, short fiction, and found sound centered around enigmatic weekly themes such as "Cringe," "Backed into a Corner," and "Should I Stay or Should I Go?" I'm curious and I'm in his thrall, wondering what will happen to the happily married woman who runs into an ex-boyfriend at a yogurt shop and can't stop thinking about him, or the teenage boy who discovers that the man he knows as his dad is not his biological father. The man who did father him is black. The boy's family is white.

Glass goes on in the dark for a few more minutes, in that familiar nasal, flat voice, the pitch slightly high, the inflections full of question marks, making him sound like a very articulate teenager or a flamboyant gay man. Then he jokes about how all of us "paid good money for this," and the stage lights go on to thunderous applause. The first thing I notice are his huge glasses, with retro thick black frames, covering nearly a third of his face. Then there's his grin, wide and smart-alecky. He has thick, mussed dark hair, streaked with gray, one of the few indications of his age: forty-six. His dark suit is wide in the shoulders, making him look like a bar mitzvah boy who hasn't quite grown into his jacket.

Of all the public radio personalities I've been in the presence of, Glass is the one whose physical appearance is most compatible with his on-air presence. He's an interplay of opposites—middle-aged yet youthful, straight yet femme-y, hip yet schlumpy. He giggles often and talks with his hands, his long fingers in the air, gesturing wildly. He digresses frequently, about everything from the Indian restaurant around the corner to the television shows he's into—*Buffy the Vampire Slayer* and *Gilmore Girls*. This last tendency, of course, is something he can't indulge in on the show, but it somehow makes sense, given the wide range of his mind. All of these qualities have generated a tremendous charisma that extends well beyond the one hour of radio Glass hosts every week into a definite celebrity status. He's been a guest on David Letterman and *The Daily Show*. He's been wined and dined by Jennifer Aniston and Brad Pitt (predivorce). He produced a pilot based on *This American Life* for Showtime and has a "first look" deal with Warner Brothers to option stories from the show for the movies. *Time* magazine named him "the best radio host in America." *People* magazine even requested his photograph so he could be considered for the magazine's *50 Most Beautiful People* annual issue. He refused.

He would have been an idiosyncratic choice for the magazine, but *People* was onto something about Glass's appeal. He's got scores of groupies—almost every straight woman or gay man I know who lis-tens to the show has had some sort of radio crush on him, and a num-ber of newspaper articles have been written about otherwise self-possessed intelligent women blushing and ooh-ing at the mention of his name. Perhaps that's because what he does on *This American Life* is the ultimate smart woman's romantic fantasy—to be with someone who is clever, brilliant, willing to be vulnerable, and *listens*, intensely and with great interest, asking questions that shape her ex-periences into stories that are powerful, fascinating, and meaningful in a way perhaps she herself never before realized.

But Glass isn't after dates (he's taken). He and the staff of *This American Life* are on a *crusade*. They're driven to portray reality in a way that radio, even public radio, for the most part fails to, because, as he puts it, most radio is too mired in the aesthetics of the news, that back-and-forth tennis game of playing sound bites from one side of an issue, then the other. There are no engaging characters, no fun, noth-ing truly unexpected, only a "fake seriousness" that offers up a world "without surprise, pleasure, humor, and joy," he said.

By making *This American Life*, "we're asserting that the world's a place where surprise and pleasure are possible," he said to his Ithaca audience. The essence of the show's crusade is "to make the kind of thing happen on the radio that doesn't happen very often—to use it to harness feelings that most people don't even try to get to in radio, to make it function like a great novel or a great movie or a great TV show."

There is something disarmingly simple about this concept, so sim-ple that it may not be obvious how truly radical it is. Gripping narra-tives have had a long history on the radio, from *The Shadow* and *War of the Worlds* to soap operas and radio plays. Around midcentury, though, television came on the scene and essentially knocked this kind of sustained storytelling off the radio airwaves. Public radio re-vived it somewhat in the 1970s and 1980s, with audio documentaries, new forms of comedy like *Car Talk,* and an esprit in *A Prairie Home*

Companion and other programs that drew on old genres like radio drama and variety shows. But only rarely has radio been a place for finely crafted and meaningful stories of personal experience. *This American Life* offers such a place—and shows us that perhaps this is what radio is *best* at. "There's an intimacy to just hearing somebody's voice, to the invisibility of radio," Glass said. "Like you're on the phone late at night with somebody you care about, and it's dark."

Glass has always had a sense for the power of narrative. On walks to school in suburban Baltimore, he'd pepper his classmates with questions, getting them to talk about themselves. He had a magic act he'd perform at children's parties, calling himself "The Magical Mystifier." Though he wasn't great at the tricks, he'd tell stories to keep the kids' attention.

Glass attended Northwestern University for a year, then transferred to Brown University because, as he told *Brown Alumni Magazine* in 2000, Northwestern students "only seemed to be interested in getting graduate degrees and making money." He said at Brown, he found "people who were obsessively studying for the sake of learning things." Glass majored in semiotics (very roughly put, the study of meaning), a program both mocked and revered for its obscurity. But he has insisted that he applies what he learned about semiotics every day, in particular the theory of Roland Barthes about narrative structure: that creating a building sequence of events, each of which raises questions about the next one, generates pleasure.

Glass started working for NPR as a summer intern in 1978, when he was nineteen. After Glass graduated from college, he worked at NPR as a tape editor and then took fill-in jobs as a production assistant. In between assignments, he'd work as a temp secretary to support himself. He went on at NPR to become a newscast writer, editor, associate producer, and producer. He filled in as the host of *Talk of the Nation* and *Weekend All Things Considered.* All the while, he was teaching himself how to structure and write good radio stories, a process he describes as taking many years. But his standards were high. He gave himself specific assignments, little tests. Every story he did, for example, had to have "some observation I'd made that no other reporter had," he told Transom.org, a web site forum for new independent public radio work. Then every story had to have someone who wasn't just a talking head, someone with a unique character he could portray in some way.

He moved to Chicago in 1989 to freelance for NPR. Chicago has been something of an incubator for iconoclastic journalistic talent, from NPR's own Scott Simon, who started the network's bureau there in 1977, to Studs Terkel and Mike Royko. Glass distinguished himself with a series of stories on the students and teachers at two inner-city schools. He also did a local show with fellow public radio producer Gary Covino called *The Wild Room* at WBEZ, NPR's Chicago affiliate. They'd crack themselves up playing extra material they hadn't been able to use in their news stories for NPR.

This American Life debuted on WBEZ in 1995, under the name *Your Radio Playhouse*, a tribute to *Pee-wee's Playhouse*. Glass soon got a request from a program director in southern California to air the show under the condition that the name be changed—and so *This American Life* was born. The show was hard to describe at first. In frustration, staff members used to say things like it was "basically just like *Car Talk*. Except just one host. And no cars." But *This American Life* did well in fund-raisers, so Glass marketed the show to other stations as a pledge drive moneymaker. He'd go out to a member station and raise double the usual amount during the hour *This American Life* was on. The program, produced by Chicago Public Radio, won over 160 affiliates on its own, then was picked up for distribution by Public Radio International, then called American Public Radio. NPR, which has a history of passing on some of public radio's best national programs—*A Prairie Home Companion*, for one—didn't make a sweet enough deal. The show's audience grew rapidly, doubling in its first year of national distribution. By 2005, it had 1.6 million weekly listeners on 490 stations. The show has been honored with the prestigious Peabody and DuPont Columbia Awards.

Putting the show together is "really a process of trial and error," Glass told the Ithaca audience. Each show starts out with a theme and about fifteen to twenty story ideas, culled from staff members and an email list of hundreds of people who've contributed to the show or have pitched ideas. After looking into prospective stories, the staff and freelancers will start production on seven or eight of them. Three or four actually make it into the show. "Basically what we're doing is industrial production, trying to make a lucky strike," he said. "The more material you do, eventually you'll find something really cool that you wouldn't have expected, a story that's so surprising you wouldn't have guessed it."

The stories on the show are preproduced, but the final run, when it all comes together with Glass's host introduction and music mixes, goes out live to radio stations. "It makes it feel like we're doing more of a radio show," Glass told the *Onion*. But he hates the tension of bringing the show together live, calling it "like flying a very complicated aircraft."

That is only one of the ways Glass struggles with his work. *This American Life* once did a show called "Jobs That Take Over Your Life." In the introduction, Glass talked about how every week he finds himself coming to terms with working on the show by going through the five stages that psychologist Elisabeth Kübler-Ross described people going through when they come to grips with death: denial, anger, bargaining, depression, and acceptance. "I realized that, if I'm having those feelings, I'm spending way too much time at my job," Glass said. By several accounts, he has the work style of an overzealous college student, often working late into the night. A *New York Times* reporter who followed him around for a few days in 1999 noted: "Glass has slept 2 hours of the past 38." It is a work style that seems unsustainable, especially for a man in his forties, but he often speaks of how much he loves what he does. "I'm at midlife and there is no crisis," he told *On the Page* magazine. "What would there be to have a midlife crisis about? I have what I want."

Glass's parents are Barry Glass, an accountant, and the late Dr. Shirley Glass, a noted Baltimore psychotherapist and the author of *Not "Just Friends,"* a book about infidelity. As he recounted in a 1996 episode of *This American Life*, his parents were completely against his choice of profession when he started interning for NPR during college. "They simply saw it the way most parents would," he said. "They saw it as impractical. They worried that I would never make any decent money, never be able to support a family." It wasn't until Glass was in his thirties and had been in radio for more than fifteen years that he found out that there was something deeper behind their protests. His father had worked in radio in the 1950s as a disc jockey. He quit the year Glass was born, for precisely the reasons he would later give to his son, and took the staid and practical path of becoming an accountant. Barry Glass didn't go back on the air until forty years later, when his son invited him to be a guest host of a Father's Day special on *This American Life*.

Glass has also done shows with his mother. In one segment on *This American Life*, he described how an ex-girlfriend called him up and read to him from an article in a women's magazine that featured his mother as a "sexpert," giving fairly racy advice. He then calls his mother to ask her about it. After Shirley Glass died of cancer in 2003, Glass wrote an essay for the *New York Times Magazine* about her work on infidelity, which questioned the conventional wisdom that a spouse's dalliances meant there was something fundamentally wrong with the marriage. He recalled how he and his two sisters "used to joke about which one of our parents must have cheated on the marriage, since the subject interested Mom so much."

Glass is engaged to his long-time girlfriend, Anaheed Alani, an editor at the *Chicago Reader*. At his Ithaca talk, he said that the Ira Glass who goes home to Alani in the evening bears little resemblance to the on-air host. "What happens is, I get very excited in my real life when I tell the story," he said. "I want to get to the details all at once, then I go on pause when I realize I've screwed it up, and I want to take it back and edit it." He imitated Alani by leaning back, folding his arms, and saying mockingly: "Master Storyteller," to the laughter and delight of the audience.

Glass is, by many accounts, a very private person. Though his radio stories, at times, have a confessional quality to them, they are thoroughly edited and scripted, right down to the "ums" and the pauses. In other words, what he says about himself is as carefully selected as the material for any other story on his show. Though I had the opportunity to see Glass speak, he refused my many requests for an interview. We had a brief telephone conversation and on-and-off email correspondence over several months. Then he sent me a final post. He apologized for the delay. "I don't want to do this," he wrote. "Not that I'm above wanting to read such a book. I'm just not sure I want to be in one."

Voice of a Sage:
Diane Rehm

Host, *The Diane Rehm Show*

There is something distinctive about public radio voices. Scanning through the dial, you can always tell when you've hit an NPR affiliate. The voices are smooth, the pace relaxed, the tone serious. They are voices of hard truths delivered gently, like a sensitive doctor carefully explaining a diagnosis.

Diane Rehm looks like a woman with such a voice. A former runway model, she is rail thin and well dressed in a maroon pants suit, the collar fashionably wide. Her hair is white-blond and worn in short, soft waves. In front of her is a laptop and a microphone labeled WAMU, the Washington, D.C., NPR affiliate where her daily call-in program, *The Diane Rehm Show,* is produced. When the show's theme music starts, she picks up the pages of her script and starts to read.

But the voice that comes out is not smooth. It's a voice with a dry tremor. It's haltingly slow. At times it creaks or even breaks. It's the voice of a woman much older than Rehm, who is sixty-nine. It's a voice that carries with it an unspoken request: *be patient with me.* And patience is a risky request in radio, as listeners who don't happen to feel patient, who are irked by the slowness, the creaks and the breaks, can simply press the scan button and move on to sing along with classic rock or catch up on the latest sports scores. For some, patience is beside the point. Rehm's voice simply isn't pleasant. Harry Levins, a journalist for the *St. Louis Post-Dispatch,* went so far as to say, cruelly, that her voice had "the quality of a fingernail being dragged across a chalkboard."

I've found that being patient, even for just a few minutes, is well worth it. I begin to give myself to the sound of Rehm's voice, her thoughtful and patient questions to her guests and callers, the reflective way she considers the topics of the day, which range from the impact of Wal-Mart on American life to therapeutic cloning to the myth of the perfect mother. The tremble stops sounding wrong. Her voice is still the voice of an old woman, but an old woman I want to keep listening to. A sage.

As Rehm put it, "people say to me that at first they thought, 'My God, what is this woman doing on the air?' And then, they continue to listen to the program for the content. Then they find my voice becomes soothing."

Rehm has spasmodic dysphonia, a rare voice disorder caused by involuntary muscle spasms in the larynx, or voice box. She would barely be able to speak at all but for regular injections of Botox into her vocal cords to stop the spasms. The Botox at first paralyzes these muscles, leaving her unable to talk at all for a week or longer. Then, she typically can be on the air for several months before her voice becomes too shaky and she needs another injection.

When Rehm was diagnosed with SD, as she refers to the disease, in 1998, she was terrified the Botox treatments wouldn't work and she would never be able to talk on the air again. But even more threatening than the loss of her career was the prospect of being silenced, a state she has dreaded since childhood. Her mother often insisted on it in their home, ordering Rehm to shut up or lower her voice. Neither of her parents, Christian Arab immigrants from Turkey, ever

asked for her opinion. They forbade her to protest any of their decisions and followed the old idea that children were to be "seen and not
heard" to extremes.

This strict environment was devastating to the bright, inquisitive
young Rehm. "It's as though I don't fully exist in silence," she wrote in
her 1999 memoir, *Finding My Voice*. "As I grow older, I become increasingly aware of how difficult a factor silence has been in my life,
and the extent to which the sounds of radio have helped me address
that difficulty."

Growing up in Washington, D.C., Rehm found consolation in listening to *The Lone Ranger, The Green Hornet, Our Gal Sunday,* and
other adventure shows and soap operas. Her first job after graduating
from high school was with the Washington, D.C., highway department, where she delighted in becoming the radio voice for the highway workers' supervisors, telling them about new repair orders or
reassignments over a two-way transmitter. She then held secretarial
jobs with the U.S. Postal Service and the Department of State. As a
yo ng mother in 1965, she took a course in fashion modeling and did
a few fashion shows and modeled for local businesses.

In 1972, the era of consciousness-raising groups and Betty Frei-
dan's *The Feminine Mystique,* Rehm took a class at George Washington University called "New Horizons for Women," also known as
Feminism 101, where her classmates encouraged her to try out
broadcasting—a career Rehm hadn't even considered before. She decided to volunteer for Irma Aandahl, the host and producer of *The
Home Show* on WAMU, a public radio station on the campus of
American University.

On Rehm's first day, Aandahl was out sick, and the substitute host
asked Rehm to join her on the air to interview the guest, a representative of the Dairy Council, there to champion the benefits of milk,
butter, and eggs. Having read a good deal about nutrition in her efforts to prepare healthy meals for her family, Rehm challenged the
guest's statements about the benefits of dairy. At the end of the

ninety-minute program, as Rehm wrote in her memoir, "I was exhilarated. I felt as though I had crossed into another world."

Her volunteer work led to a part-time job as the assistant producer of the program, whose name had been changed to *Kaleidoscope*. In 1979, after stints in health reporting for television and a closed circuit medical radio service, she took over as host when Aandahl retired. Though Rehm often filled in on the show, she felt very insecure about taking over for a popular host who'd attracted a loyal listenership. She spent hours preparing for each program, certain she was never doing enough. There were tensions in her marriage, too. She and her husband, John Rehm, then a Washington attorney, were at odds over her new professional role. No longer could she tend to home and husband as she had when she was a stay-at-home mother, and the change disoriented both of them. In an era when changing gender roles fueled a rising divorce rate, Rehm very much wanted to save the marriage. Her first marriage, begun when she was nineteen, ended in divorce, and she was leery of a second one; she also loved John very much and wanted their relationship to work.

Instead of maintaining the traditional newscaster's barrier between her on-air life and her personal life, she did something bold. She tore the barrier down. She put her husband on the air, and the two openly discussed their conflicts in a series of programs they cohosted on marriage and family issues. Topics included "What Happens When Wives Return to Work?" and "Dependence and Independence." John admitted that he missed having Diane iron his shirts and cook dinner every night. Diane described her feelings of abandonment when John went through periods of hard work and emotional withdrawal. They continued to struggle with their relationship throughout the series. At times, the two walked into the studio so angry at each other that they weren't speaking.

"And then we'd have this wonderful rapprochement," Rehm said. "We'd sort of look at each other, and perhaps start out rather formally, and then it would open up. At the end, he would get up and come over and embrace me, and I would embrace him, and we knew we had done it again."

Her show was renamed *The Diane Rehm Show* to keep in step with the growing number of talk shows on commercial radio that were named after and defined by their hosts. The show attracted high-profile guests, including Audrey Hepburn, Jimmy Carter, and Tom Clancy. Rehm also developed a reputation as a balanced alternative to the spate of new, in-your-face, opinionated talk show hosts like Rush Limbaugh and G. Gordon Liddy. She gained widespread national media attention after writing an op-ed piece in the *Washington Post* saying that talk show hosts should not take political positions, and debated other hosts on this subject, including Limbaugh himself, on national television and the lecture circuit.

Objectivity is not the only quality that sets Rehm apart from her brash counterparts. She is also unfailingly civil and gracious. "She is a lady," said Colette Dowling, a former guest on the show and the author of *The Cinderella Complex* and other books on women's issues. In person, Rehm is warm and forthcoming. But after I'd remarked on her graciousness, she insisted that she was no saint. "I'm very opinionated," she said. "I swear all the time!"

She is not afraid to be speak out, in particular when it comes to the management of her show and WAMU. She told me about the time when *The Diane Rehm Show* had the opportunity to be the first live call-in show to have on author Salman Rushdie, then making his first tentative steps back into the public eye after a *fatwah* was issued against him for writing *The Satanic Verses*. But the American University administration, fearful of the campus's safety, told Rehm to cancel the show twenty minutes before he was supposed to go on the air. "I said, 'If they cancel Salman, I'm walking out, and I'm not coming back.' And Salman Rushdie came on. You have to have the courage to stand up for what you believe in," she said. In 2003, she was one of the few WAMU staff members to speak out to the media about problems with the leadership style and spending practices of WAMU station manager Susan Clampitt, who was eventually fired.

The Diane Rehm Show began national distribution by NPR in 1995, after Rehm herself raised the $240,000 dollars needed to distribute it. This time of great triumph was also a time of great anxiety, as what had once been an occasional mysterious vocal tremor began to occur more frequently and more severely. At times she sounded as if she were being strangled on the air, and she could barely concentrate on her guests out of fear of what her voice would do. Though WAMU's then-general manager, Kim Hodgson, and several people in the NPR system expressed concern about the tightness in the voice, no one asked her to leave the show, a testament to the tolerance of public radio (despite the show's steadily rising audience numbers, it is highly unlikely that she would have been allowed to stay on the air on commercial radio).

Finally, in 1998, Rehm decided to take a leave of absence from the show. At first believing the disease might be psychosomatic, she followed an intensive schedule of therapies with a psychologist, a psychopharmacologist, and a speech therapist. "I sat at home for four months, in a chair in the living room, reading and meditating and thinking," she said. "It was really a chance for me to think about what it meant for me, to be so silent and to be without the main muscle I had used all my life."

Her convalescence also led to a rejuvenation of her spiritual life. Rehm had been raised in the Syrian Orthodox church. She sang in the children's choir, attended Sunday school, and sought refuge in prayer, asking God to help her be good so her mother would not be angry at her. As an adult she became an Episcopalian. In her struggle to restore her voice she found herself again praying for help and submitting to weekly "laying on of hands" healing rites from the bishops.

But two months into Rehm's leave of absence, her voice was no better. She was almost ready to give up her search for a cure. But John urged her on. "If it hadn't been for my husband, I sure wouldn't be sitting here now," Rehm said. "He just kept saying, 'We've got to get to the bottom of this!'" In desperation, she got a referral to the neurology department at Johns Hopkins University Hospital in Baltimore, where Dr. Paul Flint gave her the diagnosis of spasmodic dysphonia and recommended the Botox regime she still uses today.

The first round of Botox left her voiceless for two weeks, a time she used to work on her memoir. She also kept an online diary about her experience with SD for the web magazine *Slate*. Just as she had taken her marital problems to a receptive public back in her early years as a radio host, she now described her struggle with SD to the then new and thriving community of the Internet. There is a determinedly optimistic, sweet quality to her writing. "The absence of my voice has shifted my way of thinking, in that I now have a greater appreciation for silence," she wrote in her electronic journal. "Of course, my voice is absolutely necessary if I am to continue my work for WAMU and NPR. But there's a curious contradiction going on. The less I say, the more I hear."

She was back on the air weeks later. One of the first programs she did was on spasmodic dysphonia, with a panel that included all of her therapists. She's been able to maintain her presence on the show with regular Botox injections and a roster of substitute hosts, which has over the years included Melinda Penkava, journalist Steve Roberts (Cokie's husband), and others. Today, she describes herself as "becoming more comfortable" with her voice. "Harry Belafonte said to me, 'Your voice is magnificent,'" Rehm said. "And here's poor Harry. He's got this totally hoarse voice. I mean, for him to say that to me! I just thought, my God, Diane. Stop even thinking about your voice."

Rehm published *Finding My Voice* in 1999. The memoir is not just about overcoming SD. It is deeply personal and self-analytical. She describes in great detail her struggles with her childhood and her marriage and her anxiety about reconciling her success in radio with her insecurity about her ability to do the job right. She reveals that at the age of nine she was sexually molested by a congressman, whom she will not name, who promised to make her a child star. Her second book, *Toward Commitment: A Dialogue about Marriage*, written with her husband and inspired by the radio programs she did on marriage in her early days at WAMU, is similarly forthcoming; she and her husband openly discuss their sleeping arrangements (though their marriage still has "fire," they sleep in separate beds) and how they deal with finances, religion, work, and a number of other hot-button marital issues. The two books, along with her public speaking on marriage issues and SD, put her in the somewhat unusual position of being both an objective and probing newswoman/host and a public figure who insists on being intensely personal. There is nothing cheaply confessional about what she is doing, though. Rather, she sees getting personal as an elevated state, critical not only to her own development as a human being but also to how the public sees her.

"I think this country has become too focused on superficial images, on the superficial relationship that people have with people on the radio, with people who write books, with people on television," she said. "We have a relationship with the facade as opposed to the real human being. But a perfect facade is like a piece of glass. It reflects. It doesn't tell you much, except what you want to see. A personal human being relates to other human beings, which is why I get personal."

Radio of the Restless:
Neal Conan
Host, *Talk of the Nation*

ne of my trips to NPR headquarters for this book took place during one of the coldest Januarys in memory in Washington, D.C.
For days, it was blustery and the temperature hovered around fifteen
degrees, cold even for me, an upstate New Yorker. On the street,
passersby grimaced into the wind, occasionally glancing at each other
in empathy and disbelief. On one such morning, as I made my way
through Chinatown to NPR's main offices on Massachusetts Avenue
N.W., a man jogged past me in a windbreaker and shorts, with black
runner's tights on underneath. It wasn't until I saw him again on the
NPR elevator that I realized he was Neal Conan, host of *Talk of the
Nation,* public radio's most listened-to call-in show. Too disciplined
and restless to slump half-awake through the morning commute like
the rest of us, he had jogged the four miles from his home in Chevy
Chase, Maryland, to the Bethesda Metro stop, rode in to the Chinatown stop, then had another short run up to NPR headquarters.

There is a sense of that restlessness when Conan, fifty-six, is on the
air. A call-in show requires a host who can work with a minimal script
and respond quickly, not knowing quite what will happen along the

way. Such a host also needs to have a keen sense of timing and direction—let a caller go on too long, and the show becomes a tune away. *Talk of the Nation* is even more challenging, because instead of focusing in on a single topic each hour, the show typically covers two or three topics. That means that in the two hours of the program, Conan could be changing gears up to six times and talking to at least half a dozen guests and several callers from the listening audience.

The show I observed opened with a discussion of the politics of space exploration. Conan, who has red hair and a graying beard and was dressed casually in a Henley shirt and jeans, interviewed an NPR editor, a congressman from Texas, and two professors who study space policy. In the narrow call screening room adjacent to studio 3-A, two of the show's producers answered an onslaught of calls, quickly assessing what each caller wanted to talk about. They put the better prospects on hold and instant messaged Conan about them. The idea, Susan, one of the show's producers, explained, was to pick guests with a variety of opinions and balance opposing views. Conan chose a caller from Texas who supported the space program, but doubted the Bush administration was truly committed to it, and a caller who thought the money funding advances in the space program would be better spent on improving public schools.

Then Conan was announcing the next topic: a proposed airport screening program that would color code passengers according to their perceived security risk. The producers, though, were still being barraged with calls about the space program. They went through them rapidly, asking, "This is *Talk of the Nation,* are you calling about airport screening?" and quickly disconnecting call after call. During a brief break, Conan called into the screening room, "Anything for airport screening?" Justine, a thin woman with a harried voice that reminded me of the actress Hope Davis, shook her head, frowning. Conan began to interview the segment's guest, Ryan Singel, a contributing writer for *Wired News.* Justine continued, a little frantically, to get rid of space exploration callers. "He's got to give the number again," she muttered.

Then, with about five minutes left to the segment, she connected two callers, one after the other, who wanted to talk about airport screening. Bill, a frequent traveler from Chapel Hill, was for the proposed color coding. Mohammed from Tucson was not.

Score.

Conan punched Bill in first, who cheerily pronounced that he just got back from a Christmas trip to Europe and would love to be color coded. "To think I could just walk through and wave to everybody, that would be great!" he said.

After a quick comment from Singel, who doubted the system would be that easy, Conan wished Bill good luck on his next flight. Then he welcomed Mohammed.

"My question is, first of all," Mohammed said, "the population that's going to be targeted, obviously are people who appear to be Muslim or Middle Eastern looking, so that's the obvious population that will be targeted. And how is this different than Jews being given yellow tags in Nazi Germany? Are people thinking about what is happening to civil liberties and basic, basic human rights in this country?"

Conan turned the issue to the guest, condensing it to the relatively mild, "Would ethnicity be a factor?"

Singel began to answer, but Mohammed was still talking. "If you're a sand nigger, as people from the Middle East are called."

Susan cringed. "He didn't say that in the screen," Justine said.

Singel explained that there may be "quiet databases" that may include more information about Muslim people, but he said he "can't say that they intend to go after Muslims." Conan asked Mohammed whether he was "still skeptical."

"Well, this is a question of denomination of one-quarter of the planet's population, which is a racial issue, a social issue and eventually an ecological issue," Mohammed said. "The people in charge of the U.S. foreign policy need to look at why is the planet—most of the people on the planet—starting to hate this country? We should look at why we are hated, not to evade the question and not to target people who do have very, very legitimate grievances against horrible policies that are being practiced in the name of this noble Constitution of ours. Like when—"

With about a minute left to the segment, Conan cut in. "We're running out of time for this," he said. Then it was time to change the subject again, on to a discussion of burying nuclear waste at Yucca Mountain. The next hour featured writer Michael Pollan talking about livestock farming and Malcolm Gladwell of *The New Yorker* discussing the article he'd written about the popular Internet service Craig's List. When the show wrapped at a minute before four, Conan let out his breath and quietly gathered his notes to leave the studio. He looked like he finally could be spent. I wondered whether he would jog back home.

Conan first fell in love with public radio as a teenager in 1966. His family had just moved from suburban New Jersey to a Manhattan high-rise. His parents lived on the fourteenth floor, and his father, a doctor, had an office on the ground floor. After Conan got kicked out of boarding school, he moved in with them, but their new apartment didn't have a bedroom for him. He slept in his father's office. The only radio there was a KLH FM table radio, without the AM band with all the rock 'n' roll stations he usually listened to, so he explored what was then the new world of FM, at the time mostly inhabited by classical music and easy listening. But one night he tuned into a station where, as he recalled in his memoir, *Play by Play: Baseball, Radio and Life in the Last Chance League*, "people sounded like people," with everyday speech patterns. They made mistakes, and they had real conversations with each other. It turned out that he was listening to the first public radio on-air fund-raiser ever over WBAI, a Pacifica affiliate station.

He began volunteering at WBAI his senior year. He bugged the station management until he was given a chance to be on the air, a thirty-second station identification break. He was so terrified that as soon as he turned on the microphone, he wet his pants. "It was only a little," Conan said sheepishly during our interview in his corner office on the third floor of NPR.

He kept pursuing opportunities to be on the air, though, and slowly improved to the point where he was hired as an announcer and later a reporter and producer in the news department. Then he got a job at WRVR, where he met Robert Siegel, who would become a lifelong friend. After Siegel was hired at NPR, Conan began to freelance for the fledgling network. He started working full-time for NPR in 1977, as the producer for *Weekend All Things Considered.*

Since then, "I've done every job in this building," he said. "I've been a production assistant, I've directed a show, I've been a line producer, an executive producer, I've edited programs, I've run a desk, I've edited reporters, I've been a reporter, I've been a national reporter who flew all over the country, I've been a foreign correspondent, and I've been a host. I was news director for a while. It's the resume of a person with a short attention span." His more prominent roles have been as a reporter in Europe and the Middle East, the host of the now-defunct *Weekly Edition: The Best of NPR News,* and an anchor of NPR's live coverage of several political conventions, inaugurations, the Clinton impeachment, the September 11 attacks, and the wars in Afghanistan and Iraq.

Conan is married to Liane Hansen, the host of *Weekend Edition Sunday.* The two met while working on *All Things Considered* in the late 1970s. They wed in 1982 and have two children, Casey, twenty-five, a graduate of Embry-Riddle Aeronautical University, and Connor, twenty-two, a film major at Emerson College. The couple often goes for months without a day off together. Conan's workweek is Monday to Friday, while Hansen is at NPR from Wednesday to Sunday. Conan said they try to limit the time they spend at home discussing work, sometimes in vain. "One time, when she was doing *All Things Considered,* we were lying around at home together and I asked her what happened with this one moment in the show that didn't go well, and she just—" Here Conan clawed his hands in the air like a cat and made a nasty hissing noise. "It's like if you watch the movie *Star Gate*, that flash with the alien life-form parasite inside, and the eyes just glow orange, you know."

In 1991, the family was jolted when Conan was captured by Iraqi forces while covering the end of the Gulf War. He and his friend Chris Hedges, a reporter for the *New York Times*, were on their way into Basra to check out reports that a Shi'ias rebellion against Saddam Hussein was brewing. They were pulled over by Iraqi soldiers with AK-47 automatic rifles, held in a mud-and-wattle hut, then taken to a Republican Guard division.

Conan's first night in captivity, in a computer lab on the campus of Basra University, was horrible, more because of what went through his mind than how he was treated by his captors. "I remember lying there awake and thinking, I really screwed up," he said. "I had a wife and two children and I had gotten myself into this."

The next day, his captors interrogated him, Hedges, and four other kidnapped foreign journalists and took them north in a convoy headed for Baghdad. On the way, their vehicle got caught in the crossfire from a rebel attack. "The sound was unforgettable," he wrote in *Play by Play*, "some zipping by, others buzzing like bumblebees. It was chaos."

At home, word had arrived that Conan was missing. His son, Connor, then eight, was terrified that Saddam Hussein was going to get him next, and his daughter, Casey, then twelve, was, as Hansen put it, "in total denial." Hansen asked for a leave of absence from NPR.

"I wanted to be there for the kids," she said. "I felt I needed to spend time trying to find him. I wouldn't be able to concentrate. And I didn't want to have to be in a position to report my husband's death."

Her coworkers at NPR gave her crucial support. Noah Adams arrived bearing donuts and took the family for a walk. His wife, Neenah Ellis, helped the kids plant pansies in the yard. Cokie Roberts, whose father, Louisiana congressman Hale Boggs, was on a plane flight that disappeared without a trace in Alaska in 1972, also visited. NPR listeners in the community and across the country showed the family an outpouring of concern.

"Everyone felt they were a part of it," Hansen said. "I mean, it was like we were their family and it was such a connection. I don't think you get that any other place but here at NPR."

After five days in captivity, Conan was released to the Red Cross. He went to Amman, Jordan, filed several stories, and went home to reunite with his family. A few months later, he returned to Iraq for another reporting stint, but he's done no war correspondent work since.

Conan called getting captured "no great journalistic achievement" and pointed out that other journalists, such as the AP's Terry Anderson, held for six and a half years in Beirut, have suffered far worse. This modesty, he said, mingled with "irrational shame and guilt" about being kidnapped.

What also lingered for many years was the rush of the experience, of surviving capture and a crossfire in a war zone. It made news reporting in America in the go-go 1990s, with Whitewater, Newt Gingrich, the Monica Lewinsky/Clinton impeachment scandal, and the dot com boom, small and dull in contrast. As the years went by, Conan began to feel burned out.

So he decided he would become a baseball announcer.

It was 1997. He was approaching fifty. He wanted something that would challenge and thrill him the way he was challenged and thrilled (and terrified) when he first went on the air at WBAI. He was a devoted Yankees fan from childhood when, like so many boys, he'd announce aloud as he caught the tennis balls he bounced off the wall in the playground, fantasizing about his heroic save in the last inning of the World Series. He thought back to the last convention he'd covered, the Democratic Convention in Chicago the year before. As he wrote in *Play by Play*, "I would open the live coverage with a short setup, go over the lineup of speakers and events, exchange banter with an analyst and, once things got underway, describe the action as it unfolded before me. Substitute Wrigley Field for the United Center and the subject changes, but not the technique. The skills were transferable."

He was having a midlife crisis, yes, but he pursued baseball announcing with the same intensity he pursued news stories and promotions at NPR. His radio background did get him his first break—Baltimore sports agent Ron Shapiro, a public radio fan, convinced the manager of the Bowie Baysox, an Orioles affiliate in the Double A Eastern League, to give Conan a chance in the minor leagues. But the transition from news announcer to baseball announcer wasn't automatic. He had to learn how to keep score quickly and how to keep track of not only the Baysox players' names and records, but the names and records of the guys on every team they played. He practiced announcing by rehearsing in the stands with a tape recorder for several games, then got a chance to do it for real when the regular Baysox announcer had to attend his son's kindergarten graduation. From there, Conan anchored several more games that season and the next two.

He found announcing at an occasional game wasn't enough. He wanted to announce for an entire season, and he looked for a team that would hire him to do it. He got an offer from the Aberdeen Arsenal, a brand-new expansion team in Maryland owned by Cal Ripken in the independent Atlantic League, so small-time that the players had no clear path to rise to the major leagues. Then he had to choose: cover the 2000 Republican Convention and the presidential campaign to follow, or take a leave of absence to go on the road with the Arsenal. "Baseball sounded a lot more fun," he said.

So he took a five-month leave from NPR. He left his family, rented a room in a fan's house in Aberdeen, and announced the 140-game season for $75 dollars a night. He got on the team bus, ate countless McDonald's meals, talked endlessly about baseball, and watched the players try to pick up girls in bars after the games (he himself declined, he confessed in *Play by Play*, when Hansen asked him if he wanted permission to have sex on the road). He also watched the team lose, time and again, ending the season with a dismal record.

The experience gave him "a chance to recapture himself," reawakening his passion for radio and connecting him to his family in new ways. When a newspaper story about his stint in baseball announcing was published in the *Washington Post,* he found himself talking with his teenage son Connor about the last time he was in the media eye, when he was kidnapped.

"It was the first time Connor felt comfortable asking me what had happened," Conan said. "It was the first time he felt that I was available to answer the questions, I guess. He asked me what it felt like to have an AK-47 in my face. And so we were able to talk about it then."

Revived and reenergized, Conan returned to radio in time for the end of the 2000 presidential election, an off-the-field experience in play-by-play if there ever was one. He had a strong desire to continue being on the air every day, to continue to experience something more like the suspenseful, moment-by-moment feeling of baseball announcing.

That opportunity came when Juan Williams left the host seat of *Talk of the Nation* to become a senior political correspondent. The show has 2.5 million listeners, a huge change from the local public radio station that broadcast the Arsenal game to an audience so tiny that when Conan tried to give away game tickets once, no one called. Still, he says, radio, like baseball, is ultimately "a humbling business."

"You fail, as a hitter, seven times out of ten and you're considered really good," he said. "In radio, you have to make snap decisions and if only half of them are wrong, you're doing well."

Daniel Schorr, Senior News Analyst,
National Public Radio
(Associated Press/Wide World Photos)

Bob Edwards, Host, *The Bob Edwards Show*
(XM Satellite Radio/John Harrington © 2004)

Cokie Roberts, Senior News Analyst,
National Public Radio
(Steve Fenn, ABC News)

Left to right: Linda Wertheimer, Senior National Correspondent,
National Public Radio; Cokie Roberts, Senior News Analyst, NPR;
Susan Stamberg, Special Correspondent, Morning Edition; Nina
Totenberg, Correspondent, Legal Affairs, NPR
(Peter Steinhauer)

Steve Inskeep, Host, *Morning Edition*
(Steve Behrens, *Current* newspaper)

Renée Montagne, Host, Morning Edition
(Steve Behrens, *Current* newspaper)

Scott Simon, Host, *Weekend Edition*
(Photograph by Wally Skalij. *Los Angeles Times*, © 2005.
Reprinted with permission.)

Liane Hansen, Host, *Weekend Edition Sunday*
(Goodman/Van Riper Photography)

Robert Siegel, Host, *All Things Considered*
(Steve Behrens, *Current* newspaper, © 1998)

Michele Norris, Host, *All Things Considered*
(Mike Lynaugh Photography)

Melissa Block, Host, *All Things Considered*

Kai Ryssdal, Host, *Marketplace* and *Marketplace Money*
(American Public Media)

Juan Williams, Senior Correspondent,
Morning Edition
(University of Michigan Photo Services)

Jacki Lyden, Correspondent and Host,
National Public Radio
(Will O'Leary)

Taping *Wait, Wait . . . Don't Tell Me!* at Bank One Auditorium are (from left) Carl Kasell, Judge and Newscaster, National Public Radio; Peter Sagal, Host; and guest panelists Mo Rocca, Amy Dickinson, and Charlie Pierce.

Ira Glass, Host, *This American Life*

Diane Rehm, Host,
The Diane Rehm Show
(Cindy Bertaut)

Neal Conan, Host, *Talk of the Nation*
(© 1997, *Washington Post* photo by Bill O'Leary.
Reprinted with permission.)

Ira Flatow, Host, *Talk of the Nation:*
Science Friday
(Chang W. Lee/*New York Times*)

Terry Gross, Host, Fresh Air
(*The Post-Standard* and
photographer Frank Ordoñez)

Michael Feldman, Host, *Michael Feldman's
Whad'Ya Know*
(Public Radio International)

Ray, left, and Tom Magliozzi, Hosts, *Car Talk*
(Associated Press/Wide World Photos)

Garrison Keillor, Host,
A Prairie Home Companion
(Associated Press)

Brooke Gladstone, Host, *On the Media*
(Jennifer Sloan)

Bob Garfield, Host, *On the Media*
(Chris Cassidy)

Tavis Smiley, Host,
The Tavis Smiley Show
(Courtesy Public Radio International)

Kurt Andersen, Host, *Studio 360 with Kurt Andersen*
(Public Radio International)

Steve Curwood, Host,
Living on Earth
(Linda Haas)

Bill Littlefield, Host, *Only a Game*
(Mike Ostow, © 2001)

Marian McPartland, Host, *Piano Jazz*
(RJ Capak Photo-Video)

David Dye, Host, *World Cafe*
(Elena Bouvier)

Nic Harcourt, Host, *Morning Becomes
Eclectic* and *Sounds Eclectic*
(Larry Hirshowitz)

Nick Spitzer, Host,
American Routes
(Public Radio International)

John Diliberto, Host, *Echoes*
(Public Radio International)

Fred Child, Host,
Performance Today and
Creators at Carnegie
(Alex Irvin)

Korva Coleman, Host, *Performance Today* and
Symphony Space; Newscaster, NPR News
(Alan Heck)

Christopher O'Riley,
Host, *From the Top*
(Pubic Radio International)

Bill McGlaughlin, Host,
St. Paul Sunday
(American Public Media)

Walking around the World:
Ira Flatow

Host, *Talk of the Nation: Science Friday*

Ira Flatow has reported from the South Pole, interviewed Nobel Prize laureates, and hosts a weekly call-in show, but he is most remembered for a radio segment he did more than a quarter century ago about what happens when you chew wintergreen Lifesavers in the dark.

A mother from Baltimore had written to Flatow about her children's claim that wintergreen Lifesavers sparked in the dark when they ate them. She asked him to investigate. He and then–*All Things Considered* host Susan Stamberg brought two packs of the candy and a portable tape recorder into a dark closet at NPR. When he bit down on the hard candy with an audible crunch, Stamberg squealed with her trademark élan, "I saw it! I saw a flash of a kind of greenish light!"

Flatow asked listeners if they knew why the flash occurred, and he received a deluge of responses. He later could report that when sugar is crushed it gives off a high voltage discharge, which charges the nitrogen in the air and produces the light. Smashing a sugar cube (or a cherry Lifesaver, for that matter) with a hammer had the same effect, as he demonstrated in a reprise of the segment a year later.

The Lifesaver story was a watershed moment for NPR. The segment was cozy and a little wacky, a couple of buddies ducking into a closet for a bit of nerdy fun. It was theatrical, with Flatow playing the scientific straight man to Stamberg's high-pitched exclamations. It was great radio. The sounds of the creation of a sugary spark and the reaction to it were far more evocative than an image of the same could be (just imagine a brief, tiny green glow in the dark in the middle of your television screen—not very exciting). There were some amusing incidentals, too. Two coworkers ducking into the company closet created a mild suggestion of mischief, and corporate officials at Kraft refused to give NPR a comment for the story, as if the spark was some sort of scandalous revelation that threatened candy sales. Years later, though, the company would celebrate the trick in a commercial.

For Flatow, fifty-six, the main delight of the experience was that the segment was about science, and it got a rise out of people. The Lifesaver story received more listener mail than anything that had been aired on NPR up to that point.

"It could have been a really boring story," Flatow said. "If I had gone on the radio that day and said, 'Hey, we're going to talk about triboluminescence,' radios would've clicked off around the country."

Making great radio about science is still Flatow's life work. He hosts the NPR call-in show *Talk of the Nation: Science Friday*. A driving force behind the success of the show is Flatow's knack for finding good science talkers, people who can explain what they're doing effectively in layman's terms, placing their research in a broader context.

"Scientists often say they learn more and more about less and less," he said. "I like people who think about how they fit into the rest of the world."

He also enjoys what he calls "kooky" scientists who take unconventional approaches to their research and thinking. "A lot of the difference between being a crazy person and winning the Nobel Prize is that you happen to be right," he said.

Science Friday, as the show is generally known, is broadcast out of a rented studio at Sirius Satellite Radio in midtown Manhattan. The show is one of the geekier tenants at Sirius, which brims with the high-tech cool that comes with being the next big thing in radio listening. When Karen Visgoth, one of the show's producers, met me in the lobby, she told me that Eric Clapton had been spotted there the week before, a fact repeated to me later by a couple of other staff members.

A few minutes before *Science Friday* went on the air, Flatow came into the control room. In a burgundy button-down shirt and a tan sweater vest, he seemed relaxed, and so did his staff, a contrast to the quiet prebroadcast tension typical of shows airing out of NPR's head-quarters in Washington, D.C. Flatow chatted with a science writer he'd met at a convention and invited to observe the show. She had the glow in her eyes of a groupie finally let backstage, and Flatow regaled her with a story about the time the primatologist Jane Goodall was a guest. A listener called in to ask her whether she believed in Yeti, also known as the Abominable Snowman, widely viewed as a Himalayan myth. She replied that she did—and that she hoped new technology for DNA analysis of fur fibers and other leavings would help re-searchers find him.

"You could have blown me away with a feather," Flatow said. "You know, she's a world-class scientist. It makes you think twice."

That day's show featured a discussion of the search for water on Mars, concerns over genetically engineered organisms, a cosmology news update, an astronomer's preview of the spring sky, and an effort to create a genetic map of the ecosystems of the sea. As a host, Flatow is a kind of friendly science mensch, knowledgeable but never snobby. Though he's not afraid to throw in an arcane question from time to time, he keeps the conversation from wandering too far into obscurity.

He also brings an unabashed enthusiasm to his job, and that makes it easy to get pulled into the show, even if you're not sure you can be, the way I felt when Flatow introduced genomics pioneer Craig Ven-ter, who is traveling the world in his yacht, collecting microbes in order to sequence the genomes of the microbial ecosystems of the sea. I grew more intrigued when Flatow compared Venter to Darwin, "sailing the seas in the name of science."

"Traveling the world filtering seawater sounds pretty nice," Flatow said. "And it may be fruitful—Venter and his colleagues say they've already discovered a million new genes and thousands of new species of microorganisms."

It's not often you hear someone gush about filtering seawater. But this is the kind of person Flatow is. He is a man who can't hold a handful of soil without thinking of the millions of germs and DNA parts therein, who can't make it from the driveway to the front door on a clear night without gazing up at the stars and the planets, and who causes you to wonder if you shouldn't be living the same way— even if you never before thought of filtering seawater as fun, or never thought of filtering seawater, period.

When Flatow was a kid growing up on Long Island in the 1960s, he built crystal radios and oscilloscopes from Heath kits and made his own punch card reader, used in the early days of computing. His basement was full of old televisions, which he took apart and put back together again until he was skilled enough to fix his family's black-and-white. His interest in science and engineering came from his father, uncle, and brother, all "great tinkerers," Flatow said. He didn't realize it was unusual for a yeshiva boy (his family was "semi-Orthodox" and he attended a Jewish elementary school) to tinker until Ketzel Levine, NPR's gardening expert and an old friend of Flatow's, teased him about the elaborate backyard urban garden he designed and planted when he was living in the Capitol Hill neighborhood of Washington, D.C. "She'd say, 'You couldn't have done this!'" Flatow laughed. "I asked her why, and she said, 'You're Jewish. No Jewish boy can do this sort of thing.' I had no idea about the stereotype."

The other passion of his childhood was radio. At night, he'd jump into bed and turn the lights out to listen to WOR in New York City. He'd catch *The Dick Clark Show*, then Jean Shepherd's forty-five-minute monologues, scriptless, conversational musings about childhood, family, and society, which he claimed were fictional, though he always delivered them in first-person. "I was transfixed," Flatow said.

Flatow didn't imagine himself on the radio, or as anything but a straightlaced future engineer, until his junior year in high school. His English teacher, impressed by an in-class reading he'd done from *Death of a Salesman*, suggested he try out for the school play, *Rally 'Round the Flag, Boys!* He did, and he got the lead.

"Here I was, this very close, staid little engineering science geek guy, with a pocket protector and everything," he said. "And I turned out to be a ham. I got bitten by the theatrical bug, and my hamminess took off."

He attended the State University of New York at Buffalo to study engineering, but he didn't enjoy the major and the school didn't have a strong drama program. He tried the campus radio station, WBFO, at first staying behind the scenes to run the sound board. But the anti–Vietnam War fervor of the late 1960s was sweeping the campus, so he volunteered to be a reporter. "They literally threw a tape recorder at me and said, 'Go cover this demonstration in Niagara Square,'" Flatow said.

Flatow's boss at WBFO was Bill Siemering, who went to Washington, D.C., in 1970 to start *All Things Considered*. Siemering hired Flatow as a tape editor when the program went on the air the following year. Soon after he arrived, Mike Waters, another former WBFO employee and one of the original hosts of *All Things Considered*, told him they were going back to Buffalo to throw a barrel over Niagara Falls with a tape recorder inside to find out what it sounded like.

"It was all about, 'Let's find something different that we can sound! Let's find a different way to tell a story with as much sound as we can!'" Flatow said.

The adventure was typical of the capers at NPR in the 1970s, a time of rich experimentation, when radio serials like *The Shadow* were more likely to be the inspiration for the show than news magazines like *60 Minutes*. The network was a highly idealistic place, with the spirit of inquiry of a liberal arts college humanities seminar and the ballsy ambition to reinvent radio. In this charged new environment, Flatow was taken under the wing of Josh Darsa, a chain-smoking

producer who came from CBS News, where he'd made his name as
the first U.S. television reporter to interview the Beatles, and a trio of
rising female political reporters known as "The Fallopian Jungle":
Cokie Roberts, Nina Totenberg, and Linda Wertheimer. "We went
out to lunch all the time. I was like their adopted kid," Flatow said.

Flatow's main job was to cut tape (the term for editing the magnetic
reel-to-reel recording tape with a razor blade, in the days before the
process was done on computer) for the documentaries Darsa produced. Back then, documentaries ran every evening on *All Things
Considered,* on subjects as varied as a blind man who fell onto the subway tracks in New York City and survived by feeling his way under the
platform; the euthanasia of dogs in dog pounds, with the poignant and
controversial sound of a dog being put to sleep; and the life of Groucho Marx, produced after his death in 1977. Hard news, also known as
breaking news, did not have as much of a presence on the show as it
does today. "In the early days, news was something that happened in
the program, but it was not the reason for the program," Flatow said.

Amidst all this idealism, though, loomed daily deadlines.

"We would be in this little booth, sometimes for twenty-four, thirty-
six straight hours, to get the tape finished for six o'clock," Flatow said.
"Sometimes, it would literally be one minute to six and we'd still be
sitting there with a razor blade. And, a minute after six we're supposed to be on the air and sometimes we weren't on the air and Mike
Waters would be trying to fill until we're done, and every minute that
he fills is another minute I gotta pull out of the reel because the piece
has to end at 6:30!"

Flatow was also becoming the scientific brains of the network.
When Mike Waters interviewed a scientist or a science writer, Flatow
whispered follow-up questions into his headphones, à la Holly Hunter
in *Broadcast News.* Soon Waters suggested that Flatow go on the air as
a science reporter and substitute host. His old high school hamminess,
combined with what he'd learned as a tape editor and a producer
about constructing stories with vivid scripts and the use of sound,
made him a charming, funny, and adventurous communicator of the

whys, wherefores, and latest developments in science. He had Susan Stamberg slosh her arm in a fish tank filled with oil and water to demonstrate the two don't mix and recorded the sound of one of the NPR toilets flushing while observing that the water swirls clockwise. In a memorable 1979 series on Antarctica, he recorded the sound of his footsteps crunching on the frozen landscape as he walked around the bamboo pole marking the South Pole. Huffing and puffing in the forty-degrees-below-zero air, he announced that "you could claim that just by circling the Pole, you have walked totally around the world."

In 1981, he moved to NPR's New York bureau, where he worked for five years. He left NPR in 1987 to work in television and write his first book, *Rainbows, Curveballs, and Other Wonders of the Natural World Explained.* He hosted *Newton's Apple,* a popular-science series on PBS and did a stint as a science reporter for CBS News. Flatow said that though CBS supported his work, he had to contend with a certain amount of confusion and insecurity about how science news should be presented. He remembered being called into his producer's office one morning, only to find him pacing nervously.

"He said, 'I want to ask you a question,' and I said, 'I've been around, let me guess what that question is,'" Flatow said. "I said, 'Because I'm your science reporter, and this is television, and it's commercial television, you want me to look like a science reporter should, right? You want me to wear a white lab coat when I'm on television, right?' His eyes light up and he says, 'How did you know that?' And I said, 'I'll make you a deal. If your business reporter wears a green eye shade, and those little sleeves, and everything else, I'll wear the white lab coat.' And he looked at me, I had on my suit, and he said, 'What you have on now is just right.' He admitted he was being silly."

Flatow returned to NPR in 1990 with an idea for a weekly call-in show about science. He thought NPR could have something to offer in the Rush Limbaugh–driven resurgence of call-in radio shows nationwide. Flatow's idea didn't come to fruition until after the Gulf War. During the war, NPR started airing a daily afternoon call-in show for listeners to ask questions about unfolding events. After the war was over, stations wanted NPR to put together a permanent call-in show, and so *Talk of the Nation* was born, with general interest topics from Monday through Thursday and Fridays reserved for Ira Flatow and science. While *Talk of the Nation* broadcasts out of Washington, D.C., *Science Friday* is based in New York. Most of the week, Flatow works from his office near his home in Stamford, Connecticut, and his staff works out of an office in back of a bridal shop on 45th Street. "You have to walk through the mannequins and everything to get to our little spot back there," he said.

Flatow is married to Miriam Flatow, who has worked in theater and dance administration and costume design and "is a real Gilbert and Sullivan expert," Flatow said. "She knows every single word." The couple has three children: Sam, twenty-one; Anna, eighteen; and Abigail, fifteen. None of the kids, Flatow said resignedly, has caught the science bug.

"I once had a psychologist on the air and during the break I said, 'You know, why is it that my kids don't have this interest?'" he said. "She said, 'You know why? You don't realize it, but you're the professor, you're their teacher, and no one ever wants to do what their teacher did. You're an evangelist for nature and explaining the beauty of it. You're just preaching too hard. You have to back off a bit.'"

Perhaps with his kids, but nowhere else. Flatow is busy brainstorming for a new project: a twenty-four-hour cable news science channel. "There's so much going on in science," he said. "You've got great personalities, you've got great research going on all the time, all kinds of socially relevant and politically relevant topics."

But Flatow said science in the media is still a hard sell, despite what he feels is its obvious appeal. He points out that *Science Friday* has one and a half million listeners every week. And whenever he is a guest on other local call-in shows, which usually cover topics other than science, "the switchboard lights up," he said. "The announcer looks at me like, 'What are you selling here? What magic do you have?' I say, 'I have no magic. People love to talk about science.'"

Teacher: Terry Gross

Host, *Fresh Air*

Terry Gross almost had a career as a junior high school teacher. It was 1973. She had recently graduated from the State University of New York at Buffalo. She took a job as an eighth-grade English teacher in a local school. She was, by her own account, a hippie with frizzy hair and purple corduroy jeans. Several of the students were taller than she was. They knocked over bookshelves when supervisors came to the classroom and spread rumors that she was a heroin addict. She was fired after six weeks.

It is mind-boggling to think of all the radio we would never have had, had she fallen in love with blackboards and grammar lessons and asking kids to read the first page of chapter two out loud—the interviews with Nicolas Cage, Johnny Cash, Marilynne Robinson, Chris Rock, and more than five thousand other significant voices on the cultural and political landscape. It is hard to imagine a world where her unmistakably breathy and enthusiastic announcement, "I'm Terry Gross, and this is *Fresh Air*" would not go over the airwaves every weekday to four and a half million listeners.

Fresh Air sets the gold standard for the art of the interview. The show does everything public radio does well: it's interesting, relevant, civil (most of the time), and even-handed (most of the time). But then there's a realm that is Gross's alone. She isn't really an interviewer. She has conversations. She listens incredibly well and responds to details that intrigue her, willing to pursue the unexpected instead of merely checking off a list of questions. She keeps a sense of wonder in her conversations, without sounding at all naive. In the end, the interview feels like an experience, a journey, not a confrontation or a fact-finding mission. I listen to *Fresh Air* with a level of absorption that I don't find on any other radio program.

In the public radio world, Gross is still a teacher. Everyone I know in the field wants to Make Radio Like Terry Does. I know I do. I've analyzed her questions, the way she guides the interview from topic to topic, her choice of guests. Though a colleague once teased "Nice Terry Gross imitation!" on an author interview I did, I'm sure I've largely failed to achieve anything close to her level. But it's never been a waste of time to try.

I met Terry Gross in 1992. She was the featured speaker at a fund-raising reception for NPR affiliate KWMU in St. Louis. At the time, I had a graduate assistantship in the news department of WSIE, another public radio station across the Mississippi River in Edwardsville, Illinois. I had come to the reception with several other women who were also just starting out in radio. We all idolized Gross and hoped for a few pointers.

Gross is short, about five feet tall, and that is what hits you first. In a photograph a friend took of the two of us talking, I am slouched over my drink, as if trying to get to eye level with her. But Gross is not just short, she is barely there. She is thin, with a boyish figure and close-cropped gamine hair that's caused lots of speculation about her sexuality (she is straight). She is pale and wears large glasses with pronounced frames. She has a bookish, yeshiva boy air, as if she doesn't get outside very often, her days too filled with study, though instead of bending over the Torah and the Talmud, she is speed-skimming novels and newspapers, listening to music, watching DVDs of films and the latest dark-natured original series on HBO, preparing for her interviews. She looks in the photograph as if she would rather be doing these things than talking to me and my friends, who were trying to make it in public radio and wanted to find out how she did.

Gross once told a group of journalism graduate students at the University of California–Berkeley, "I work in a medium where I get to be totally invisible, and I get great pleasure from that, being a pretty self-conscious person." At the beginning of her career she even refused to have her photograph taken, wanting to honor this invisibility. But by the time we met, she was too well known, too sought after, to hide. If indeed on that day she felt timid, she pushed herself past it. She answered our questions graciously, if a bit flatly, her slight Brooklyn accent more apparent than it was on the air. She even offered to listen to demo tapes of our own radio efforts. I'm not sure who took her up on the offer. I was too scared. What my friends and I wanted was to *be* her, to spend our days absorbed in the finest offerings of American culture, to ask Jodie Foster with sensitivity and an utter lack of pretense what it was like to seduce Robert De Niro's character in *Taxi Driver*, to boldly yet gently press James Baldwin on why he's spoken out on civil rights issues but not on gay rights. We wanted to laugh the way Gross laughs, with genuine delight and surprise, emotions rarely expressed in the overly scripted media universe we were trying to break into.

Terry Gross, fifty-four, grew up in Brooklyn. She has said that she loved musical theater and listening to the antics of deejays like Murray "the K" Kaufman on rock 'n' roll radio, but there were very few women on the air at the time and she never imagined she would have a career on the radio. She wished she could be a writer or a lyricist, but never thought she actually could be one, so she turned to teaching. But after her teaching debut flopped, radio saved her. One of her roommates, she told us, was a host on *Woman Power*, the feminist radio program broadcast on WBFO, the NPR affiliate at the University of Buffalo. The roommate came out as a lesbian on the air, much to everyone's surprise. Her lover, who also worked on the show, decided that now that their relationship was out in the open, she would move to WBFO's lesbian-feminist program. Gross took her place on *Woman Power.* The first show she did was about the history of restrictive women's undergarments, such as the bra and the girdle, and consisted of her reading summaries of research she'd done on the topic and playing every song she could find that mentioned clothing. Despite this awkward start, she quickly fell in love with radio and learned on the job how to interview guests, edit tape, and relax her voice so she didn't sound like Minnie Mouse on the air.

She went on to host *This Is Radio*, a daily afternoon interview show. WBFO's program director, David Karpoff, soon moved on to WHYY (then WUHY) in Philadelphia and created *Fresh Air*, a show inspired by *This Is Radio*. Gross went to Philadelphia to host *Fresh Air* in 1975, after it had been on the air for about a year. The program, broadcast from two to five every afternoon, was live, local, and more politically oriented than it is today. Until Danny Miller, then a Temple University student and now her executive producer, showed up to offer his services as an unpaid intern in 1978, Gross had no staff. That meant that she did everything. She scheduled interviews, met the guests, did the interviews, and played records in between. The show went national in 1985. It aired once a week at first, then became a daily show in 1987.

Gross approaches her interview subjects with great care and preparation. She crafts her questions and talking points to communicate, without showing off, that she knows and respects her guests' work and lives, an approach that's important in getting guests to trust her and open up. She reads, listens, and watches as much as she can in advance, her research obtaining a sometimes scholarly thoroughness. I've heard her bring up thirty-year-old newspaper articles and deeply obscure bits of trivia—she's even had guests express amazement at the depth of her preparation. She herself has said she never feels completely prepared, having only about two to three hours to get ready for each interview.

With prep time, staff meetings, edits, and taping interviews, Gross's days can be extremely long. She has said she works until dinner and then works until bedtime. She and her husband, Francis Davis, a jazz writer and contributing editor for *The Atlantic Monthly*, do not have children. "I always felt like I couldn't imagine doing the show and having children," she told the *Detroit News*. Her social life has also been limited by work. She told an audience at a 1998 speech at the University of California–Berkeley that "the paradox of my life is that while I'm home preparing to be a sensitive interviewer, I'm a lousy friend." She told Scott Simon on *Weekend Edition* that she meets few people outside of work. "My life is intellectually adventurous, but in the physical world, I'm almost always in a chair reading or watching or listening," she said.

Her interviews with creative guests—artists, writers, actors, and so forth—are often biographical, her questions geared toward exploring their inner lives and imaginations and giving a sense of who they are as people. She has written in *All I Did Was Ask: Conversations with Writers, Actors, Musicians, and Artists*, her 2004 collection of interviews from *Fresh Air*, that she "violate[s] decorum" all the time in her interviews, asking a guest about his religion or sexual fantasies in a way she never could in normal social discourse. She's gotten author John Updike to talk about his stutter and his psoriasis and vibraphonist Gary Burton to talk about coming out as a gay man in the jazz world. She takes advantage of the fact that the interviews are prerecorded and edited, telling artists that they have the right to turn down questions they feel are too personal, or to start over if they're not comfortable with how they've expressed themselves.

She's tougher on political figures. They don't get the same right of refusal when personal questions are relevant to issues in the public eye. She pushed Nancy Reagan to answer questions about social issues such as AIDS and homelessness during her husband's presidency, while all Reagan wanted to do was promote her ghostwritten autobiography. She asked Newt Gingrich about a published report that he'd had oral sex with his girlfriend in a car, which Gross felt was relevant because of Republican reaction to the then-ongoing Monica Lewinsky scandal in the Clinton administration. Monica Lewinsky herself walked out of her interview with Gross after being asked about giving the president oral sex while he was on the telephone in the Oval Office.

Though some of her guests come to the WHYY studios, most of them speak with Gross from a remote location, typically at their local public radio station, using a satellite hookup or a digital telephone line. She likes being with her guests in person, but also enjoys the "pure radio" of not being able to see them face-to-face. "Anything they want to communicate to me has to be with sound," Gross said in an interview on WAMC Northeast Public Radio in Albany. "Maybe that means they have to work a little bit harder to make sure they're communicating, through their words or their laugh or their sound, what it is they want to communicate, which would be good thing, because it means the listeners would be in on it and not just me."

Orville Schell, the dean of University of California Graduate School of Journalism and a China expert who's been interviewed several times on *Fresh Air*, has compared the experience of being interviewed by Gross in a studio far away from her to Freud's preference for sitting behind his patient's couch so he wouldn't be able to influence them with his facial expressions and body language. "Far from impeding her ability to establish rapport, distance has, counterintuitively, enabled Ms. Gross to create a sense of closeness and engagement that has become a hallmark of what many see as the best interview show in broadcasting," he wrote in a 2001 *New York Times* article. "As with Freud, Ms. Gross's ability to draw her subjects out seems to increase in direct proportion to her separation."

Musa Mayer, a breast cancer patient advocate and author who has been interviewed twice by Gross from studios in New York City, agrees that "there's a disinhibition that happens" because she and Gross aren't sitting face-to-face. More important for Mayer, though, is Gross's approach to asking questions. "I know I can count on her to get to a deeper level and to pick up on surprising insights," Mayer said. "Very often what happens to me with radio interviewers is they have their own agenda and that's all they want to talk about and they don't really listen. With Terry, you feel like you've been understood, like she hasn't just read the first page of your book and then pretty much nothing."

Not every guest has been so pleased. Some have walked out on her. *Rolling Stone* editor Jann Wenner left after she asked him about accounts that he exaggerated subscriber numbers in the magazine's early days to attract advertisers. Lou Reed did the same when she asked him how he felt about being middle-aged. More recently, right-wing Fox News host Bill O'Reilly terminated an interview after Gross asked him about whether he used his television program to settle scores with his critics.

Her 2001 interview with Gene Simmons, the bass player with the rock group Kiss, is probably her most infamous. She wanted to talk to him about the glam makeup he wore onstage and what it was like to grow up as an Orthodox Jew and then transform himself into a seventies pop icon. He parried sarcastically with her, making sexual insinuations including the oft-quoted line: "if you want to welcome me with open arms I'm afraid you're also going to have to welcome me with open legs." Gross called him "obnoxious," setting aside her usual polite detachment. "By the time the encounter was over, we sounded like two first-graders calling each other names," she wrote in *All I Did Was Ask*. She and her staff decided to air the interview anyway, on the grounds that even if it was a train wreck as an interview, it made great radio drama. Simmons's appearance inspired three thousand emails and the attention of the *New York Post*, *Entertainment Weekly*, and a number of other national newspapers and magazines.

For all the interviews she's conducted, Terry Gross is not always comfortable being interviewed herself. Though she has consented to a number of interviews over the years in connection with speaking engagements and the publication of *All I Did Was Ask,* she describes herself as a private person, having been brought up by parents who, as residents of a crowded Brooklyn apartment building and as Jews who lived through the time of the Holocaust, carefully guarded their own personal lives. Gross declined to be interviewed for this book after repeated requests, to my great disappointment. A small consolation is the thirteen-year-old photograph of the two of us together at that reception in St. Louis, talking about radio, my head bent toward her, listening closely.

King of Quips:
Michael Feldman

Host, *Michael Feldman's Whad'Ya Know?*

It's fifteen minutes before air time on a Saturday morning in July, and Michael Feldman is warming up the audience for the live broadcast of *Whad'Ya Know?*

"Where are you guys from?" he asks.

"Arizona!" someone shouts out.

"Arizona," Feldman scoffs mildly. "No one's really *from* there."

He paces in front of the show's stage set, which looks like the last afternoon of a Midwestern yard sale. There's a statue of a cow, about half of life size, its flank bearing the slogan: "Wisconsin: America's Dairyland." A knee-high Del Monte plastic banana leans against an orange vinyl booth seat. There's also a green sea creature blow-up doll, a varnished wood wagon, a Bakelite radio, and an applause meter, ranging from "tea party" to "kegger" to "japatui," a Wisconsin expression of uninhabited enthusiasm.

A woman shouts out that she lives in Florida, but originally came from New York.

"See, she's free to admit it," Feldman says.

Then he takes a step back and looks out at the audience. There are about three hundred people here, a full house in the lecture room at Monona Terrace, a convention center overlooking Lake Monona in Madison, *Whad'Ya Know?*'s hometown. On tour, Feldman packs venues that seat several thousand. So this mix of locals, some of them who faithfully attend every Madison broadcast, and tourists, eager to see the face behind the voice (and arguably Madison's most famous resident), feels chummy and intimate. They're primed for more teasing, but his mood has shifted, become more contemplative.

"You are here in the audience with no background, no future," he says. "You can live in the moment. Abandon all distractions: family problems. Work. Medication."

It is as close to seriousness as Feldman, fifty-six, gets in front of an audience, meaning that it's probably still a state of mock seriousness. He doesn't really mean it the way, for example, a Zen meditation teacher saying the same sort of thing would mean it. But he means it in a Michael Feldman way. That's to say that in the relative levels of joking around that Feldman bounces through in the course of his weekly radio program, this one may rate, were there a meter to measure it, "least insincere."

In any case, the audience seems all too ready to be in the moment and have a little fun. Feldman points out the applause sign, and everyone claps heartily when it lights up. He asks for a volunteer to read the infamous disclaimer statement for the quiz (which, for the uninitiated, starts out: "All questions used on *Whad'Ya Know?* have been painstakingly researched although the answers have not. Ambiguous, misleading, or poorly worded questions are par for the course. Listeners who are sticklers for the truth should get their own shows"). Dozens raise their hands. One boy who looks to be about ten shouts "Me, me!" as if Feldman were giving away tickets to Disney World. He picks someone else, a guy named Jeff from Middleton, Wisconsin.

Just before ten o'clock, Feldman settles down into the booth. He has small, bemused eyes and sports a goatee. He looks quite a bit like the comedian Robin Williams, though Feldman's style is as under-whelmed as Williams's is revved up. To Feldman's right is his backup band: bassist Jeff Hamann, with gangly long limbs and dark hair slicked back lounge lizard–style, and pianist John Thulin, with short salt-and-pepper hair and a long oval face. To Feldman's left is his an-nouncer, Jim Packard, a veteran Madison radio man with an upturned nose, a prominent chin, and a reddish complexion, which clashes with his bright orange shirt.

The on-air sign lights up.

"Stephen Hawking now says black holes are neither black nor holes," Feldman says. "This is quite a startling development, ending all hope for a parallel universe with a parallel Michael Feldman with good eyes, taller, maybe thirty-two years of age. This is what I call stunned disbelief."

He gets a titter of laughter.

"Never start off with a Stephen Hawking joke," he says.

"No," Packard shakes his head. "It disappears into the cosmos."

"Will you make a note of that?"

"Yes, I will."

"Well, whad'ya know?" Feldman asks resignedly.

"Not much. You?" the audience choruses, perfectly on cue, as au-diences have done for the past twenty years *Whad'Ya Know?* has been in existence.

Michael Feldman's Whad'Ya Know? is part stand-up comedy, part quiz show, and part late night television–style talk show. The pro-gram starts with "All the News That Isn't," an opening monologue of quips inspired by current events. Feldman will do a couple of offbeat interviews; in the first hour of this morning's show, it's Dan Hill, the author of *Body of Truth* and an expert on body language, and in the second hour, he talks to Don Gorske, the Fond du Lac prison warden made famous in the documentary *Super Size Me* for consuming twenty thousand Big Macs. The "Town of the Week" segment features a telephone interview with a town resident, typically the first person reached by a show staff member calling random numbers in the local phone book. In "Thanks for the Memos," Feldman reads bizarre office memos sent in by listeners, such as "Please refrain from leaving undergarments or sports gear in or around the lavatory facilities. It can be very dangerous, as I'm sure you'll all remember. Last month Mrs. Wicker tripped on a piece of male undergarment and bruised her leg."

The quizzes on *Whad'Ya Know?* have audience members and callers competing for prizes—usually trinkets and gift packages of Wisconsin cheese—over an offbeat variant of the sorts of questions heard on *Jeopardy!* Feldman is a slyly gentle host. On this broadcast, the two contestants—Rhoda, a retiree on the phone from Oregon, and Katie, a college student chosen from the live audience—debate the answer to the question of whether 10, 25, or 60 percent of eighteen- to twenty-four-year-olds are "jealous of celebrities." They decide on 25, but Feldman holds off on the "wrong answer" buzzer, repeating the question a second time. He waits until Rhoda muses, "60 is like two-thirds . . . should we go with 60?" and quickly dings the "right answer" bell.

Feldman isn't really after the competitive spirit; he's too eager for opportunities to banter with contestants and the audience. And they eat it up. When Rhoda gushes to Feldman, "I just can't believe this. I listen to your show all the time!" Feldman returns, "I can't believe it either. That we'd meet like this. Because I've fantasized about this for years, that some day you would call, and here you are."

Feldman will also spend quite a bit of time on the show just roaming through the aisles with his microphone, drawing audience members out with everything from a comment about their clothing to questions like how much beer fits in a sousaphone. His style is drawn in part from *Tonight Show* creator Steve Allen, whom Feldman watched on *The Steve Allen Comedy Hour* back in the 1960s, when he was in junior high school.

"He'd have guests, but he'd go in there and work the audience pretty much by the seat of his pants," Feldman told me. "He's really an innovator in that kind of talk format."

What's funny about *Whad'Ya Know?* can be difficult to pinpoint. Feldman is not loud or shocking. He's not particularly hip. His oldest daughter, Ellie, fourteen, won't even deign to come to the show. "I don't think she's ever heard of me, to tell you the truth," Feldman said. From listeners, the show elicits very mixed reactions—from great adoration to those who simply don't get it. Feldman probably would be completely lost on Comedy Central, and in fact attempts to get him on television, one by the Disney Channel and two by other syndicators, failed miserably. He speaks in an offhand, Wisconsin-accented undertone, at times almost a mutter. In high school, he wasn't the popularity-hungry class clown. Rather, he'd crack jokes quietly to the person in front of him and to either side, hoping girls would notice him. Like another one of his influences, Groucho Marx, Feldman gets a lot of his laughs from innuendo. When a phone trilled from the audience during his Madison broadcast, he called out, "All right, whose cell is that? Huh? Man, put it on vibrate. You'll have a good time, we'll have a good time."

Feldman's humor draws on two seemingly opposing American comedic traditions: the folksy, relaxed humor of the heartland (typified by his rival, Garrison Keillor) and the bawdy, fast-paced gags of Catskill comedians. His brother Howard, an attorney, calls the hybrid "the Milwaukee School of Comedy," originating with the 1950s television writer Nat Hiken (*Sergeant Bilko, The Phil Silvers Show*) and spoofmaster brothers David and Jerry Zucker (*Airplane, The Naked Gun*), all Milwaukee natives.

"You get kind of a laid-back Jew," Feldman said. "A self-effacing, laid-back Jew."

But not too laid-back. He calls himself "one big anxiety, Mr. Anxiety." He says he's always felt like an alien in the Midwest, where the norm is still considered to be white and Christian. He's always either explaining to fans that he's a Milwaukee native and no, he did not grow up in New York, or he's being embraced as a fellow outsider. Years ago, a listener in a yarmulke greeted him at the Rapid City, South Dakota, airport one April with a bag of matzohs.

"It's hard to get matzohs in the Black Hills during Passover, apparently," he said.

In person, this alien anxiousness, which some have described as Woody Allen meets the heartland, comes across as skittishness. He tends to quip rather than converse. When I showed up for our interview, arranged by a member of the show's staff, after his Madison show, he told me he didn't realize I was coming and suggested I go with him to lunch at the Great Dane Pub and Brewery, where the cast and crew eat after every Madison broadcast. He asked my husband, who was planning to stroll our two-month-old daughter around during the interview, to join us, too. So I found myself sitting on a stool across from Feldman in a noisy bar, my daughter napping in her stroller behind me while I worried she'd wake up and cry. My husband sat beside her, talking to the band members. Two other visitors, who worked at public radio affiliate WNIJ in Rockford, Illinois, were there wanting to talk to Feldman as well. It was, to say the least, not the most conducive environment for an interview. I suggested doing the interview after lunch, but Feldman shrugged and said, "We can just talk right here." It wasn't until later that I realized it might not have been a question of his being too busy to talk later. Maybe he wanted the crowd, the sense of an audience, the sense of me as just another audience member he could banter with.

This is just speculation, of course. In the end, he covered quite a bit of ground in the interview, quip by quip.

Feldman likes to refer to himself as a "twenty-five-year overnight sensation." He got his start in radio in 1965, when he was still in high school. The youngest of four sons of David Feldman, a Milwaukee accountant, and Geraldine Feldman, a stay-at-home mom, Michael won contests at two different local rock stations to be a guest deejay.

"I wrote a letter saying I was the Diogenes of Milwaukee and I went down to Bradford Beach and practiced elocution with pebbles in my mouth," he said. "Both stations bought it so I got to host two shows. I played 'What Kind of Fool Am I' for the Milwaukee Braves. That was their last year in town."

When he asked the manager at one of the stations about a career in radio, the man told him to forget about it and go to college, "apparently because he'd ruined his whole life by being in radio, as most people in it do," Feldman said. He took the advice, enrolling in the University of Wisconsin. He had two brothers who were doctors and one who was a lawyer, and he was in the process of applying to law school when a friend of his asked him if he was sure he wanted to be a lawyer.

"I never really thought of it. I just thought, well, at a certain point nothing else works, you become a lawyer," he said. "So I took all the applications, put them in a bowl, and burned them. And I let the ashes sit in the bowl on my kitchen table for about a week. Every time I passed it, I would say, law school, there it is."

Instead, after college he ended up teaching high school English for six years in Kenosha, Wisconsin. Then he returned to Madison to take a job at Malcolm Shabazz City High School, an alternative school. Radio's allure didn't fade. In an effort to get himself out of what he called his "annual Christmas depression," Feldman started volunteering at WORT, Madison's community radio station. At first, all he did was deliver the station newspaper. Then he started filling in on the air, which led to a regular Friday night gig called *Thanks for Calling*.

"It was for whoever was undateable or at home or nonambulatory on a Friday night," he said. "I remember some very sad people calling in, thinking I was sympathetic, but I couldn't really do much for them."

He went on to host a daily morning comedy show from Dolly's Fine
Foods, a twenty-four-hour diner. "It wasn't fine. It wasn't food," he
told *People* magazine. "But there was a Dolly." The show aired live in
the early hours before he had to go in to teach. He sat in a booth behind the jukebox, playing music. In between sets, he'd talk to customers on the air, many of whom were weary or wasted stragglers
from the night before. Once, a drunk began to act up, and then held
on to the jukebox to keep the dishwasher from taking him outside.
The dishwasher proceeded to pull both the man and the jukebox out
the door. Feldman dutifully reported the goings-on to his listeners,
right down to the temperature outside once the drunk was finally
thrown out.

Feldman left WORT to go to Wisconsin Public Radio to host a Saturday program called *High Noon.* When that folded, he reprised his
Dolly's days in a Saturday morning show from a bar called Club de
Wash, which at that hour served drinks to nurses and other night shift
workers. He met his wife, Sandy (frequently referred to on *Whad'Ya
Know?* by the pseudonym "Consuela"), a fan from the audience, during the show's run. The marriage, his second, proved to be far more
enduring than the show, which ended when he was recruited by
WGN, a commercial station in Chicago, for a morning host gig. His
cohost was a former traffic reporter, and the two didn't get along. "We
had totally different ideas about what radio was about," he's said. "She
thought radio was about her and I thought it was about me." After six
months, the station fired them both.

He ended up back at Wisconsin Public Radio, pitching the idea for
Whad'Ya Know? as a national program with guest interviews and
quizzes, building on the wry style and audience rapport he'd developed from his earlier shows. The game plan wasn't too specific, but
WPR's general manager, Jack Mitchell, was a long-time fan of Feldman from his morning show at Dolly's and didn't need high concept.

"It was just everything I could do in a two-hour period," he said.
Over the years, that pretty much describes it. He's telephoned the

mother of an audience member named Hankus to rib her for nam-
ing him after a cartoon called "Hankus the Horse." He's asked writer
David Foster Wallace, the erudite author of the gargantuan novel
Infinite Jest, if he ever threw anything away. He's watched befud-
dled as a psychologist guest who studies the cognitive skills of chim-
panzees came onstage with one clinging to her leg. In an era of
consciousness-raising about the challenges of balancing work and
family, Feldman joked frequently about bringing up his two daughters, Ellie, born in 1991, and Nora, born in 1993. He even changed
Ellie's diaper onstage.

Today *Whad'Ya Know?* has about 1.4 million listeners. He calls the
success of the show's freewheeling format "kind of a fluke." However
original the show is, though, it's been subjected time and again over
the years to the dread "Garrison Comparison." *A Prairie Home Companion,* produced in neighboring Minnesota, has always trumped
Whad'Ya Know? in the ratings. So Feldman tends to end up being
called that *other* guy from the Midwest hosting a live radio show—despite the fact that the programs are quite distinct. *A Prairie Home
Companion* is largely scripted and relies on Keillor's storytelling
prowess, radio drama, and a variety of musical acts. *Whad'Ya Know?*
is mostly improvised, relying heavily on Feldman's spontaneous repar-
tee with the audience.

The rivalry has stayed on a slow simmer for years. Years ago, Feldman attended a live *Prairie Home Companion* taping in Madison and
introduced himself to Keillor, telling him all about the show he was
doing from Dolly's. All Keillor did in reply, Feldman has said, was ask
where the men's room was. In a *Milwaukee Journal* interview, Keillor
said he'd never heard *Whad'Ya Know?* and described Feldman as "an
insult comic" and "not my cup of tea."

Feldman, it should be said, is far more apt to take potshots at his
Minnesota neighbor than vice versa. At the Madison broadcast, when
he finds out his guest, author Dan Hill, is on the telephone from St.
Paul, Feldman wonders, "Is he there for Garrison's show? Maybe we

scooped him" (A *Prairie Home Companion* goes live on the air on Saturday evenings). Later in the show, an audience member asked Feldman whether other public radio personalities "looked like how they sound."

"Nothing like they sound!" Feldman said. "Garrison, for example. Short. Red hair. He has curly red hair. Thick glasses. A rather large shnozola."

"He's changed since I've seen him, then," the woman said, likely a veteran of public radio live tapings (Keillor is very tall, with dark brown hair, though he does have substantial glasses and a sizable nose).

"That's not him. That's his stage persona that's entirely different. He's inside that suit."

A more recent rival has been Peter Sagal, host of NPR's *Wait Wait . . . Don't Tell Me!* As Feldman tells it, in 1996 NPR tried to acquire *Whad'Ya Know?* from its long-time distributor, Public Radio International. Feldman said that when negotiations favored PRI, "NPR said, well if you don't come with us we're going to schedule a quiz show opposite you on the weekends." *Wait Wait* was launched in 1998, with a recommended air time opposite *Whad'Ya Know?*—prime public radio real estate following the popular Saturday morning lineup of *Weekend Edition* with Scott Simon and *Car Talk.* At the time, Feldman quipped to *Current,* a trade newspaper for public broadcasting, "It's quite a leap of faith to do a quiz show with a wisecracking Jewish host. I don't know why they think it would work." It did work—*Wait Wait* today has slightly more listeners than *Whad'Ya Know?* But many stations do air both shows, simply rescheduling one or the other from its recommended air time.

It's difficult to tell whether Feldman's jealousy is real, or just another aspect of his Woody Allenesque inferiority/superiority complex persona. Once he's done playing the underdog to Keillor or Sagal, he might transform into the hard-driving egotistical host, chastising the members of his backup band for interrupting him too much, or firing his producer, Todd Whitter, on air. Feldman in fact regularly cans Whitter during the *Whad'Ya Know?* broadcasts, once so convincingly that Whitter's mother called, concerned. "My mother was pretty sure it was for real," Whitter said. "I told Michael, maybe you want to make this a little more jesting?"

The reality is that Feldman is quite close to his cast and crew. When Whitter's daughter was born in 2004, Feldman gave him and his wife a week's worth of meals prepared by a professional chef. He's known announcer Jim Packard since his Dolly's days, when they'd run into each other on their daily walks along the railroad tracks that run through Madison. Packard, a talk show producer and substitute host at Wisconsin Public Radio, has been with *Whad'Ya Know?* since its beginning. So has Lyle Anderson, who is in charge of taking listener calls and finding local residents for Feldman to speak with about the "Town of the Week."

The closeness among the cast and crew may be one reason why the show works without rehearsals. Feldman and his researcher, Diana Cook, prepare extensively to come up with quiz questions and get the background on tour locations and the town of the week, but production meetings are an anathema. "We've only had one, ever, and Michael didn't show up," Packard said. "I get the script about twenty minutes before the show. Sometimes I'd like more time to prepare, but it somehow works well."

Particularly for Feldman. "I have to be in the moment," he said. "I'm out of the moment the rest of the week. For two hours, I can be in the moment and actually listen to what people say and how they react. It's a nervous reaction, mainly, what I do. There's really no thought involved at all."

A Funny Person Who
Reads a Lot of Newspapers:
Peter Sagal

Host, *Wait Wait . . . Don't Tell Me!*

Peter Sagal, the host of NPR's radio game show *Wait Wait . . .
Don't Tell Me!* is giving Helen Thomas, the eighty-four-year-old
dean of the White House press corps, a quiz about Britney Spears.

One of the questions is to identify which gift Spears gave Justin
Timberlake as a token of their love when the two were boyfriend-
girlfriend: "A: matching $10,000 gold-plated toilet seats engraved
with their photographs. B: a singing Billy Bass specially programmed
to sing In Sync's 'Bye Bye Bye.' Or C: his own chocolate factory,"
Sagal reads, his words crisply enunciated, bouncing a little in his seat
as he emphasizes a word or a phrase.

Thomas, who is on the telephone from Washington, D.C., chooses
B. "I would hate to think of either one of the others," she said in her
phlegmatic little-old-lady voice, familiar to anyone who's watched a
White House press conference on television.

"So just out of a hope for sanity, you're choosing the singing Billy
Bass?"

Thomas giggles. "Yes, but I'm sure it's probably not true."

"Well, I'm going to give you a chance to change your choice," Sagal offers hopefully, his eyebrows raising.

"No, that's all right."

"It was the toilet seats," he says, with a mock sadness.

"Oh . . . "

"Now you have one more chance here, one more chance to face up to the American people and find the truth—"

"You can tell the American people I'm a total failure!" Thomas cries, and the two burst into laughter.

Getting a woman renowned for her boldly antagonistic questions of presidents from JFK to George W. Bush to speculate on the frivolous escapades of a pop star is typical of the ironic fun Sagal, forty, stirs up on *Wait Wait . . . Don't Tell Me!* His approach blends a pundit's knowledge of current events, quick wit, and the stage presence of a trained actor. The result is an Ivy Leaguer's comic riff on the suspense and staginess of 1930s radio quiz shows like *Information Please. Wait Wait* takes guests, call-in contestants, and a compulsively clever rotating panel of journalists (Roy Blount Jr. and P. J. O'Rourke are among the regulars) through a series of games and questions meant to test their wits and their knowledge of the week's news. NPR newscaster Carl Kasell is the judge, scorekeeper, and straight man to Sagal's antics. When I visited a taping of the show in July 2004, the cast of the show was brought together virtually, with Sagal in Chicago and the panelists at radio stations in their homes cities, joined by live-quality, high-speed telephone lines. Since May 2005, the show has been taping live on Thursday evenings in front of an audience at the Bank One Auditorium in Chicago, with the entire cast on stage.

Wait Wait is produced by NPR and its Chicago affiliate, WBEZ, but the show doesn't sound very NPR. What I mean to say is, *Wait Wait* is *funny.* It's smart, too, of course. But the show gives its news junkie listeners some relief from the seriousness of NPR's daily diet of

thoughtful reports, up-to-the-minute newscasts, and probing interviews. "They need a break, a laugh—that's what we do for the public
radio listener, in public radio style," Sagal said.

The irony of Sagal's un-NPR comic persona is that off the air, he is
a screenwriter and playwright whose work takes on suburban violence
and the Holocaust denial movement, the kind of serious subject matter likely to catch the attention of a NPR arts reporter. His only background in public radio was all the hours he'd spent procrastinating by
listening to NPR instead of writing. His main qualification for the job
was "being a funny person who reads a lot of newspapers," he told me
over lunch at Capi's Italian Kitchen, a bustling, cafeteria-style restaurant in Chicago's Navy Pier, a few floors down from the WBEZ studios. To get there, we'd had to elbow our way through the Pier's
Family Pavilion, a kitschy complex of shops, restaurants, and muse-
ums that was even more crowded than usual because a downpour had
just moved in off of Lake Michigan. He, like others on the WBEZ
staff, was a little embarrassed about the pier (Ira Glass calls it a "cut-
rate amusement park")—it was neither the bohemian nor the academic sort of setting public radio stations tend to be in.

Sagal told me he was a shy and awkward teenager who discovered
he felt more comfortable on stage than off. So he became a "drama
geek" in high school in his suburban hometown of Berkeley Heights,
New Jersey. While an undergraduate at Harvard, he moved on to directing. "I could always imagine a performance better than the one I
was doing," he said. "My best performance was always my first reading, that first superficial read. But sustaining the character was tough.
I couldn't do the transformative work."

In 1982, while working a summer job between semesters writing
for *Highwire*, "an intelligent magazine for high school kids," he got his
first experience of being on the radio. A local radio show, *Dr. Rick's
Love Talk*, invited him on to talk about teenage sexuality. "My reading
was extensive, though I hadn't done a lot of field research!" Sagal
quipped. He had recently befriended Keith Fleming, the nephew of

prominent gay writer Edmund White. Fleming had opened Sagal's eyes to gay rights, and he ended up spending much of his on-air conversation talking to Dr. Rick about the importance of tolerating homosexuality. Sagal wasn't invited back. "It was the first incident in a long lifetime of pretending to know more about something than I actually do," he said. "Now, I can talk about any subject for thirty seconds! The trick is not understanding a topic, but understanding what someone expert on the topic would say." The skill has come in handy on *Wait Wait*, where the show guests will banter about anything from the Kyoto treaty to whether Martha Stewart would be allowed to get her hair highlighted during her prison term.

After college, Sagal moved to Los Angeles to break into screenwriting. In the time-honored tradition of the Hollywood wannabe, he took a number of odd jobs. He was an extra in a Michael Jackson video (though he ended up on the cutting room floor), a ghostwriter for a former adult film actor, a travel writer, and a staff reporter for a motorcycle magazine; he used to ride himself, but quit on the order of his wife. He was also the literary manager at a regional theater, a job that required him to read and recommend plays submitted by aspiring playwrights. Plenty of them were bad, but the best writers—future Pulitzer Prize–winning playwright Paula Vogel among them—inspired his own writing. In 1992, he won a Jerome Foundation fellowship at the Playwrights' Center in Minneapolis. There, he met his wife, Beth, an actress, when she had a role in one of his plays. After three years in Minneapolis, he and Beth moved to Brooklyn, where Sagal continued to knock on the doors of the theater world.

His plays have been staged at the Stella Adler Theater in Hollywood, Long Wharf Theater, Actors Theater of Louisville, Seattle Repertory, and Florida Stage. Among his most critically acclaimed works are *Mall America,* a comedy/drama about the aftermath of a shooting spree at the Mall of America near Minneapolis, and *Denial,* a play about the relationship between a Holocaust denier and the Jewish lawyer who defends him. I happened to have seen the premiere of *De-*

nial at the Long Wharf Theater in 1995. The play was intense and deeply intelligent, with gripping rounds of verbal sparring and a daringly empathetic portrayal of the Holocaust denier. I told Sagal how memorable the play was, and he thanked me, seeming at once flattered and a little astonished, as if I'd touched on a previous lifetime.

And in a way, I had. He told me that though *Denial* achieved considerable critical attention, a somewhat sour review in the *New York Times* killed the play's chance of making it to Broadway. He'd been trying to make it in the theater world for more than a decade, and he was starting to get burned out. "What's frustrating is that I kept imagining there's a progression to your career, a certain threshold from which you proceed and move on," he said. "But that's not the case. You have success, then it's still what have you done for me lately?"

Public radio gave him a new and far less precarious occupation. Dan Coffey, public radio's "Dr. Science," was the original host, and Sagal was initially hired to be a panelist. When Coffey didn't work out, Sagal replaced him. That holy grail of the starving artist—a regular salary and health insurance benefits—came just in time. He and his wife had recently had their first child, and two others would follow by the time *Wait Wait* was five years old.

After years in the cutthroat theater business, he found public radio a far gentler profession. "Competition" came to mean little more than a barb or two from Michael Feldman, the host of *Whad'Ya Know?*, a weekly comedy quiz show distributed by Public Radio International. NPR initially recommended its affiliates schedule *Wait Wait* in the same late Saturday morning time slot that *Whad'Ya Know?* was broadcast live. When Feldman found out about that, he quipped to *Current*, a trade newspaper for public broadcasting, "It's quite a leap of faith to do a quiz show with a wisecracking Jewish host. I don't know why they think it would work."

Despite some similarities in concept, the two shows have very different zeitgeists. *Wait Wait* follows a detailed script (though with plenty of room for improvisation), is more news-oriented, and is edited considerably after the show is recorded. *Whad'Ya Know?* is live, with minimal scripted elements and more improvisational comedy. Feldman's approach is Marx Brothers meets the Midwest, whereas Sagal has called himself "the Regis Philbin of the snotty, arugula-eating set." Over the years, the rivalry has faded. Feldman has even been a guest, though a somewhat cantankerous one, on *Wait Wait*. Both shows have done well, each attracting more than a million and a half weekly listeners, and many stations reschedule one show or another from its recommended time so they can air both.

Though *Wait Wait* does tour occasionally, Sagal stays as close as he can to his wife and family at home in Oak Park (which he has described as an "un-suburban suburb"). He has three daughters: Rose, seven; Grace, five; and Willa, two. Sagal's own father, a chemical engineer and manager at AT&T, had to work long hours and travel. "I didn't like it when he was not there," Sagal said. "In general I leave work and go straight home. We brought our children into the world. I can't not be there."

There has been a price to the stability Sagal enjoys as the host of *Wait Wait*. It's difficult for him to find the time to write. When he took the job, he figured he only wrote about two hours a day anyway, a schedule he thought he could maintain while doing the show. But that didn't quite come to pass. "I realized, it's not the two hours," he said. "It's the rest of the time wandering around thinking about stuff."

He does still take on the occasional outside project. He was one of the screenwriters for Miramax/Lion's Gate's *Dirty Dancing: Havana Nights,* released in 2004 to lukewarm reviews. Far more rewarding these days is the response he gets from public radio listeners about *Wait Wait*. "I don't know if I have fame, but whatever it is I don't understand why people complain about it," he said. "It's tremendously gratifying to know people enjoy what I do. It's worth getting up in the morning."

Public Radio's Grease Monkeys: Tom and Ray Magliozzi

Hosts, *Car Talk*

No one thought *Car Talk* would work.

In the mid-1980s, a show with a couple of wisecracking mechanics answering callers' questions about their cars was not very "public radio." It just didn't fit in in the land of Beethoven, the St. Paul Chamber Orchestra, and Linda Wertheimer.

And then Susan Stamberg took a listen.

In 1987, Stamberg, often referred to as the "Founding Mother" of NPR, listened to a tape from WBUR in Boston of Tom and Ray Magliozzi, two brothers with thick Boston accents, degrees from the Massachusetts Institute of Technology (MIT), and a gift for comedy and diagnosing auto repair conundrums. She loved it, but at first, no one else did. Not NPR's news director, not her producer, not ever her husband, who was a car fanatic. The brothers themselves weren't even enthusiastic about her idea to get them a regular spot on her show, *Weekend Edition Sunday,* because she wanted to interact with them. "They were brothers, and they'd grown up talking to each other," Stamberg remembered on *The Bob Edwards Show* in 2005. "Who needed some woman to come in there?" But then they found out that Stamberg drove a 1974 Dodge Dart, a model Tom had a particular fondness for. "Then the world was mine!" she laughed. "They knew I'd be okay."*

So she convinced the powers that be at NPR to let her give Click and Clack, as the brothers call themselves, a try. After several months as a regular segment on *Weekend Edition Sunday, Car Talk* made its national debut as a full-length show of its own. It stood out on public radio, then known primarily as a place for classical and jazz music and interviews with poets and Ph.D.'s. Public radio had always had its witty elements—in particular Stamberg's own antics, which included listener contests and game show–style skits, such as one in which contestants competed to see if they could identify all the tax shelters available to rich people. But Tom and Ray completely sidestepped the public radio bread and butter of current events and music and used America's love-hate relationship with the automobile as raw material for comedy. And while most of the public radio clock was relentlessly sincere, *Car Talk* was all about teasing. The brothers made fun of callers about what cars they drove and how they drove them, towns they lived in, their spouses, and how they spelled their names. The brothers ribbed each other and their off-air staff. They even teased NPR, with sign-offs like, "Even though Terry Gross throws a fit when she hears this, this is NPR, National Public Radio."

But before the blockbuster audiences, before Susan Stamberg, before WBUR, the Magliozzis were just a couple of Italian American broth-

---

*It should be noted that there are other versions to the story of how *Car Talk* went national. The *Car Talk* web site credits *All Things Considered* host Robert Siegel, who heard the show while on vacation in Massachusetts and decided it was national material. NPR Vice President of Programming Jay Kernis claims credit for noticing the show as well. Jane Christo, then the general manager of WBUR, was the reason the tape got to Susan Stamberg in the first place. She saw the show's national potential and persisted in bringing the show to the attention of various people at NPR, according to the show's executive producer, Doug Berman.

ers growing up in Cambridge. Tom got his degree down the street at MIT in chemical engineering and economics in 1958 and became an engineer. Ray, eleven years younger, started out studying mechanical engineering there, but ended up with a degree in the humanities. He graduated in 1972 and moved to Vermont to teach eighth grade. The following year, Tom quit his engineering job and spent his time hanging out in Harvard Square, wondering what to do. Their mother pestered Ray to "do something about your brother, he's become a bum," Ray told the *Washington Post* in 1999.

Tom already had an idea of his own: a do-it-yourself car repair shop. He could rent out repair bays to customers and give them advice on how to fix their own cars. Ray wasn't taking to teaching eighth-graders, or the cold Vermont weather, so he came back to Cambridge to start the Good News Garage with his brother. The business had a fumbling start. The customers weren't very successful at fixing their own cars, and the brothers ended up doing all the work. Then, in 1977, Tom and Ray were invited to participate in a panel of car mechanics for a call-in show at WBUR, the public radio station based at Boston University. As legend goes, Ray decided he had better things to do and the other mechanics never showed up, so Tom ended up having the whole show to himself. He was good enough to be invited back the next week, this time with brother Ray in tow. They arrived at the station to find that the program director who'd organized the show had been fired. All he left was a note that said, "Have fun, and try to watch your language."

For the next ten years, the duo had a local weekend radio gig they named *Car Talk*. They called themselves "Click and Clack, the Tappet brothers," a knock on the locally popular sports talk show *Clif and Claf,* featuring the irreverent banter of two sportswriters, Clif Keane of the *Boston Globe* and Larry Claflin of the bygone *Boston Herald-American.* Though the Magliozzi brothers often sounded alike, there were some subtle differences: Tom tended to be more rambling and philosophical, while Ray was more matter-of-fact. At first the brothers worked for free, then for a small stipend. Business also improved at their garage. They had long since given up on the do-it-yourself angle and become a more traditional repair shop. By the mid-80s customers had to wait a month to get an appointment for a tune-up.

But the brothers' Boston popularity was nothing compared to what was to come. Once *Car Talk* went national, it quickly became a hit. After only a few months on the air, the Magliozzis had a guest spot on *The Tonight Show with Johnny Carson,* or actually Jay Leno, then a guest host with a lot in common with Click and Clack—he was a Boston native *and* a former grease monkey. The brothers also launched a syndicated newspaper column on car repair that appeared in more than three hundred newspapers. The show won a Peabody Award, and it's been featured on *CBS Evening News,* the *Today* show, *60 Minutes,* and *Late Night with David Letterman.* It is the most popular entertainment show NPR offers, with 4.2 million listeners on nearly six hundred affiliate stations. *A Prairie Home Companion,* distributed by American Public Media, is the only other public radio entertainment show to rival those numbers, with more than 4 million listeners on 558 stations.

Off the air, Ray continued to run the garage, and Tom got his doctorate in marketing and became a business consultant. Along with *Car Talk's* executive producer, Doug Berman, they formed Dewey, Cheetham, and Howe—yes, it's a real company, though not a law firm—in 1992 and decided to produce their show independently after their contract with WBUR ran out. The purpose was to work for themselves. "They consider themselves temperamentally ill-suited to working for large companies, since they can't keep their mouths shut," said Berman in an email. The move also got them away from some of the limits of nonprofit radio. They've developed a number of for-profit spin-off ventures, including web site advertising and "the Department of Shameless Commerce," which vends *Car Talk* paraphernalia, including regularly issued theme CDs and a half a dozen show-related books. Dewey, Cheetham, and Howe is currently exploring the possibility of developing an animated PBS television series based on the show. It's not known how much money the company is worth, but in 2001, the *Boston Herald* reported that "according to sources, Christo seriously regrets handing over ownership of *Car Talk* to the Magliozzis. When the auto repair show premiered . . . who knew the funny brothers had a lock on such a hit?"

The *Car Talk* web site has a featured link with cars.com, a web site that offers a guide to pricing new cars, surrounded by plenty of car advertisements. But whatever their gains from these links, Click and Clack are unafraid to take aim at automakers on the show. They have joked that the Ford Festiva should be sold with a funeral wreath. Tom once made a crack about a tailgate problem on the Dodge Caravan and joked that Chrysler had "paid off" investigators to prevent a recall. When a Chrysler rep demanded a correction, Tom gave one— but only sort of. He said no money changed hands, but then laughed loudly and joked that Caravan passengers were only being ejected through the back doors, "not the sunroof and side doors."

Car Talk airs in most markets on Saturday mornings, and the most widespread misperception about the show is that it's a live broadcast. It's actually taped on Wednesdays. Callers leave messages about their car problems on the *Car Talk* voice mail. Out of the thousands of messages left each week, about a dozen or so are picked by *Car Talk* producers to get a funny, interesting, and varied mix of car and car-related problems. Click and Clack's responses are not scripted or rehearsed, though. "They know absolutely nothing about the calls before they hear them on the show," Berman said. "Absolutely nothing."

After the recording session, the show is edited for clarity and length. About 30 percent of the callers are cut. Melissa Hart, who was a caller on the show in 2003 to ask a question about her Isuzu Amigo, made it into the final version of the show. In an article in the *Christian Science Monitor,* she expressed her amazement at how polished she ended up sounding on the air. "The magic of sound editing had turned me darn near eloquent as I explained my dilemma," she wrote.

I can offer up just a few details about what Click and Clack have been up to lately, other than the obvious: they are still teasing and guffawing their way through *Car Talk* every week on NPR. Tom, sixty-eight, is semiretired from marketing consulting and teaching. He's married to Joanne and has a son and two daughters. Ray, fifty-six, works a few days a week at the Good News Garage. He's been married to his wife, Monique, since 1970, and the couple has two sons. He loves to garden and once told the *Boston Globe* that he uses only organic fertilizer because he suspects his pet border collie died from repeated exposure to lawn chemicals. The Magliozzi brothers declined, through an email from their executive producer Doug Berman, to be interviewed for this book. For the past five years or so, they have very rarely granted media interviews. I've even tried to call *Car Talk* a few times, hoping for some idea of what Click and Clack are like in action (not to mention some help with my own car repair dilemmas), but I've never gotten a call back. Too bad I can't get my hands on a '74 Dodge Dart.

A Prairie Home Whirlwind:
Garrison Keillor
Host, *A Prairie Home Companion*

Garrison Keillor is a man of many paradoxes. A monologist and best-selling writer, his vision of small-town America is both deeply nostalgic and deeply ironic. He has been at times fiercely partisan, openly railing against the conservative direction of America, yet in his storytelling seeks a universality beyond politics. He has a voice, as one critic put it, "like a down comforter," yet his stories have moments of cutting wit and mocking insight that sting like the cold air that comes in when your partner lifts the covers too abruptly. He is not beautiful. He is a lanky six feet four inches, with slumped shoulders, amphibian eyes, a waddled neck, and a wide, boxy forehead. Yet he has tremendous charisma, his prominent eyebrows expressive, his bangs hanging over his forehead in a sweetly boyish way. He's even been named one of *Playgirl* magazine's "Ten Sexiest Men in America."

Keillor, sixty-three, is also a very busy man. He hosts *A Prairie Home Companion* live most weekends, publishes about a book a year, and involves himself in any number of outside projects at a given time: a syndicated newspaper column, a new radio show, a voice-over for a Honda commercial, a traveling gospel group, a film based on *A Prairie Home*

Companion. Yet he knows how to make time stop. During his monologues, he stands alone on a darkened stage, the spotlight on him, his
glasses pushed up on his forehead, his eyes closed, pacing back and
forth like an evangelical minister. He holds no script, and he's not reciting anything from memory. His tales about the fictional town of Lake
Wobegon come from some primal place inside himself, the place early
man used to tell tales before there were computers, typewriters, pens,
pencils—only firelight in the evening and a circle of listeners, huddled
for warmth and for what would one day be called mythology.

Keillor packs theaters around the country for stagings of his radio
show, performing in front of thousands. Yet he is intensely private. He
did not respond to my many requests for an interview. He has been
quite press shy since a flurry of media attention in the mid-1980s,
much of it quite positive, some of it dishing about his love life. He will
occasionally emerge for interviews in connection with publicity for
one of his books or projects. Reporters seeking a more in-depth portrayal of him have not had much luck, including Minnesota writer
Michael Fedo, the author of the 1987 book *The Man from Lake
Wobegon.* As Fedo sought out others to talk to about Keillor, Keillor's
lawyers sent letters to performers, musicians, former teachers, and
others, asking them not to speak to Fedo. St. Martin's put out the
book anyway. Keillor kept jabbing back, at least figuratively; in the
epilogue to his novel *WLT: A Radio Romance,* he writes about an
unauthorized biographer who is hit by a truck and becomes a cata-
tonic vegetable. More recently, Keillor threw his legal weight around
again, threatening to sue a Twin Cities–area blogger for marketing
and selling T-shirts that said "A Prairie Ho Companion" during the
local filming of Robert Altman's movie based on *A Prairie Home Companion* in 2005.

Garrison Keillor grew up in Brooklyn Park, Minnesota, then a small
town, now a thriving suburb, on the Mississippi River outside of Minneapolis. His birth name was Gary Edward (later changed to the more

literary Garrison), and he was the third of six children of John and Grace Keillor. His father was a railway mail clerk and a carpenter. Though Keillor's monologues frequently play on the Scandinavian roots of rural Minnesota culture, the Keillors are of Scottish descent

Keillor was raised in the Plymouth Brethren, a religious sect that does not allow tobacco, alcohol, dancing, gambling, and movies. He sung hymns with the Brethren on street corners and at the Minnesota State Fair while a sect member preached the gospel to passersby. Listening to the radio was permitted, and Keillor told *Newsday* that his first memory of the radio was of hearing an announcer proclaim the end of World War II on the family's Zenith console. The radio became an entryway into the world outside the strict rules of the Brethren. He listened to *Let's Pretend, Fibber McGee & Molly, Amos & Andy,* and the amateur talent shows and quiz programs hosted by Cedric Adams on WCCO in Minneapolis. He went to high school in nearby Anoka, where he wrote for the school newspaper and the yearbook and composed cutting lampoons of high school life, which circulated in an underground manner around the school.

In 1960, he started college at the University of Minnesota as an English major with a journalism minor. He was an announcer at WMMR, a closed-circuit student radio station, then started working for KUOM, the university's educational and classical music radio station, which had a professional staff with a handful of hired students. He became one of the hosts of *Radio Free Saturday*, which had a more freestyle format than the rest of the week, with interviews and a wider variety of music. Keillor pushed the envelope further than most. He played *Sgt. Pepper's Lonely Hearts Club Band* in its entirety when the album was released, upsetting the university broadcasting director, who proclaimed he never wanted to hear rock 'n' roll on the station airwaves again. Keillor also first began to experiment with humor. One afternoon he broadcast a fake hot-air balloon traffic report, describing the local traffic conditions while running a loop of a recording of the airy hiss of a hot-air balloon in the background.

Keillor was also the fiction editor of *The Ivory Tower*, the university's literary magazine. He fashioned it after *The New Yorker*, the magazine he idolized, and wrote a "Talk of the Town"–style column called "Broadsides." He met his first wife, Mary Guntzel, a music major, at school, and the two married in 1965. Keillor graduated the following year, receiving two major poetry awards on campus: the Academy of American Poets Prize and the Fanny Fay Wood Poetry Prize.

After college, Keillor rode a bus to New York City to try to convince magazine editors at *The New Yorker, The Atlantic, Time,* and other glossies and publishing houses of the time to give him a job. In a 2003 interview on *Fresh Air*, he told Terry Gross, "They all did me the great favor of turning me down, which as you look back was the best thing that could have happened to you. Instead of getting a job as you were hoping as a researcher at *Sports Illustrated* and to go to work in the hive of Time, Inc., and spend the next thirty years filing clippings, instead you were released out into the world to be a writer, which was exactly the right thing, except you weren't smart enough to know it at the time."

So instead of making their way in the Big Apple, he and his wife moved into an old farmhouse outside of Freeport, a town that would become part of the basis for the fictional Lake Wobegon. The town is in Stearns County, about ninety-five miles west of the Twin Cities, and is the closest anyone has been able to determine to the physical location of Lake Wobegon. Marine on St. Croix in eastern Minnesota also inspired aspects of the fictional town, including a grocery store that was run by a man named Ralph, as in Ralph's Pretty Good Grocery. Both towns had Chatterbox-like cafés.

While living in Freeport, Keillor wrote short stories and worked as the morning music host at KSJR in Collegeville, the original station of what would become Minnesota Public Radio (MPR). As at KUOM, he showed a quiet rebellious streak. He shifted the format of his show from classical to bluegrass and other forms of music. When station management complained, he quit to write full-time. He had already sold his first story to *The New Yorker* the year before, a three-hundred-word parody called "Local Family Keeps Son Happy." It was about a couple so worried that their teenage son would get into a car crash that they hired a prostitute so he would stay home.

Keillor found he couldn't support his family—which now included his baby son, Jason—solely by writing, so a few months after leaving KSJR, he took a job at KSJN in St. Paul, the station that would become home base for MPR. He was the station's morning host from 1971 to 1982, though he left for several months in the mid-1970s to again attempt writing full-time. He mixed the Grateful Dead, Beach Boys, Rolling Stones, and country tunes in with Brahms and Haydn. He had eccentric habits, such as playing a song over and over again, trying to catch the words, or, if he got distracted, letting the needle run off the record. He got into tiffs with management over donors who threatened to hold back their contributions if he stayed on the air, but he refused to change.

He called his show *A Prairie Home Companion*. He told Steve Inskeep on *Morning Edition* in 2004 that he got the name from the Prairie Home Cemetery in northern Minnesota, a graveyard founded by Norwegian immigrants. "It took them a long time to establish a cemetery out there on the prairie because these Norwegians assumed they were going to make their pile and then go back home," Keillor said. "They didn't intend to stay here. The cemetery was their acknowledgment that this was their home, their life." Though he first began to mention Lake Wobegon back when he was working in Collegeville at KSJR, much more of the social and commercial landscape of the town and the show surfaced on KSJN, including the fake commercials for Powder Milk Biscuits.

Keillor got the idea to do *A Prairie Home Companion* as a radio stage show when he went down to Nashville in 1974 on assignment from *The New Yorker* to cover the last performance of the Grand Ole Opry in the old Ryman auditorium. He copied from the Opry the variety stage show format with live musical performances in front of an audience. He also tapped into other aspects of broadcasting history. Breaking for a story in the middle of a music program was a practice common in radio in the thirties, forties, and fifties and was used by Gene Autry and Smilin' Ed McConnell. Another inspiration was *The Bell Telephone Hour*, a television show in the 1960s that featured a diverse group of musicians, from jazz clarinetist Benny Goodman to gospel singer Mahalia Jackson to classical pianist Van Cliburn. Keillor's show, of course, would have a decidedly Minnesotan twist, with comic stories from Lake Wobegon, the town he'd been dreaming up in his head and talking about on the air for years.

The first three broadcasts of *A Prairie Home Companion* were prerecorded in May 1974 at the Walker Arts Center and broadcast the following month on MPR, then known as Minnesota Educational Radio. The first live broadcast of the show was July 6 of that year, from the Janet Wallace Fine Arts Center at Macalester College in St. Paul. Tickets cost a dollar for adults and fifty cents for children. Only twelve people attended. But the show caught on, and four years later, the production moved to its current home in the World Theater, now the renovated Fitzgerald Theater, in St. Paul.

In 1980, MPR began offering the show to a national audience. NPR, in one of several of the network's infamous no-thank-you's (*This American Life* was another one), turned down MPR's efforts to get it to distribute the program. In response, MPR banded together with four other public radio stations to form American Public Radio (now called Public Radio International), a new organization to distribute *A Prairie Home Companion* and other programs to stations. The show is now handled by American Public Media, the national distribution arm of Minnesota Public Radio, which also handles *A Writer's Almanac*, a daily five-minute program Keillor narrates on literature and history.

National distribution sent *A Prairie Home Companion* toward its glory days. Though the show never lost its Minnesota flavor, the program proved itself to have an appeal far beyond the Midwest, with significant audiences in New York, Los Angeles, Chicago, Boston, and Dallas. In 1985, *Lake Wobegon Days*, Keillor's chronicle of the town he'd brought to life on the show, was published and became a number one best-seller. After more than a decade of hosting *A Prairie Home Companion,* he and the show were suddenly in the media spotlight. *Time* ran a cover story on him. *Newsday Magazine* called him "America's Hottest New Storyteller." *The Mother Earth News,* in a mocking take on *Playboy*'s celebrity interviews, did a "Plowboy Interview" with Keillor.

But 1985 was also the start of cataclysmic shifts in Keillor's personal life and the beginning of the end of the first era of *A Prairie Home Companion.* Keillor and his first wife, Mary, had divorced in 1976, long before the *Prairie Home Companion* juggernaut hit full steam. He lived for years with the program's producer, Margaret Moos, in St. Paul. In 1985, he went to his twenty-fifth high school reunion in Anoka, where he saw Ulla Skaerved, who was a sought-after and viva-cious exchange student from Denmark during his senior year. The two began a romance and soon announced their engagement. Moos took a personal leave of absence from the show. The *Minneapolis Star Tribune* ran a story about the impending nuptials and Moos's depar-ture, which was then picked up by newspapers across the country. Keillor was very upset by the onslaught of media attention to follow, particularly in the *Star Tribune* and the *St. Paul Pioneer Press.* Cover-age included the publication of his salary ($173,186 in fiscal 1986) and the address of the home he, Skaerved, his son Jason, and her three children moved into.

Keillor announced in February 1987 that *A Prairie Home Compan-ion* would be ending that June. The program had 1.9 million listeners and was the center of a $100-million-a-year media industry and mail order catalogue. He told *Monitor Radio,* a now defunct public radio news program, that his "running disagreement with the two papers in town over what constitutes private life" contributed to his decision to stop the show. "When I came home and found a picture of my house in the paper, with the address and everything, I thought to myself, I can't really live here."

Minnesota Public Radio hired Noah Adams away from *All Things Considered* to host *Good Evening*, a program meant to take *A Prairie Home Companion*'s place. Keillor spent a summer in Denmark, then moved to New York, explaining that his wife wanted to live there. After years of selling stories and essays to *The New Yorker*, he joined the magazine's staff and worked out of a tiny office there, fulfilling a dream he had ever since he was thirteen and a teacher gave him a copy of the magazine.

But his new life and surroundings were far from Lake Wobegon. He's called living in New York "like living in a foreign country, without the benefit of a language barrier." Two years after ending *A Prairie Home Companion*, he revived the show as *The American Radio Company*. The show was based at the Brooklyn Theater and made frequent forays around the country. "I've never looked forward to performing as much as I have now," he told the *St. Petersburg Times*. "I need to get out of New York. I need to get out and see some streets with houses on them."

His disappointment with life in New York culminated in the announcement in 1992 that *Vanity Fair* editor-in-chief Tina Brown, who had a reputation for putting profits and trendiness ahead of literary quality, would be taking over the helm of *The New Yorker*. "I packed up my office and moved my books out," he told Terry Gross on *Fresh Air*. "It took me five minutes to think about it and I did it." In 1993, he left New York to move to a historic log cabin in the woods of western Wisconsin, outside of St. Paul. He explained that his voice was starting to become tainted with a New York accent, and he could no longer come up with stories about Lake Wobegon unless he lived closer to its real-life model. Another factor in his decision to move may also have been the breakup of his marriage to Skaerved, which he was so reluctant to speak about that she wrote a caustic letter in 1993 to the *Minneapolis Star Tribune* accusing him of "building on the illusion" that they were still married. "The truth is that the marriage ended two years ago, when you moved in with another woman."

Minnesotans were slow in welcoming their native son home. A local television panel debated, "Does Garrison Keillor deserve a second chance in Minnesota?" A *New York Times* article on Keillor's return described guest James Earl Jones proclaiming, after a round of thunderous applause, "What a great audience!" Keillor told him, "For you, not me." Later, he said, "Minnesotans, bless their hearts, are an earnest people. They believe the harder that they clap for James Earl Jones, the more it demonstrates they're not racists."

But in retrospect, the hiatus years seem as if they did very little to break Keillor's long-legged stride. *A Prairie Home Companion* (the new name never caught on, so the old one was eventually restored) celebrated its thirtieth anniversary in 2004 and has more than four million weekly listeners. Keillor even lives in St. Paul again, in a French chateau-style home in the Cathedral Hill neighborhood. He got married again, to Jenny Lind Nilsson, a violinist who has collaborated with him on a few writing projects. Their daughter, Maia, was born in 1999.

In the late 1990s, he wrote a syndicated advice column for Salon.com under the name "Mr. Blue," dispensing wisdom on such matters as why boyfriends don't call enough, whether a writer should date another writer, and what to do if you find pictures of your girlfriend kissing another man. He stopped writing the column after a heart operation in 2001, telling his readers, "It was exhilarating to get the chance to be useful, which is always an issue for a writer (What good does fiction do?)." He has since resumed writing for Salon, but this time around the subject is politics.

A movie adaptation of *A Prairie Home Companion,* directed by Robert Altman, was filmed in St. Paul in 2005, with a limited release planned for 2006. Keillor wrote the screenplay and stars as a radio host addressed as "GK." Cast members include Meryl Streep, Kevin

Kline, Woody Harrelson, and Lindsay Lohan. Other recent projects include hosting a new radio program, *Literary Friendships.* In 2005, he began writing a syndicated newspaper column for Tribune Media Services, released a children's book and CD called *Daddy's Girl,* compiled the poetry anthology *Good Poems for Hard Times,* and invested in a restaurant in Avon, Minnesota.

The list of Keillor's activities is fairly astounding—particularly at sixty-three, with a weekly live show to get on the air, a young daughter, and a heart problem in his not-so-distant past. As I worked on this chapter, I smiled to come across an article by a reporter for the *Minneapolis Star Tribune,* Deborah Caulfield Rybak, trying to get a quote or two from Keillor after a taping of *Literary Friendships.* "When asked about his work schedule, he pulled back into himself so rapidly that one could almost hear the whoosh of air," she wrote.

But she finally got her answer. "You have to keep up a certain pace, otherwise you drift," he told her.

That word, *drift.* I've always found it a lovely word, the state I fall into while hiking in the woods, enjoying a glass of wine, or reading. It's happened, in fact, many times while listening to *A Prairie Home Companion.* So I found, if not a paradox, a certain sad irony in his use of that word, and an urge to tell him—if we ever do meet—that drifting may not be so bad.

The Last Toy
in the Cereal Box:
Brooke Gladstone and
Bob Garfield

Hosts, *On the Media*

On the Media's Monday morning meeting is finally getting started, an hour late, turning it into a noon meeting, for reasons no one really seems to know. Six staff members are crowded into the office of Brooke Gladstone, the show's cohost and managing editor. The walls are a light purple, and on the shelf behind her desk is a bottle of Listerine and a black and white photograph of her twin daughters, huddled in winter jackets.

A starfish-shaped speaker phone is perched on the edge of the desk. That's Bob Garfield, on the line from Fairfax County, Virginia. He cohosts the show remotely, taping interviews and writing reports from his home office and telecommuting to meetings. He's just gotten back from a trip to Jordan, and he's working on a story about limits on freedom of the press there.

"Hello, Bobby!" Gladstone calls into the speaker with a tongue-in-cheek, boisterous cheeriness. "I hear you have a couple of fabulous pieces on the ball."

"Kind of simmering," Garfield says flatly.

"I expect you to be more enthusiastic," Gladstone teases.

A little girl's voice calling "Daddy?" can be heard over the speaker phone.

"Hi, Ida!" Gladstone calls out. It's Garfield's four-year-old, popping into his office. We hear the sounds of him shooing her out, and he and Gladstone agree on a deadline for the piece.

"Fantastic," she says, twirling a strand of her dark, wildly curly hair. She wears black like a college art major: black sweater, black skirt, black boots, black and blue plaid tights. Her face is round, she wears no makeup, and she's given to little nervous habits: in addition to hair twirling, she bites her nails. Her eyes wander frequently to her computer screen to monitor incoming emails.

The staff throws around several story ideas: religious broadcasters and indecency lawsuits, two new books on the Washington press corps, and the Committee to Protect Bloggers. Tony Field, an associate producer, pitches an idea about the increased use of television in the Mexican school system. Educational TV, supplemented by poorly paid teachers' aids, is essentially replacing teachers in one-fifth of the middle schools there, he explains. "A lot of Central America is interested," he says.

"Sounds horrible to me," Garfield says. "But it's not really a media story."

"It's not?" Field asks.

"My initial reaction was like Bob's, but then when Bob said it, I started to disagree," Gladstone says. "It depends on why we are thinking of this. If it's a crisis of education, it's not a story for us."

"Got it," Garfield cuts in.

"Can I just finish a goddamn sentence? If it's about TV and education, it could be a story."

Garfield argues that it's an old story of television's failure as an educational tool. "When has it ever worked in education? Ever?" he snipes, and the idea is thus killed.

Gladstone, concerned, says to Field, "You don't look happy."

"No, no, it's fine," he says, and they move on to a discussion of new, higher fees for Freedom of Information Act requests.

What is and isn't a story about the media is frequently a topic of debate behind the scenes at *On the Media*, a weekly show of interviews, reports, features, and commentary produced at WNYC, a public radio affiliate housed in New York City's municipal building in lower Manhattan. The show defines its subject matter rather loosely, covering the persecution of journalists in Zimbabwe one week and vanity license plates the next. The distinctive, wry style of Gladstone and Garfield pulls the diverse material together. They are public radio hosts who refuse to use, as *Slate* magazine's Jack Shader once put it, the public radio "microphones [that are] specially fabricated to decant all emotion from the voices of their reporters." Gladstone and Garfield are unafraid to sound vehement, self-deprecating, funny, delighted, or even caustic.

They are also unafraid to show and even outright state their biases, but they insist these biases are more about journalistic principles than partisan politics. They'll attack the Bush administration's record on the freedom of the press, then turn on the White House press corps for not insisting on it themselves. "Press freedom is what [*On the Media*] seeks to guard under any administration," Gladstone once announced, addressing listeners who accused the show of Bush-bashing. Lefties, it should be said, don't escape criticism, either. Garfield called Michael Moore's film *Fahrenheit 9/11* "more polemic than journalism, picking and choosing facts and footage that served the filmmaker's point of view and discarding facts that are inconvenient."

Gladstone and Garfield were invited to host *On the Media* in early 2001 as part of WNYC's effort to revive the floundering show, which started as a local call-in in 1995 and then went national as a magazine-style show two years later. It had a small staff, not much money, only about eighty affiliates, and was "kind of a dead shark," Gladstone said. Then Dean Cappello, WNYC's vice president for programming, shored up more funding and convinced her and Garfield to host.

Gladstone, at the time a media reporter for NPR, was intrigued by the idea of doing a show of commentary and analysis. She was also eager to leave a beat that required her to, as she told the independent public radio web site Transom.org, "do a three-and-a-half minute piece every time [former *New Yorker* editor] Tina Brown passed wind." Another plus was working with Garfield, whose work she had edited while on staff at *All Things Considered.* The two had also collaborated on a public radio spoof called *Pledge This.* "He is an original," she said. "There's no one who sounds like him, nobody who approaches a story like him, no one who can range from mocking self-abnegation to righteous indignation within the range of a single piece."

The *On the Media* relaunch was by any measure a success. The show is one of the fastest-growing programs in public radio. By 2005, the number of listeners was more than 765,000, with 206 station affiliates. Also that year, the program won a Peabody Award. "*On the Media* reminds us that the messenger is always part of the message and must be examined as such," the judges said.

Gladstone admits her rapport with Garfield has gotten "trickier" since they started working together on *On the Media.* "He likes to think of me as a meddling, control-freaky older sister," she told me, then pointed out that he is only three months younger than she is (they're both fifty).

Garfield juggles the show with a regular columnist job for *Advertising Age* and frequent public speaking gigs. As managing editor of the show, Gladstone is hands-on all week and has the final say in most decisions. "I think he loves that when he's not around, and he's not so happy about it when he is around."

Garfield describes his relationship with Gladstone as "80 percent harmonious." He said 10 percent of the time, they disagree and eventually work things out (see above). The other 10 percent of the time, "we treat each other horribly, like brother and sister fighting over the last cereal box toy," he said.

But the moments of tension do pass. As Gladstone put it, "I just think that, ultimately, we have so much respect for each other, it seems to trump that occasional power struggle."

Brooke Gladstone

After the Monday staff meeting, Gladstone and I went to lunch at Shore, a quiet tavern a couple of blocks away from the municipal building. She explained that she's using our interview as a rare excuse to take it easy, to have a little holiday, especially since a Nor'easter was on the way and everyone was going to try to get home early.

We studied the menu, glad to be out of the March cold. "They have fish and chips," she said suggestively. Once I admitted I was tempted, she urged me on with the conspiratorial tone of a close girlfriend who knows your nutritional weak spots. "Come on. It's a holiday," she said. "I'll have it, too."

The waiter arrived. We got the fish and chips.

Gladstone told me she grew up in Syosset and Huntington, Long Island, one of six children of a woolens wholesale merchant turned stockbroker. "I always told my parents they should have stopped after two, had a son and a daughter, which I think was quite generous given that I was the third," she said. "But no, my mother really liked babies. She once said she lost interest when we began to talk."

As a teenager, she discovered WBAI, the counterculture Pacifica affiliate in New York City. She loved listening to *The Outside,* a freeform show of music, satire, and comedy hosted by Steve Post, "a crotchety outrageous personality" (and now a colleague at WNYC) who held court on the airwaves Saturday nights from midnight until 5 a.m. When Gladstone was only thirteen, she had the chance to be on WBAI herself, filling in for a friend who had a fifteen-minute show called *High School Blues*. "I remember being asked about abortion, and I pontificated," she said.

When Gladstone was sixteen, in 1971, the bottom dropped out of her father's stockbroker business. He struggled for a while, driving a truck, then sold their Long Island home at a loss and, just in time for her senior year in high school, moved the family to Morrisville, Vermont, a small rural town an hour south of the Canadian border. "We tripled the Jewish population," Gladstone said. "And I had wire-rimmed glasses, which weren't regarded as real by my classmates. And I wore black all the time, and I was really into my nihilistic period, and we were just weird."

Her parents went through several jobs and attempted to start a number of businesses, among them a clothing store and a restaurant, none of them successful for long. Her parents eventually moved to Florida, then spent their last years in Mexico, "where they were very happy," Gladstone said. "They were always seventeen. They were the most well intentioned, loving seventeen-year-olds you can imagine, but they were always seventeen."

Gladstone went to the University of Vermont and majored in theater. She had a few dinner theater and summer stock roles during and after college, then realized she "didn't have the intestinal fortitude" for life in the theater. "When I had the right part, I was really good," she said. "But when it wasn't the right part, I was okay. And I realized I was limited in my range, and I wasn't as expert and instinctive in my craft to really succeed as an actress." The "right parts," she added, tended to be "prostitutes and mother-in-laws—there's something earthy, a sense of humor, a kind of irreverent quality, I think, that seems to be necessary for me to succeed."

After college, she waitressed in a Washington, D.C., bar called Columbia Station. She started dating (and eventually married) one of her customers, Fred Kaplan, a journalist who now writes the "War Stories" column for Slate.com. He helped her break into freelance writing. She wrote for trade publications for the strip mining and cable industries and then worked as an editor for the short-lived *Washington Weekly,* a free alternative newspaper.

Gladstone was working for *Current,* the trade newspaper for public broadcasting, during NPR's 1983 budget scandal. As she covered the network, she became intrigued with the process of making radio. She watched reporters pull together interviews and ambient sound, organize the material, and produce their reports, a process she described as "directing your own little one-act play."

"I was just so awestruck," she said. "I never imagined for a moment, for a *moment,* that I would ever get to work there."

She became friends with Scott Simon, NPR's Chicago bureau chief, who was brought in to Washington to cover the budget story from an outsider's perspective. Five years later, Simon was hosting *Weekend Edition* and needed an editor. He ran into Kaplan and asked about Gladstone—could she do it? She had just finished taking a year off to stay at home with her infant twin daughters and had a new job writing speeches for a union. She promptly quit to work for Simon. Public radio, she discovered, "was the exact right combination of information and presentation and narrative and all the stuff I loved about theater, news, and narrative." She worked as a senior editor for *Weekend Edition* for three years, then did the same job at *All Things Considered.*

In 1991, Gladstone received a Knight Fellowship to study Russian at Stanford University. The following year, she, Kaplan, and their daughters moved to Moscow. He was named Moscow bureau chief for the *Boston Globe.* She planned to file stories for the *Globe* and the *San Francisco Examiner.* But she also toted along a tape recorder her cousin, Ketzel Levine (the NPR correspondent best known as the network's gardening expert), had given her, so she put together a radio piece on Moscow's obsession with dubbed-over Mexican soap operas.

Finally the "little one-act plays" of public radio were her own. She enjoyed radio reporting so much that she all but forgot about her newspaper contacts back home. During the next three years in Moscow, she covered the insurgency at the Russian Parliament, the legalization of homosexuality, orgasmic faith healers, the rewriting of school textbooks, and the rise of the Russian mob. I remember much of her reporting from that time. She had a distinctively theatrical delivery and an arch way of capturing the chaos and absurdity of post-Soviet Russia. Her work stood out on the public radio airwaves, like Ethel Merman stepping on stage to perform a show tune in the middle of a concert of Baroque music.

In 1995, Gladstone's family returned to the United States and settled in Brooklyn. Gladstone was the media correspondent for NPR for the next six years, until WNYC came calling with the offer to cohost *On the Media.*

She described herself as working "stupidly hard" on the show. On Thursdays, the day before the show is distributed to stations, she and much of the staff will stay at work until 2 a.m. or later. "I work immoderately, and then I kind of collapse," she said. "It's not sustainable and not mature. It's like I still work like I'm in college."

I asked her whether she thought the professional and financial roller coaster of her parents' lives had anything to do with her work style. "You've got to wonder," she mused. "If there's a lasting impact it's that I don't have the confidence that . . . you know, if I don't work as hard as I can, that I'll get stuck on a curb somewhere with a bottle of Thunderbird in a brown paper bag. There's this sense that somehow, if you want to succeed, you can't let up. Whether it comes from the fact that there was rather a lot of financial insecurity in my background or whether it's just a fundamental lack of confidence or maybe just an inborn modus vividness, that I can't say."

Gladstone's twin daughters are now twenty, both college students. Sophie attends Vassar College and Maxine is at Oberlin. Gladstone told me that at times she felt she "missed out on a lot of the kid stuff" while they were growing up. Working on *Weekend Edition,* she remembered, would leave her busy through Saturday, then exhausted most of the rest of the weekend. When she was an editor on *All Things Considered,* the weekday schedule was more family-friendly. "But then I was so stressed out after every show that sometimes, in order for me not to yell at [the kids], I would have to stop at the bar next door, have a shot of scotch with a colleague, which would waste twenty minutes, but would keep me from yelling," she laughed. Her years as a reporter in Moscow and New York City were more flexible, and by the time she started hosting *On The Media,* the girls were in high school and busy with their own lives. "I feel like we have a really close relationship, even if I wasn't there as much as I wanted to be," she said. "So I think that all told, it all worked out in the end for us."

After our meal, Gladstone and I lingered over coffee in the warm, empty restaurant. We knew that outside the wind would be strong, the first snow flurries of the coming Nor'easter stinging. Our conversation had turned to gossip about the public radio world, things we made each other promise we wouldn't repeat, nothing too juicy really, just another indulgence, like the fish and chips we'd both managed to finish. I asked her if there was anything else she wanted me to know about her before we parted ways, and she grew serious.

"There was one thing I wanted to say," she said. "And that is that, when you've been doing radio for a while, it becomes, somehow, the way that you experience the world."

She told me that when her mother was dying a few years ago, she felt she had to bring her tape recorder along to her mother's bedside to record her last days. Gladstone was so frantic about it that she had her senior producer run the equipment down to her home in Brooklyn just before she left for the airport. She didn't understand why at the time, but later she realized the tape recorder had become "like another limb," she said. "Or another sense. You know, you have your five senses and then you have your radio sense, and it combines all the others and makes sense of things."

Bob Garfield

Long-time listeners to public radio may remember Bob Garfield as the NPR's "roving reporter" of the 1980s and 1990s, the guy who told the stories of some of America's greatest unsung eccentrics. There was the Texas woman who made her beloved seven-hundred-pound pig a cause célèbre after the city of Houston evicted him from her home. There was Norman Bloom, the homeless "Numbers Man" who frequently called in to Larry King's radio show to expound on his belief in a unified explanation of the universe based on arithmetic. And there was Garfield's own Kafka-esque quest to get an invitation to bowl in the White House bowling lanes. He recounted these strange sagas in one of radio's most ironic nasal voices, somewhat reminiscent of that of David Schwimmer on *Friends*, but, thankfully, far more wise and world-weary.

Now Garfield is on to more serious radio fare as the cohost of *On the Media:* the ethics of white-owned newspaper chains publishing broadsheets geared at minority populations, the question of whether government employees can be prevented from speaking to the media, and the increasingly cutthroat competition among magazines devoted to the care and feeding of ferrets.

Okay, so he's not always so serious.

The ferret piece broadcast the first week Garfield did the show, back in 2001. "It's still my favorite thing I've done," he said.

Garfield's sense of sarcasm and the absurd came from being the son of a mother who was "very critical of everyone and everything around her" and a "kind of goofy" father. "There's a long tradition in the Garfield family of finding fault with others," he told me in a telephone interview from his home office in Virginia. "I just am the first person to figure out how to cash in on it."

Garfield grew up outside of Philadelphia. His goofy father had a distinctly ungoofy job: he was an engineer at a plant that manufactured paper plates and cardboard boxes. "My theory is, he was a very creative guy, but he was the ninth of nine children and he was pushed into doing what he did by his pushy, very pushy older siblings," he said. "I think he would have been a textile designer if he'd had it his way. But he had this creative side that he turned to hobby stuff. He made little sculptures, acted up at cocktail parties, stuff like that."

I asked Garfield whether he felt he was living the creative life his father didn't have. Garfield told me that he felt lucky to be able to do exactly what he wanted to do in his career. "I've had moments where I feel that I've avenged his bondage at the hands of his family, let's put it that way," he said.

As an undergraduate English major at Pennsylvania State University in the 1970s, though, Garfield had no idea what he wanted to do with his life until a professor insisted he try an internship at a local newspaper. Garfield went to work at the *Centre Daily Times*, a twenty-five-thousand-circulation daily in Bellefonte, Pennsylvania. "And I was there twenty minutes before I understood with absolute clarity that this was how I was going to spend my life," he said. "It was the ambiance, the fact that you could say 'fuck' in the newsroom. The skepticism, the whole package, it totally corresponded with my world view of curiosity, irreverence, casualness."

Garfield went on to become a business reporter at the *News Journal* in Wilmington, Delaware. In 1982, he began writing a regular column on the ad industry for *USA Today*. Three years later, he was hired by *Advertising Age*. There he wrote "Garfield's AdReview," a weekly column of advertising criticism, and, for four years, a weekly syndicated column about American eccentrics.

In 1986, he began doing radio versions of those columns for *All Things Considered* and went on to do some 150 stories for NPR over the next twelve years. Brooke Gladstone edited many of them. "I was such an admirer of his pieces before I started working at *ATC*," she remembered. "Then when I became his editor, he was happy because I got his work, a quirky sense of humor that almost always hits, but sometimes doesn't, and you need to pull back a little here, change wording there, maybe eliminate a joke that just isn't gonna make it, and he trusted me because we had a similar sense of humor." Transcripts of several of his radio pieces on "bizarre Americana," along with a number of his columns, were published in his 1997 collection, *Waking Up Screaming from the American Dream*.

Garfield's power in the advertising world has become formidable in the two decades that he's been writing "AdReview." In 2003, he published *And Now a Few Words from Me: Advertising's Leading Critic Lays Down the Law, Once and for All*, a collection of his columns, and he's a much sought-after speaker on the advertising world. His writing can be caustic and slaying, with barbs like "the concept just plain sucks." He's also a wry and often hilarious social critic. In a column about an ad for Always menstrual pads, he wrote: "Being ashamed about your period is like being ashamed of respiration. ('Oh, I am soooooo embarrassed. Let me just disappear into the powder room to breathe. And please don't tell Walter! It makes him very queasy')." And he can be influential. Coke changed its slogan back to "Always Coca-Cola" after he trashed the new "Always and only (Coca-Cola)" slogan as "gilding the lily."

I told Garfield I thought I detected a common theme in his work on eccentrics and advertising: an intrigue with big ideas that don't work. "I've never actually made that connection," Garfield told me. "The phenomena probably have different provenances: one is rooted deep in the human soul, and one is rooted in vanity and arrogance. But I could be wrong. They could actually come from the same chromosome."

Garfield has had his own share of big ideas that haven't worked. *Waking Up Screaming* includes an essay about his own efforts to launch a quiz show on public television. He's also tried to sell a screenplay to Hollywood, a saga he documented in a radio essay for *On the Media*. "I constantly have ideas, and I constantly pursue them, and failure is a way of life for me as well," he said. "People notice what has worked, but nobody knows the incredibly long list of efforts of mine that have just come to nothing."

When Garfield started cohosting *On the Media* in early 2001, he thought the show would have plenty of "Garfieldian quirky oddball stuff" and the spirit of the program would be "a little less sober" than the typical public radio fare. Then came the September 11 terrorism attacks, the Patriot Act, and the wars in Afghanistan and Iraq. "September 11th changed everything," he said. "The reason [*On the Media* has] grown in distribution and listenership I think has almost nothing to do with the irreverence factor and everything to do with it being sort of the last defense against tyranny."

Garfield lives with his wife, Milena, a theater producer from Belgrade, and their four-year-old daughter, Ida. He has two other daughters from a previous marriage: Katie, twenty-three, a staff member at *The Week*, and Allie, twenty, a sophomore at James Madison University. Working out of his home has its advantages, he told me. He can take a break to spend time with Ida if he wants to. But work and family also mix in unintended ways. Ida's shouts and squeals may be audible, say, during an interview with a U.S. senator. "So more than once a week, I have to press the pause button and scream upstairs at the top of my lungs, TISINA, which is Serbian for silence," he said.

Garfield, in fact, has had to pull away, apologetically, from our telephone interview a couple of times to exchange a word or two with his wife. Near the end of our conversation, he excuses himself again and doesn't bother to cover the phone. "Darling, my love, precious, shut up, please darling!" he calls.

Then he's back. "She sometimes goes days without speaking to me, except when I get on the telephone and then she just wants to chat!" he said. "I have kind of an eccentric wife."

Somehow, I wasn't at all surprised.

Coloring the Invisible:
Tavis Smiley

Host, *The Tavis Smiley Show*

Tavis Smiley doesn't sound like a public radio host.

He'll welcome a familiar guest as "brother." His speech is salted with "ain't," "right quick" and other slang. He speaks in a blended accent that comes from his native Mississippi and central Indiana, where he grew up. He is blunt and bold. He's pressed Secretary of State Condoleezza Rice to respond to hip-hop artist Kanye West's claim that "George Bush doesn't care about black people" and quizzed the CEO of Greyhound about how the closing of several stations nationwide will affect blacks.

In the supposedly invisible world of radio, Smiley, forty-one, insists on color. The voices of his guests and commentators on *The Tavis Smiley Show* are often, though not always, black. He'll regularly readjust the focus of news interviews to the particular concerns of black Americans. The show stands out in the world of public radio journalism, which usually insists on pristine objectivity from its hosts. With Smiley, there's no hiding his politics. Though he doesn't preach on his show à la Rush Limbaugh and his guest list is as likely to include Kay Bailey Hutchinson as it is Barack Obama, Smiley is a long-time activist.

He's written about his Democratic populist views in ten books published within twelve years, including *Hard Left* and *Doing What's Right: How to Fight for What You Believe—And Make a Difference.*

The Tavis Smiley Show began in January 2002 as a daily program, the first regularly scheduled black-oriented show NPR had ever produced. In December 2004, just before the show's third anniversary, Smiley chose not to renew his contract with the network, citing disappointment with management's efforts to expand marketing and outreach to broader audiences. He told *Time* magazine: "It is ironic that a Republican president has an administration that is more inclusive and more diverse than a so-called liberal-media-elite network." An NPR attorney told the *New York Times* that Smiley would not negotiate with the network after his agent issued a list of demands. In January 2005, NPR started *News and Notes with Ed Gordon*, another African American themed show, to replace *The Tavis Smiley Show.* The following April, Smiley's show relaunched as a weekly two-hour program from NPR's rival distributor, Public Radio International.

Public radio is just one of the very many things Tavis Smiley does. He also hosts *Tavis Smiley*, a nightly program on public television. He runs the Tavis Smiley Foundation, a nonprofit organization with a mission of encouraging and empowering black youth, and the Smiley Group, a communications company. He is a philanthropist who gave one million dollars to Texas Southern University in 2004 for its communications program and a new building to put it in: the Tavis Smiley School of Communications and the Tavis Smiley Center for Radio, Television, and Print Media. He's also a widely sought-after inspirational speaker whose "empowerment cards" offer advice such as: "Create something new today just for the fun of it. Don't burden yourself with deadlines or fixate on dollars and cents. Let the child inside you play."

But Smiley does have quite a few deadlines himself. My request for an interview with him was met with a response from his assistant that because he was working on a tight schedule to finish two books, he wouldn't be available for several months, well beyond my own deadline.

Tavis Smiley is the oldest of ten children. A native of Mississippi, Smiley grew up mainly in Kokomo, a small industrial city in central Indiana. His father, Emory Smiley, was an air force officer. His mother, Joyce, was a part-time Pentecostal evangelical minister, and the family was very involved in the New Bethel Tabernacle church. The couple had six sons of their own and became the legal guardians of the two sons and two daughters of Joyce's sister after she was murdered.

In his book, *Keeping the Faith: Stories of Love, Courage, Healing, and Hope from Black America*, Smiley wrote about his parents with great admiration: "Never did I hear my parents complain, not even once, about the extra responsibility they had taken on, despite the fact that my parents' income hadn't increased and the space in the trailer we lived in hadn't gotten any bigger." Yet he has also described an incident of disturbing physical abuse when he was in the seventh grade. His father, believing Tavis and his sister had disrupted a church service, whipped them with an extension cord so harshly that, after a teacher discovered their wounds, they were hospitalized for seven days. The two were taken out of their parents' house and sent to separate foster homes. After several months, Tavis returned. His sister stayed in foster care and went on to struggle with a crack addiction for many years. He has "repaired" his relationship with his parents. "I believe we have to forgive in order to live," he wrote.

As a teenager, Smiley volunteered for the Sunday school superintendent at his church, Douglas Hogan, who was also a member of the city council. The experience introduced Smiley to politics and led him to consider it as a career. He attended the University of Indiana on a debate scholarship, interned for Los Angeles mayor Tom Bradley for a semester, and became an aide. He ran for a seat on the Los Angeles

City Council in 1991, when he was twenty-six. He finished fourth out of fourteen candidates.

After the election, he started doing a radio commentary called *The Smiley Report* on KGFJ, a black-owned station in Los Angeles. He recruited the sponsors himself. In 1996, he became a regular commentator for *The Tom Joyner Morning Show*. From 1996 to 2001, he hosted *BET Tonight with Tavis Smiley* on Black Entertainment Television (BET). He was fired after selling an interview he did with former Symbionese Liberation Army member Sara Jane Olsen to ABC, though he did offer it first to BET and CBS. The firing was met with consternation among Smiley's growing number of fans, who speculated that BET's purchase by Viacom might have played a role in his dismissal.

Tavis Smiley and NPR joined forces a few months later. NPR executives had been meeting with the management of thirty-eight black-oriented public radio stations for years, batting around proposals for programming that would appeal to their audiences. The result was a plan for a current affairs program with a recommended air time after *Morning Edition*, and Tavis Smiley was offered the signature host job.

At the time of Smiley's departure from NPR, nearly three years later, *The Tavis Smiley Show* had eighty-seven member stations and more than one million weekly listeners. Twenty-nine percent of its listeners were black, compared to 6 percent of the overall public radio audience for news and talk programming. As of October 2005, sixty stations were airing the Public Radio International relaunch of *The Tavis Smiley Show*.

In 2004, *The Tavis Smiley Show* was one of several public broadcasting shows analyzed for the "political ideology" of their guests by a secretly hired consultant to Kenneth Tomlinson, then the chairman of the Corporation for Public Broadcasting. (Tomlinson stepped down after the CPB's inspector general delivered a report critical of his leadership.) The analysis found that less than half of the guests on *The Tavis Smiley Show* were "liberal." In an editorial in the *Washington Post*, Smiley said the debate over ideological balance misses the real problem: "Why isn't the debate over how public broadcasting can become more inclusive of folk of different ages and national origins, of various ethnic groups, faiths and cultures—over how it can be used to introduce Americans to new ideas, and to each other?"

A View from the Tower:
Kurt Andersen

Host, *Studio 360 with Kurt Andersen*

In 1986, in the middle of Ronald Reagan's second term, *Spy* appeared on the newsstands. The magazine was somewhat inscrutable to me at first. It was like *Mad* magazine for politically savvy grownups, and I, a freshman at Oberlin College, wasn't one yet. All the truly hip people at school were reading *Spy*, though, and I came to understand the satire and enjoy a few laughs at "Separated at Birth," "the Spy List," and the jokey advertisements and fake letters to the editor of *The New Yorker.*

Nearly two decades later, I am watching Kurt Andersen, one of the founders of Spy, conduct a conversation about fairy tales for his Peabody Award–winning public radio program, *Studio 360 with Kurt Andersen*. He sits in a studio alone, a bottle of Poland Spring water at his elbow, twiddling his pen. He is tall and slim and wears a sweater and jeans. His dark hair, graying above the ears, is cut nearly razor short. His nose and chin are prominent and his eyes are wide. His guest is Gregory MacGuire, the author of the novel *Wicked*, on which the hit musical was based. MacGuire's voice is piped into the studio through a live-quality telephone line from Los Angeles. He tells

Andersen that he started *Wicked* after finding himself wondering about history's worst demagogues and the nature of evil.

"You started out wanting to explore, inspired by Saddam Hussein and Hitler, the nature of evil, and then you turn the Wicked Witch into a kind of victimized, free-spirited left-winger. How did that process happen?" Andersen asks carefully, his voice a little halting.

"It's like the process by which any parent grows to love his or her new child," MacGuire begins, a bit preciously, and explains that, despite his original intentions, he "began to like her" in the process of writing about her every day.

After they discuss MacGuire's work, their conversation focuses on the show's three feature stories. The first is about the history of the Nutcracker Ballet, the second about how author Salman Rushdie, while in hiding from a *fatwah* against him, used a modern-day fairy tale to communicate with his young son, and the last about the public's reaction to an artist's cute, creepy, and provocative creature sculptures in the 14th Street subway station.

Studio 360 is some of the things *Spy* was. It's smart and clever and questioning and meant for audiences with those same tendencies. But though there are moments of levity, most of the show is quite serious. Some of the shows turn out to be "totally serious," Andersen told me after the taping. He has rarely in his life, he said, taken to projects that were so serious. "I'm fifty and not thirty-two. Maybe that's the difference."

Studio 360, distributed by Public Radio International, explores themes in art and culture—loneliness, Freud, color, death, farming, and dreams have all been subject matter for the show. Each program starts out with a radio essay by Andersen, then moves into an interview with a guest. Susan Sontag, Margaret Atwood, Woody Allen, Verlyn Klinkenborg, and Thomas Lynch are among those who've been on the show. The interviews are interwoven with three feature pieces on various aspects of the week's theme. The format is part *Fresh Air* artist interview and part public radio news magazine, but the show usually has little to do with the week's news, instead emphasizing concepts in "high and low culture," as Andersen puts it. The feature pieces are also different from the standard sound of NPR reports. Reporters can use the first person, for example, and may speak of their own personal experiences as they delve into their topic.

The show is produced at WNYC in New York, whose offices are in a tower on top of the municipal building, a grand Renaissance Revival landmark on One Centre Street in lower Manhattan. Andersen and I spoke in his thirtieth-floor office, which has a spectacular view of the Brooklyn Bridge. The round shape of the tower was one of the inspirations for the somewhat enigmatic title of the show. "It's the 360 degrees of taking a theme and looking at it from all sides," he said.

Inasmuch as *Studio 360* is unlike *Spy*, and inasmuch as Andersen is at a different stage in his life, there are ways that his work on the show reminds him of those heady early years at the magazine. He became the host of *Studio 360* before it had a name or a concept, beyond the broad notion of being about arts and culture. He and the show's staff spent a year working out what the program would be before it went on the air in 2000. "This is a very different thing in every way imaginable [from *Spy*], but in terms of having a core group of people who kind of click and move as one, it's sort of comparable," he said. "And I didn't expect to experience that twice. I was really lucky."

Andersen grew up in "the western suburboid edge" of Omaha, Nebraska, in the 1960s. His parents were a lawyer and a "literate, intense reader/writer housewife." He was the youngest of four children. Once he hit adolescence, "the age when you hate things," he chaffed at his surroundings. "I hated being in the suburbs, I hated being surrounded by nothing but white people, I hated everything about it," he said. "That being said, it was a great place to grow up, in a house full of books, full of music."

He realized he wanted to be a journalist when he was eight. He published an essay about Thanksgiving in the local paper, with his by-line and photo. "So there was this essay with my picture, and it was almost like my consciousness just snapped on," he said. "I thought, oh, okay. I get this. It was fantastic."

As an undergraduate at Harvard University, he was an editor of *The Harvard Lampoon*. After graduation, he started his journalism career at NBC writing radio copy for Gene Shalit. At *Time* magazine, Andersen wrote about national affairs and criminal justice issues and then became the magazine's architecture and design critic for eight years. He struck up a friendship with Graydon Carter (now the editor of *Vanity Fair*), and the two spent lunches brainstorming about a magazine of political satire and humor.

They took the plunge in 1986 and started *Spy*. It was a time, Andersen remembered, when the media landscape was far different than it is today. He and Carter at first hardly thought about advertisers or audience demographics, factors impossible to ignore in launching a glossy today. And the whole idea of media that satirized the media was just beginning to percolate, with *Saturday Night Live*'s "Weekend Update" and David Letterman. "No one criticized the *New York Times* in 1986," Andersen said. "It was a scary and brave, if I may say so, thing to do, as opposed to today when any blogger with a stuffy nose can write a critique of the *New York Times* or anybody else."

The idea quickly attracted readers and financial backers. Andersen and Carter were able to raise $6 million in six months. "The combination of nonfiction and a satircal-humorist point of view didn't exist beyond us, frankly," he said. "So we were fortunate in being, if not the only game in town, one of the few games in town, and therefore had this big impact."

Andersen and Carter sold *Spy* in 1991, and the magazine folded seven years later. Andersen now sees the comic ethos of the magazine as a kind of cultural precursor to *The Daily Show* and the "snarky voice" of web sites like theonion.com and modernhumorist.com. "To some degree, [*Spy*] died and was composted into the media earth and grew new seedlings," he said.

After *Spy* sold, Andersen returned to *Time* as an editor-at-large and wrote a weekly column on entertainment and media. He became the editor of *New York* magazine in 1994. Two years later, he was "spectacularly fired" for covering Wall Street too aggressively. He found himself, a week after his fortieth birthday, with a year's severance pay. He started writing a novel, taking on little outside work other than writing a cultural column for *The New Yorker*. "I had an idea for a book, so it seemed like now or never, better try it and see if I can do it and like doing it rather than turn sixty and think, oh, I should have tried doing that," he said.

The result was *Turn of the Century*, published in 1999 by Random House. The novel, a best-seller, is a social satire that aims its barbs at the media, Wall Street, cyberspace, and the revved-up pace of family life in New York in the year 2000. The *Wall Street Journal* called it a "smart, funny and excruciatingly deft portrait of our age."

While doing publicity for the book, Andersen did an interview at WNYC with Leonard Lopate and noticed a Help Wanted posting seeking a host of a new arts and culture program. Sounds like a great show, Andersen thought to himself, but he had never worked in radio and it didn't occur to him to apply. A few weeks later, he got a call asking him if he might be interested in hosting. "It seemed sort of serendipitous, if not magical," he said.

Other than working for Shalit fresh out of college, Andersen had no radio experience, so he had to learn the craft of radio, from how to speak into a microphone to how to conduct an interview as a performance instead of simply a way of gathering information for a news article. He finds radio a "wonderful" medium. "The thing they all said to me when they were talking to me about this job is, you know, it's a very intimate medium," he said. "I kind of didn't know what they meant, but I now get that, because it is this one-on-one with the listener in a way that television certainly isn't. All I know is the feedback we get in the form of emails from listeners is more regularly passionate and intense and enthusiastic than any media thing I've ever done. Which is some measure of how intimate it is."

Andersen is married to Anne Kraemer, a writer who was a contributing editor at *Martha Stewart Living* and worked for many years in children's media. They live in a four-story townhouse in the Carroll Gardens section of Brooklyn and have two daughters, Lucy, fifteen, and Kate, seventeen. He spends his mornings at home, writing. His second novel, *Wonderstruck*, a historical novel set in Europe and America during the gold rush, is due out in 2006 from Random House. He also writes "The Imperial City" column for *New York* magazine and has collaborated on a number of screenplays and scripts for television, film, and the stage, including the off-Broadway revue *Loose Lips* and a screen adaptation of *Turn of the Century*. In the afternoon, he goes into work on *Studio 360* at WNYC. The routine, he said, is "kind of perfect, for me. It works well to have both the collaborative social experience and the private personal creative experience."

After a career of switching jobs every five years or so, building the ultimate journalist's dream resume, he's not planning on shifting course again anytime soon. "I have felt in the past, eh, this is great, I'm not going to put my heart and soul into it, it's probably not for life," he said. "I kind of feel like writing books and doing [*Studio 360*] could very well be for life. I hope they are, in fact."

Speaking Truth to Power:
Steve Curwood

Host, *Living on Earth*

When Steve Curwood's son was eight years old, he told Curwood, "You've got to do something about the environment."

It was 1989. Curwood was an investigative journalist who'd worked for the *Boston Globe* and NPR. At first he wanted to write a book about climate change, but after talking to experts on the topic, he decided the best way for him to take on the issue was to start a radio program. "I realized the difference I could make was in public radio," he said.

The result was *Living on Earth*, a weekly program about the environment from NPR. The show defines its subject matter broadly, from the environmental impact of Hurricane Katrina to garbage accumulation on Antarctica to a campaign to put gardens in every school yard to the history of plant-based aphrodisiacs. "One of our challenges is to keep the mix of stories sufficient so that it's not always bad news all the time," he said. "Because if you just are hearing constant bad news, it sounds like complaining and who wants to listen to that?"

Living on Earth is produced by the World Media Foundation, located on the fourth floor of an office building near the Davis Square T stop in Somerville, on the outskirts of Boston. I interviewed Curwood on an afternoon in mid-December. The office was very quiet, with few people around. Our conversation had the feeling of a meeting with a professor on the final day before winter break, when most of the other students had already gone home and there is time and space to speak in leisure.

Curwood himself actually is quite professorial. He teaches a yearly seminar at Harvard, his alma mater, and has an academic's way of explaining the big ideas behind what he's doing and who he is, with thoroughness and a tendency toward tangents, qualities rare in the deadline-driven news world. He is heavyset, with a wide, mildly ironic smile, and wore a green checked shirt under a tan v-necked sweater. He is black, a fact not always apparent to listeners, both because of the invisibility of radio and because there are no obvious markers of ethnicity in his even, calm speech.

Curwood, fifty-seven, told me that his intellectual manner comes from his mother, a sociology professor who taught at Antioch College in Yellow Springs, Ohio, and other colleges in Rhode Island and Tennessee. She also introduced him to the wonders of the natural world. She was a naturalist and a bird-watcher who often took him birding at their New Hampshire summer home. Curwood's father, a contractor, died when Curwood was very young.

He took to journalism at an early age. By the time he was twelve, he was a licensed ham radio operator and wrote for the *Yellow Springs News*. "It was great fun," he said. "I would write up this and that and go down to the newspaper, which was then set in hot type, and I would set the story in type, and golly, it would come out in the newspaper!"

He told me that the philosophical underpinnings of his interest came from growing up Quaker. He attended Westtown School, a Quaker boarding school in Chester County, Pennsylvania. "One of the things I have learned is this notion that you speak truth to power," he said. "You can't move forward as a society unless you're addressing the real problems."

His first encounter with public radio was in a radio drama group at WYSO, a public radio group that had just been built by Antioch College. He also got interested in the technical side of radio. By age sixteen, he had a first-class radio telephone license, the most advanced commercial license. Curwood worked during college as a technician at New Hampshire public television and CBS radio. A senior engineer warned him that though he'd make more money as a techie over the short term, automation would ultimately eliminate most engineering jobs. "And, you can have more fun on the other side of the glass," the engineer advised.

Curwood's first job after graduating from Harvard was at the *Bay State Banner*, a black-owned newspaper in Boston. He covered desegregation issues as part of the *Boston Globe*'s education team, which won a Pulitzer Prize in 1975 for public service. Remembering the advice of his WYSO mentor, he went into broadcast journalism. He worked a special on school desegregation for public television and then was recruited by WGBH-TV to be on their evening news. He had a young daughter by then, and his wife was back in school. He took the job in part because he wanted to take care of his daughter during the day, an unconventional rationale in the 1970s. "The *Globe* was very unhappy— 'What? You're going to work nights so you can be with your kid? This is not how you do things!'" he remembered. "WGBH was happy to hire somebody to come to work in the afternoon and evening."

He worked as a producer on *The Advocates*, a public debate show at WGBH. When the program ran out of money, he moved to Washington to work for NPR as a reporter and the host of *Weekend All Things Considered*. When the network hit rocky financial times in the early 1980s, he went back to the *Globe*. He covered a sexual abuse case and began to work on a book about it, but his publisher backed out after being threatened with a lawsuit.

That's when Curwood's son, James, piped in to redirect his career. The pilot of *Living on Earth* aired in 1990, and the program launched as a weekly show the following year. Beyond his son's naive hopes, Curwood found environmental journalism strongly compelling. "As a person of color, and a person who did a lot of investigative work at the *Globe*, I have encountered a lot of denial from the people who say one thing when something else is going on," he said. "You know, when you're a person of color they say, Gee, that place was rented yesterday. You know that it's bullshit. You know it's a lie. And when I started looking at the question of climate change, I began to realize that there was a rather large lie perpetrated around it in a very tricky kind of way."

In taking on that lie, and other issues related to science and the environment, he found that he also had to take on journalism itself. He explained all this, in his digressive manner, with a series of analogies: if one person thinks the shutters should be green and another wants them to be blue, a reporter can do a story including the opinions of each, and, as opinions, they will be equally as accurate and neither side will be "right," just different. But in science, he said, that reporter can't interview one person who says two and two is four and another who says two and two is five.

"You've got to go for what seems to be the best science and help the listener understand that this is the best we know right now," he said. "I have a hard time working with some journalists on that, because—taking climate change, for example—there are some entrenched interests who want to push skepticism. Well, the weight of evidence is nowhere near the skepticism about the greenhouse effect."

He also struggles with the impression that environmental journalism is by nature advocacy. "This is one of the biggest challenges of environmental journalists, because people have this prejudice—and I use this strong word prejudice—when somebody covers the environment, oh my God, they must be some sort of environmental activist," he said. "I'm an activist for citizens to know what the heck is going on."

He points out, too, that environmentalism has only in its most recent incarnation been considered a "liberal" movement. He quoted a line from Teddy Roosevelt's memoirs: "'The rude, fierce settler who drives the savage from the land lies all civilized mankind under a debt to him.' So Teddy Roosevelt gave us what, five national parks, a hundred fifty million acres of national forest, and this highly racist perspective," he said. "Here you have this movement that begins as Republicans who are fairly conservative and racist, and today, people's knee-jerk reaction is, Gee, the enviro crowd, they're liberals. I think both perspectives are oversimplified."

Curwood lives in the southern New Hampshire summer home where his mother, who died in 1990, took him birding when he was a boy. The property in Nottingham has thirty acres and a pond. It is an hour commute—he usually takes the train—to his office in Somerville. He blames his decision to live at "the family house" on Edward O. Wilson, a Harvard biologist who was a guest on the show in 1994. Wilson coined the term "biophilia" to describe his theory that humans have a natural need to respond to other life-forms. "When I heard about biophilia, and the fact that we really deeply connect with other species, my plan to live there in retirement really went out the window and I decided to base myself there," he said.

There are few blacks in Nottingham. When he was a kid spending summers there, he didn't face much hostility, but "people wanted to know if it washed off, the skin color." When he moved in year-round in 1996, the police in every town around Nottingham stopped him. "I have no tickets, absolutely no tickets," he said. "The all had to check me out. As soon as virtually every town had stopped me, it stopped."

Curwood's son, James, twenty-five, is a musician in New York City. His daughter, Anastasia, thirty-one, is an assistant professor of African American and diaspora studies at Vanderbilt University. Curwood is divorced from their mother. In 2003 he got remarried, to Jennifer Stevens-Curwood, an artist and real estate agent. The two bought a home in Cape Town, South Africa, after a reporting trip there and have returned several times since. "In having supported divestiture, disinvestment, in South Africa, now that things have changed, it suddenly made sense to put some money back in," he said. "And it's fun, it's a really beautiful place."

Living on Earth is broadcast on 280 public radio stations and has more than half a million listeners. Looking back on the decade and a half since the show started, Curwood has seen the program's influence increase. *Living on Earth* did environmental profiles of presidential candidates in 1992, when such articles were rare. The next election cycle, many other media outlets followed suit, and now such profiles are commonplace. "One of the biggest roles we play is other journalists pay attention to what we do, and it winds up in general journalism," he said. "I believe we've really helped to make a difference."

Book Writing in Miniature:
Bill Littlefield

Host, *Only a Game*

Bill Littlefield was never a prospect.

As a kid, he played ice hockey, tennis, baseball, and other sports. He wasn't serious about any of it. He just liked to have fun.

What he has always been serious about is stories. He studied fiction writing at Yale, and he's written two novels and three nonfiction books. As the host of *Only a Game*, a weekly program of analysis, interviews, and reports about sports, he'd rather hear the story of the writer who spent a season hanging out with the obsessed fans of the University of Alabama football team than score a postgame locker room exclusive with Green Bay Packer quarterback Brett Favre. He's after stories that will surprise him, make him laugh, teach him something he never knew before. And that means breaking open the definition of sports journalism to include the Irish soccer/football/hockey hybrid of hurling, the reenactment of ancient Olympic Games by a group of fifth graders, and a convention of baseball statistics–loving geeks.

Littlefield and I spoke in the cafeteria of WBUR, the Boston public radio station where *Only a Game* is produced. He was about to head off to the nearby town of Lowell to talk to a former head of the

241

U.S. National Women's Softball team about a proposal to eliminate the sport from the Olympics. Littlefield is a slender man with a narrow chin and large, square-shaped glasses. He wore a bright yellow shirt, with blue and white flowers, the effect quite loud, in contrast to his soft-spoken, thoughtful manner. But the shirt reminded me that, on the air, he's the guy who heartily yucks it up every week with sports analyst Charlie Pierce and won't hesitate to do an interview about people who ride roller-coasters for days at a time. Littlefield told me that he considers humor a key element of what makes a good story on *Only a Game.* "Almost any sport, almost any game, from our point of view, offers all kinds of possibilities," he said. "The challenge and the fun of what we do is, how do I find a story that's compelling and intriguing and funny that happens to be set in sports?"

Growing up in Montclair, New Jersey, in the 1950s, Littlefield was captivated by the debut of baseball great Willie Mays. "It was pretty easy to get interested in baseball when perhaps the greatest player who ever lived was beginning his career," he said. He played on local youth ice hockey and tennis teams but was outclassed once he went away to prep school at Phillips Academy in Andover, Massachusetts. "They were playing a different game," he said of his varsity league classmates. "They were half again as fast and they were just better than I was."

As an undergraduate at Yale University, he became interested in writing, but he was too shy to hand in a sample of his work to apply to take a class with renowned poet and novelist Robert Penn Warren. One of his teachers submitted Littlefield's writing instead, and he got into the class. He remembers that Warren gave him one gentle yet, at the time, difficult to take insight. "He said to me sometime late in the semester something like, 'When you have something more to write about, you may really have something going here because you've got some style and some voice, but you don't have anything to say yet,'" Littlefield said.

Littlefield didn't think sports would play a role in what he had to say until he was living in Boston, pursuing a master's degree at the Harvard University School of Education. He played softball with a community team in Brookline and wrote about the experience in an essay for the *Boston Ledger*, a now-defunct weekly paper. He became the paper's regular sports columnist and began to submit radio commentaries based on his columns to WBUR and NPR. "Eventually I made enough of a nuisance of myself that they just started buying my stuff," he said.

He did public radio sports commentaries for ten years while teaching writing and English at Curry College in Milton, Massachusetts. While on a hunt for new story ideas, he came across an ad in the newspaper calling on Boston-area high school baseball players to come to Holy Cross College on a Saturday to play for a major league scout. He showed up with a tape recorder and struck up a conversation with the scout, who'd played shortstop for the Cubs in the 1940s. It was raining and the tryouts were called off. "We just stood under a lean-to watching the rain and talking," Littlefield said. "And I got the idea that a major league baseball scout would have an incredible number of stories and would make a great narrator for novel."

That idea became the seed for Littlefield's novel *Prospect*, about a retired baseball scout whose career is revived when the black woman who helps take care of him introduces him to her talented great-nephew. It was not, he told me, his first novel. He'd written one years ago, during summer and Christmas vacations from his teaching job. On the advice of a friend, he made himself write three pages a day. "If it took half an hour, I'd be finished in a half an hour. If it took four hours, I'd wait until I had my first three pages and that's how I wrote my first book," he said. "It will never be published, but you step back from that great pile of pages and you say, Wow, okay, I can do that. That gave me the sense when I got the idea for *Prospect* that writing a novel wasn't nearly as intimidating as it otherwise would have been if I hadn't done the other one first."

He sold *Prospect* to Houghton Mifflin, and it was published in 1989. He's gone on to write another novel, *The Circus in the Woods* (2002), aimed at young adults, and three nonfiction books: *Baseball Days* (1993); *Champions: The Stories of Ten Remarkable Athletes* (1993); and *Keepers: Radio Stories from "Only a Game" and Elsewhere* (1999). He has also coedited *Fall Classics* (2003), a collection of writing about the World Series, and guest edited the 1998 *Best American Sports Writing* anthology.

In 1993, he began to brainstorm the concept of *Only a Game* with David Greene, who would become the program's first producer. The show began as a half-hour local show that July. It expanded to an hour the following January and debuted nationally in October 1994, distributed by NPR as a lead-in show to *Weekend Edition* with Scott Simon. That meant that its recommended air time was 7 a.m. Saturday. "Not my decision," was Littlefield's only comment on the early hour.

Only a Game has a tiny staff. Littlefield works with three producers, all four of them and their work stations squeezed into a narrow cubicle at WBUR. Senior producer Gary Waleik, an avid fly fisherman, and associate Producer Gabe O'Connor, who has a degree in sports journalism, are the kind of zealous sports fans you'd expect to be working on the show. Associate producer Karen Given is not. She has "zero background" in sports, as she put it. She said that perspective helps her edit the show for a public radio audience, many of whom are not avid sports fans. "I'm the one who's like, I don't understand that, that doesn't make sense to a normal person," she told me.

Littlefield says the talent on his staff makes up for its small size. "They're all brilliant," he said. "And when you've worked together for a certain amount of time, [a small staff] is probably an advantage because it's not a question of worrying what everybody's doing or making sure there's work for everybody. We all have plenty to do, and I have utter faith and trust in their decisions and how they do their job."

Littlefield may not have been a sports scout's prospect when he was a kid, but he has stayed active on the field, mainly as a volunteer coach for the soccer and basketball teams his two daughters, Amy, nineteen, and Alison, sixteen, have played on. He is married to Mary Atlee, a paralegal and administrator, and lives in the Boston area. He still teaches one course a semester at Curry College. He stopped taking on full course loads once he found his "dream job" hosting *Only a Game*. "It's the process—go down, talk to a bunch of people, lay it all out on your desk and say, 'Okay, where's the story in all this?'" he said. "That to me is fascinating. It's book writing in miniature."

PART III

Music

Grand Dame of Jazz:
Marian McPartland

Host, *Piano Jazz*

Marian **McPartland is** deliciously polite. Maybe it comes from her native England, where manners have a long and colorful history, alongside monarchies and beheadings and clotted cream scones. But she's been in the United States for more than a half century, so you could speculate that the flavor of her politeness has been spiced by the many seeming contradictions of the role she's played in American jazz: a woman in a man's world, a white playing a musical form birthed and shaped by blacks, a Brit taking on "America's classical music" with such extraordinary understanding that she can play gentle ballads with Stanley Cowell one afternoon and hold forth with Marilyn Crispell's free jazz escapades the next. She is a host who will make sure you are not too hot or too cold, make sure the drink you want—whether it be mineral water, coffee, or a glass of Courvoisier—is in easy reach. She will make sure you know how delighted she is to have you on her show, how terrific you are, how she wishes she'd known you longer, had you on her show sooner, perhaps you can come again?

Her reward is your playing, and the chance to accompany you. She has described the feeling of her first year doing *Piano Jazz*, back in

1979, as being "like a kid in a candy store," calling all the jazz piano greats she could think of to ask them to be her guests. Though today it is she who is courted by publicists and record promoters, that delight is still with her. Walking into the lounge at Manhattan Beach Studio for the first in a weeklong series of *Piano Jazz* tapings, she spots pianist Lenore Raphael's latest CD, *Reflections,* on an end table and stops short. "She's supposed to be quite something. We must get her on the show," she says.

Piano Jazz producer Shari Hutchinson hands McPartland, eighty-seven, a Styrofoam cup of hot, milky tea, the bag still steeping, and takes her black tote bag, stuffed with magazines, arrangements, and more CDs, off the crook of her arm. "Good Morning, Marian," Hutchinson says. "I brought that in for you. I thought you might want her." They speak quietly together for a few minutes. There is some concern about McPartland's stomachache, which she describes as a "rumbly tummy," and when the day's guest, singer/pianist Patricia Barber, is to arrive. They are scheduled to start at noon, but she will be late, they are sure of it. The musicians are always late. Hutchinson shows McPartland a couple of phone messages about an upcoming concert. McPartland shakes her head. "Those people again. They are having a hard time telling me what they want me to do."

Hutchinson stands close to McPartland, assuring her there will be time to return the call after the taping, or she could call from the car service on the way back to Port Washington if the session runs long. The studio is reserved between noon and four, but McPartland likes to be on her way at three to avoid the rush hour. Both women are short and formidable, but in vastly different ways. McPartland is thin and carefully put together, with black slacks, a black print blouse, and squat-heeled pumps, her ash-brown hair shaped helmet-style around her narrow face. Hutchinson is stocky, her short blond hair in tightly styled curls. She is dressed for the August heat in a sleeveless pale blue cotton sweater, her freckled face still ruddy from the hustle from hotel to studio.

I am to interview McPartland before the taping starts, but there is a problem. Even though we are in one of New York City's most acclaimed recording studios, there is no quiet place to talk—which is necessary, as I want to use the interview in a radio segment. I thought we'd be able to use the same room McPartland tapes the show in— probably the most acoustically perfect space I, in my years of working at bean-counting public radio affiliates, could ever hope to enter. But the piano tuners are at work there. Soundproofing, I discover, only works one way, at least in this case. The test-banging of each key on the two Baldwin grand pianos reverberates through half the Manhattan Beach offices. McPartland and I search through the rest, but the front lounge picks up street noise, and the other offices have ringing phones and noisy central air.

I feel ridiculous, leading McPartland from room to room, but she is perfectly game. She opens the door to the bathroom, sticks her head in, and listens. "It's quiet in here!" she giggles. She puts the toilet seat down and sits on it. I close the door, lean against the sink, and pull out my minidisk recorder. The room is narrow and cluttered with stacks of audio equipment catalogues, but at least it's clean.

Before we can start, the studio manager knocks on the door. "Come in," McPartland says. "We're just doing a little interview in here." The manager shakes her head and raises her eyebrows. "I think I have something for you," she says. She leads us to the most remote corner office, unplugs the phone, and agrees to turn down the air conditioning. McPartland has a merry look in her eye. She has, after all, almost been interviewed in a bathroom.

When McPartland first started performing, she was terribly shy. "Absolutely mute" is how she puts it. "I could barely say good evening. It was awful. I had to have it written down on a piece of paper: 'Thank you very much, ladies and gentleman. And now I'd like to play . . . '" More than sixty years later, she still shows traces of that carefully rehearsed performer in my interview with her, with frequent expressions of gratitude and generous helpings of "wonderful," "fantastic," and other superlatives. It's as if she's still genuinely amazed that she's gone from being a teenager who gazed longingly at posters advertising Duke Ellington's appearance at the Palladium, certain her parents would never let her attend, to an octogenarian who has played with and befriended more jazz greats than probably any other living musician. We don't have much time to talk before she has to be back in the studio, and her answers to my questions are nicely concise—a minute or two—which is about the length of the typical answer on *Piano Jazz*, after editing. Even though she's the one being interviewed, her host's constant internal clock is still ticking— a sense of pacing I'm familiar with from interviewing seasoned politicians and professional "spokespeople." But McPartland has, as you might imagine, much more jazz in her responses, a sense of improvisation and fun, embellished with infectiously girlish giggles, brief digressions, and the feeling that she is honestly glad that I am there to ask her to talk about her life—and if there was just a bit more time she'd want to learn all she could about mine.

McPartland was born Margaret Marian Turner near Windsor, England, in 1918. She first approached the piano when she was three, climbing onto her mother's piano bench to try to sound out a Chopin waltz. McPartland's love affair with jazz began when she was a teenager, studying piano at the Guildhall School of Music during the day and listening to jazz on the BBC at night. Her interest in the form deepened when she became involved with a boy who came to the house toting jazz 78s by Fats Waller, Benny Goodman, Lionel Hampton, Teddy Wilson, Duke Ellington, and other American jazz stars. McPartland couldn't get enough of the music. In the practice rooms of the elite Guildhall, she'd try to perfect Art Tatum runs and other riffs that impressed her, despite the disapproval of one of her professors, who once yanked open the practice room door to admonish her: "Stop playing that trash!"

She didn't. Her quick ear and talent for improvisation got her a gig with the Claviers, a four-piano vaudeville act put together by the well-known British entertainer Billy Mayerl. Her conservative parents, who'd felt they'd already compromised enough by allowing her to pursue a career as a classical musician, were shocked when their daughter announced she was leaving the Guildhall—and their home—to go on the road. Her father offered her a thousand pounds to turn down the job. She refused. "I mean, they really couldn't stop me," she said. She calls the show, which featured two women and two men playing jazzy pop on gold pianos, "actually very posh. We toured all the good theaters in England." Still, she took a stage name, Marian Page, to spare her family the embarrassment of having a daughter in show biz.

During World War II, she toured around Europe, entertaining the troops. In Belgium, she spotted cornetist Jimmy McPartland in a jam session under a USO tent. He was already a minor legend in the United States, both for his genius at Chicago-style jazz and for his swaggering, raffish presence. She had never heard of him. She boldly sat in, causing him to wonder "Who's the chick rushing the beat?" He came to know her quite well. The two performed together in a trio accompanying a juggler, a singer, and a tap dancer. The act would head out to the front every day in a weapons carrier, Marian and the other girls prettied up in beads and sequins for the soldiers. But underneath the glitter, she was getting the jazz education she'd craved for so long. "Suddenly jazz records sounded so meaningful," she wrote in her collection of essays, *Marian McPartland's Jazz World: All in Good Time.* "I was able to hear more, and get some ideas from what I heard."

Marian and Jimmy fell in love and married in Aachen, Germany, on February 3, 1945. The life the McPartlands shared is one of the most fabled love stories in American jazz. The two came from very different backgrounds. She was upper-middle-class, from an extended family that included the mayor of Windsor, knighted by Queen Elizabeth.

She spent her youth practicing classical piano eight hours a day, with a pause for tea promptly at four. Jimmy hailed from the working-class mean streets of Chicago. He was thirteen years older, divorced, and an infamously heavy drinker. What brought them together, as *Washington Post* feature writer Paul Hendrickson puts it, was "jazz, with its own inner logic. It was the music that was going to yoke them for a lifetime."

After the war, Jimmy took his bride back to America. He had an established career to return to. Marian was faced with both the thrill of being surrounded by the music she'd long adored and the daunting prospect of making her way in the jazz world at a time when few women dared to do so. Even the all-women's jazz bands that emerged during the war were falling by the wayside as clubs and dance halls made room for the men returning to their old jobs. But Jimmy was determined to open doors for Marian into the Chicago and New York jazz scenes. "Jimmy really was the person who probably helped me more than anybody because he knew everybody," Marian said. Initially, though, she was self-conscious about establishing her own identity and insisted on using her old stage name, Marian Page, when she played with Jimmy's Dixieland groups in Chicago.

Jimmy wasn't an easy partner. He'd show up for gigs drunk, and it would take him forever just to announce the song, causing the rest of the band—Marian included—to squirm. Marian tried to keep him from the liquor, but he'd wander around the bar, telling his buddies his wife couldn't stand to see him drink, and get someone to take a flask into the men's room for him. Looking back on that time, though, Marian preferred to emphasize that once he really committed to Alcoholics Anonymous, "he was sober for the rest of his life."

It didn't take long before Marian forged a place for herself independent of her husband. Her acclaim grew during an eight-year engagement at the Hickory House, a famous jazz spot in Manhattan, where Duke Ellington and many of the greats she admired came to hear her play. She was also a regular at the Embers, the London

House, and Condon's. She toured with Benny Goodman and wrote songs that were recorded by Tony Bennett, Sarah Vaughan, and Peggy Lee. She was definitively moving away from the traditional Chicago-style Dixieland swing Jimmy was famous for and had helped define. "I didn't want to play in that style all the time," she said. She wanted to experiment and keep up with the new harmonic, melodic, and rhythmic challenges posed by bebop and other emerging jazz forms. Though, under Marian's influence, Jimmy explored wider repertoires and less formulaic approaches than many of his Dixieland chums, the couple inevitably moved apart musically, with different touring schedules; they gigged together only occasionally.

Her life took a difficult turn in the 1960s. "I don't know if I would use the word 'depression,'" she said. "I felt I was not doing as well as I thought I should be doing. I was getting in my own way and needed guidance." She had Benny Goodman (with whom she's rumored to have been romantically linked) drive her to the Menninger Clinic in Topeka, Kansas, where they were touring. She stayed a couple of weeks. Back home on Long Island, she began seeing a therapist regularly. "It was a very successful thing. I got a lot out of it," she said. Despite this rocky time, and the drug and alcohol addiction that plagued her husband and so many other key figures on the American jazz scene, she insisted that there is no inherent "dark side" to the jazz life. "I never thought of it that way," she said. "There were people of course who were in bad shape like Charlie Parker. I think it's funny calling it the dark side. There are too many people I know who are on the light side."

Marian and Jimmy divorced in 1970, but the two remained close. They continued to share their Merrick, Long Island, home for many years. Even after she moved to Port Washington, he would often come to stay with her. "The divorce was a failure," Marian often says. On Jimmy's seventieth birthday, she threw him a party. As he cut the cake, he said, "I suggest that all married people get divorced and begin treating each other like human beings." In 1990, he was a guest

on *Piano Jazz*. He blew his horn and sang to Marian flirtatiously, causing her to explain, "In case you're wondering what's going on here,
we're having laughs and enjoying ourselves. My guest today is Jimmy
McPartland, a gentleman well known to me, of course." A year later,
Jimmy was diagnosed with lung cancer. In his waning days, Marian
thought it was time they made their love official, again, and they remarried. He died two weeks later. "Jimmy was a great part of my life,"
she said. "I can't believe it's been so long since he died. It seems like
yesterday. His spirit is still in the house."

Piano Jazz was launched in 1979. McPartland had a regular gig then
at the elegant Cafe Carlyle on Madison Avenue, and William Hay of
South Carolina Educational Radio (SCER) stopped by to ask her to
do a thirteen-week radio series. SCER would produce it, and NPR
would distribute it. The show would be taped mainly in New York,
and SCER's staff would do the footwork and the postproduction from
the station's Columbia offices, an arrangement that's held to this day,
as it is, as producer Shari Hutchinson puts it, "more economical" than
doing everything from New York.

Piano Jazz was originally conceived as a series for pianists only.
The format was simple: McPartland would open the show with a signature flourish from her composition "Kaleidoscope," then she
would interview her guest for a few minutes. The guest would play a
solo, then they'd talk some more, then the two would play a duet,
then more chatter, then McPartland would solo, then the pattern
would start again. In the beginning, funds for the show—mainly from
Exxon and the National Endowment for the Arts—were scarce. For
studio space, McPartland and her guests had to rely on the kindness
of the Baldwin Piano Company, an underwriter of the show to this
day. *Piano Jazz* was recorded in the company's Manhattan showroom.
McPartland and her guests had their pick of ten gleaming new pianos; the eight not chosen were simply rolled to the side. Her first

guest was mentor and friend Mary Lou Williams, who, back in 1958, was at her side in Art Kane's famous "Great Day in Harlem" photograph of the New York jazz world. "I loved her creativity. She always wanted to be on the edge," McPartland says. Other early guests included Eubie Blake, Billy Taylor, Hazel Scott, Bobby Short, and even the famously reticent Bill Evans. The first season won a Peabody Award, the first of several broadcast honors the show would win, including an International Radio Festival of New York gold medal and a *JazzTimes* Readers Poll award.

The "pianos only" restriction helped launch McPartland's reputation for raising the profile of the jazz piano duet, an often-neglected jazz instrumental format, into what jazz writer Marshall Bowen calls "something of an art form." But after *Piano Jazz*'s first producer, Dick Phipps, died, Shari Hutchinson was promoted from sound engineer to producer, and she had no qualms about opening the show up to other kinds of musicians. In walked Dizzy Gillespie, Tony Bennett, Joe Williams, Rosemary Clooney, Gary Burton, and others. Hutchinson remembers the first show she produced. "The guest was Sarah Vaughan! I was so nervous!" she said. But the experiment worked. Vaughan's duets with McPartland, Hutchinson says, "were beautiful." The singer even sat down at the piano for a couple of numbers, a rare treat, but playing the piano would no longer be obligatory for guests on *Piano Jazz*.

Along with encouraging McPartland's innovations, Hutchinson provides a steadying hand in the production of *Piano Jazz*. She's the one in charge of making sure each show has the feeling of an intimate, live performance, minus headphone feedback, screwups, cursing, and dead-end chatter. She may, however, preserve the more interesting flubs, like the time McPartland welcomed the shy Tommy Flanagan by asking him, "How are you doing?" and he only nodded. She had to remind him this was radio and he had to say something. Hutchinson handles moments like these by being eminently straightforward, her directives called out in a stern southern accent that defies any north-erner's stereotypes of honeyed graciousness and leisure. Yet her man-ner toward McPartland also has a certain daughterly intimacy, a connection Hutchinson describes as "more than just producer and host." The two talk on the phone almost every day. Hutchinson knows what makes McPartland giggle and what makes her curse. She knows McPartland will want a strawberry milkshake, made with skim milk, for lunch. She knows about her small vanities, such as how she hates to wear headphones because they mess up her careful hairstyle. Hutchinson waits until the last moment to remind McPartland to put them on, at which point she quips, "There goes the hair."

Other changes have evolved during Hutchinson's tenure. The show occasionally tests the waters with guests from outside the jazz world, including classical pianist Ruth Laredo, Sting, Steely Dan, and Willie Nelson. "We had never met before," McPartland said about Nelson, "but we hugged and kissed and we were great pals right away. He did a wonderful show." She picks guests from other musical genres on the basis of their ability to improvise. "There is a lot of jazz in people who are not thought of as jazz musicians in the commercial sense. Donald Fagan, in his early days, was really into jazz. On the show, all he wanted to do was play Louis Armstrong and Duke Ellington."

Over the years, McPartland's identity has become much more about being the host of *Piano Jazz* than being a solo pianist. She has said on more than one occasion that she doesn't feel she has a real style of her own. "But in a way, I think that's a plus because if I was committed to a certain style I really wouldn't be able to do *Piano Jazz*," she said. "You can imagine how silly it would be, playing in an Erroll Garner style when I had someone like Ravi Coltrane on the show!" She's even set out to prove herself in the classical music world. When a friend told her she couldn't read music well enough to play with an orchestra, she set out to learn Grieg's Piano Concerto in A Minor and performed it with the Rochester Symphony Orchestra.

McPartland can seem blithe about her chameleon abilities, but she does not hide the fact that the challenge of improvising with so many different musicians over the years still gives her a little stage fright. "Oh, I get nervous all the time," she said. "I don't mean nervous to the extent that I'm going to mess up, although I get close once in a while. But I think you have a sort of nervous edge, perhaps because it is all so improvised. The talk is as much improvised as the music. I have to be thinking ahead while the guest is talking. What am I going to play next? How are we going to get into that tune, or are they going to take a left turn and go into a whole other subject? Sometimes it's tricky, but mostly it works, and if there's any bad stuff we can cut it out. Thank God for tape!"

Despite the strategizing going on in her head (or perhaps because of it), McPartland's interview style comes across as fairly laid-back. Her questions are rarely precise, and she digresses often into reminiscences about musicians and gigs from her past. She is also given to certain preoccupations, which come up regularly in her conversations with guests. For one, she is a firm believer in the importance of jazz standards, even in the repertoire of freeform musicians. "I think it's fine to write your own material," she said, "but I'll always want to hear maybe one or two standards so you know something about the person, so you know where they've come from." Other favorite topics include: her husband's influence on her career, the first night Duke Ellington came to the Hickory House to hear her play, composer Alec Wilder's underrecognized work, and her regret over the fact that Miles Davis was never a guest on her show. She simply couldn't work up the nerve, even the time she rang his hotel room by mistake at the North Sea Jazz Festival (she was trying to reach Herbie Hancock). They chatted about her husband—"he was always fond of Jimmy"—but she was too daunted to use the opportunity to issue an invitation. The overall effect of these asides is that she doesn't seem prepared in the way that, say, Michele Norris or Terry Gross do, their precise questions buttressed with facts, dates, or quotes that make it clear they've done their homework.

McPartland does prepare, of course. She listens to her guests' latest recordings, bones up on their biographies, practices their compositions, and discusses with Hutchinson what she'll ask them. But what comes across on the air is the feeling that McPartland's life is her homework, a life packed with gigs and introductions and encounters with an extraordinary range of musicians and musical styles. She doesn't need the studied, impartial precision that other hosts may demand of themselves. McPartland's guests are her colleagues, and *Piano Jazz* is at its best when it sounds like what it is: two musicians in a recording studio, finding ways to connect personally and musically. As Hutchinson puts it, "I think the way she approaches it is as if you're having a conversation with someone in their living room. As if you're sitting there talking to a friend. It doesn't always follow a logical pattern. Because it's supposed to be an intimate conservation, no one cares about that. And that's Marian's approach."

For some, though, this style takes a bit of getting used to. A listener in Amherst, Massachusetts, says the first few times she heard *Piano Jazz*, she found herself tuning away impatiently. "It seemed to me [McPartland] was going on and on, saying absolutely nothing." But then she gradually got used to "this bizarre interview style," realizing that "she ends up creating an environment in which her guests really open up."

When Patricia Barber finally arrives, "opening up" seems to be the last thing on her mind. She gets to Manhattan Beach, as expected, late, about a quarter to one, a backpack slung over her shoulder. She is tall and pale, with the slightly bleary-eyed look of a musician unused to being in public this early. In a whispery alto mumble, she asks her publicist from Blue Note Records to hunt down an espresso. Hutchinson overhears, and tells the publicist there's an Au Bon Pain on the corner.

Barber has a reputation for being haughty, intimidating, and whip smart—a "bop intellectual," according to *New York Times* critic Margo Jefferson. But whatever braggadocio Barber has or is rumored to have, there's no evidence of it on the *Piano Jazz* set. She chatters nervously, confessing how she reacted to the invitation from McPartland, whom she calls "the Johnny Carson of the jazz world," to do the show. She'd rushed over to see Judy Roberts, her Chicago mentor and friend, who'd been on *Piano Jazz* several seasons before. "I went in, she was playing, well, we might not want to talk about this. But anyway, I said, 'Oh my God oh my God, I'm not really a solo pianist.' And she said, 'You know what? You could go in there and vomit and she'll make you sound good.'"

"Oh, that's an awful thing to say!" McPartland exclaims. "It has nothing to do with me making you sound good. You will sound good on your own."

"I thought that was the ultimate compliment," Barber says, her eyebrows raised mischievously.

"Then you expect something from me that I can't possibly give, you know. A lot of what I do depends very much on what you get from the guest."

"Right, but it can't be a fluke. Your shows always sound good."

After nearly a quarter century of hosting *Piano Jazz* and more than six decades of playing jazz, McPartland has achieved a kind of "Grand Dame of Jazz" status, an ability to forge connections across the race and gender divides that have at times plagued the jazz world. Documentary filmmaker Burrill Crohn, who worked with McPartland on his 1981 film *Women and Jazz*, credits some of this ability to the era when she entered the jazz scene. "Swing was much more integrated. It wasn't until after World War II that sociological pressures like black liberation started to split the jazz world." Even then, McPartland was undaunted. "Musicians recognized a classy lady when they saw one,"

Crohn said. "She had no attitude whatsoever. She didn't go out of her way to make connections. It was just natural."

As for being female, McPartland remembers all too well the days when somebody would call a musician for a job, then hang up when he found out the candidate was a woman. Then there were the old condescending comments—"a good woman drummer," "not bad for a girl." More pointedly, in a 1952 issue of *Down Beat* magazine, jazz critic Leonard Feather wrote: "She is English, white, and a woman—three hopeless strikes against her." Though these days no critic would dare dismiss McPartland, or any other woman on the jazz scene, quite so blatantly, she says that while she doubts male chauvinism will ever completely go away, there have always been women able to overcome it. "Mary Lou Williams and Melba Liston did. In fact, when they rehearsed with a band, they were so tough, the men were afraid of them!" McPartland believes women in jazz today are less distracted by discrimination. "I haven't heard anything about it lately. It's all very positive."

That may be in part because the *Piano Jazz* stage is so integrated. For both female and male musicians, the show, with its exposure to public radio's cultured, CD- and ticket-buying minions, is a prime gig. But unlike a lot of prime gigs in the jazz world, you are just as likely to hear women as you are to hear men on the show. Few have done more than McPartland to get their jazz sisters in the limelight, from flagship guest Mary Lou Williams to the highly modern sounds of saxophone player Jane Ira Bloom. Shari Hutchinson calls McPartland's efforts "inexhaustible." "She has lived through many different decades of women's movements, and she is truly a role model for women."

These days, McPartland is also getting attention for her longevity. In 2003, she turned eighty-five. Her birthday celebration at Birdland was a gala affair, with performances by Billy Taylor, Phil Woods, Jason Moran, Chris Potter, and Regina Carter. *The Today Show* featured McPartland—along with Helen Gurley Brown, of all people—on a series called "Ladies in Their Eighties." *Piano Jazz*, with a twenty-fifth anniversary in 2004, has also enjoyed remarkable staying power as the longest-running jazz show on NPR, keeping its head above water in a time when the network has made what many jazz lovers see as ruthless cuts in programming. In 2002, NPR canceled two critically acclaimed shows, *Billy Taylor's Jazz at the Kennedy Center* and *Jazz from Lincoln Center*. The documentary series hosted by Nancy Wilson, *Jazz Profiles*, continued to air only in reruns. McPartland calls the shows "very high caliber" and the cuts "a shame," but she still believes NPR has a firm commitment to jazz. "I can't say why [they're cutting other jazz shows]. As far as we're concerned I have enough to do thinking about my own show. They're not anti-jazz because they're very pleased with what we're doing."

There is an undeniable self-centeredness to a statement like this— and likely some political savvy, given *Piano Jazz*'s long and close partnership with NPR. McPartland is a woman who doesn't want to lose out. Despite her celebrity and her age, she still carries within her the focused ambition of the wide-eyed British lass she once was, determined to make it on the America jazz scene. Each *Piano Jazz* taping, each performance is never quite enough. There is always someone else out there to play with, someone new to get to know, from Kyrgyzstanian teen wunderkind Eldar Djangirov to Latin jazz innovator Chucho Valdes to twenty-something crossover sensation Norah Jones. When McPartland is not out performing or taping the show, she's practicing and preparing, arranging future gigs, responding to the constant stream of requests from music educators, other musicians, and journalists, and listening to tapes and CDs from the many artists petitioning to get on *Piano Jazz*. Ask her about anything outside the music world, and she speaks vaguely of having a few other interests: taking walks, riding her stationary bike, protecting the environment. "It's just getting so bad. So many birds and animals are extinct," she said. She'll give even fewer details about her personal life. She lives alone, and though she will admit to having had other relationships, she won't provide details. She will only insist that Jimmy "was the most significant person in my life."

Though McPartland is long past the age when most of her contemporaries in the Long Island suburbs traded in the working life for a set of golf clubs and a condo in Florida, she resists any notion of slowing down. When I asked her about whether she has any thoughts of retirement, I got a playful reprimand: "Oh God! Why did you have to bring that up? People used to ask Duke Ellington that, and he'd say, retire to what? I feel the same way. I mean I suppose if I, well I don't know, I can't think of losing my brains or something like that, but if that happened that would be a drag. But as far as I know, I'm in good health, and it certainly is more fun to work than it is to be sitting at home watching the neighbors over the fence."

Not Indie Cool:
David Dye

Host, *World Cafe*

David Dye is interviewing the band Wheat, a trio of slacker-handsome men in their thirties from the Boston suburbs. They're in the cramped recording studio of WXPN, the Philadelphia public radio station where Dye's show, *World Cafe*, is produced. The studio used to be a record library, and vinyl albums, their spines worn with use, still fill the shelves along the walls. The staff tried clearing the records out years ago during a vinyl purge, but the acoustics of the room suffered, so everything was hauled back in. It's April 2004, and the whole operation is scheduled to move into new digs later that year, a change everyone on staff is talking about with great anticipation.

But the current set-up works for Wheat, which made a name for itself in the nineties as a melancholic, lo-fi indie group. Their latest album, *Per Second, Per Second, Per Second . . . Every Second*, is distinctly more catchy and playful. In other words, more pop. Dye is calling the band on it, gently.

"A lot of people point to this record as a change for you guys," he says. "Um . . . it's a little more accessible, and I think that's a good thing. Did you see it that way when working, or were they just songs?"

"I think they were just songs," Scott Levesque, the lead singer, says. He has a heavy mop of curly dark blond hair and speaks with a Boston accent so thick he almost sounds British. "I think with each record you get closer and closer to the things you hear in your head, to get them on tape, to try to capture them. And of course as you progress through life things change."

The band launches into "Closer to Mercury," a cut from the album. Levesque closes his eyes as he sings, one hand rising and falling and cutting through the air as if he's conducting himself, his high vocal stylings reminiscent of U2's Bono: "I would've walked behind / I would've walked beside you / I would've told you every lie / I would've done that just for you." Ricky Brennan strums upbeat guitar licks and harmonizes on the chorus. Percussionist Brendan Harvey keeps the beat with a plum, a palm-sized purple shaker, a thin silver bracelet jiggling on his wrist. They're all hungry-thin, as if they frequently forget to eat. Dye, fifty-five, nods to the song, his eyes half-closed in concentration. He's stocky and has thick white hair and a full beard. He's a mercifully solid presence next to the band's gauntness. He looks as if he spends time in the earthly world of laundry, city parks, and lunch, along with the constant stream of sound, much of it ephemeral, from the music scene he captures on *World Cafe*, his daily program of contemporary alternative music and interviews.

"David Dye / he's a nice guy," Bruce Springsteen once sang in a Philadelphia club, when he was just getting his start in rock 'n' roll and Dye was a young Philadelphia deejay who gave him his first radio interview and quite a bit of airplay. Some three decades later, The Boss is a megastar who rarely gives interviews. Dye is one of the most sought-after radio hosts in the world of Triple A (Adult Album Alternative) radio, and he's still a nice guy. So nice, in fact, that even after the hundreds of interviews he's done with performers from Ani DiFranco to Moby to De La Soul, his approach remains without hubris or attitude. He is openly admiring of his guests, at times awkwardly so, as if he was just another eager fan. He even stammers sometimes. Over lunch in a Thai restaurant near the campus of the University of Pennsylvania, WXPN's landlord and licensee, he told me that he grew up in a family "where people were not forthcoming, people didn't ask questions," so bringing up potentially sensitive subjects—such as why Wheat went pop—still makes him nervous. "It's an ingrained fear of asking something that's going to set someone off emotionally," he said. "And I have to get over it. It's my job."

This sense of responsibility has pushed him into delicate territory. He was one of the first people to ask Norah Jones about Ravi Shankar, her estranged father. He talked to Patti Smith about her return to music after mourning the deaths of several loved ones. He survived a session with the curmudgeonly Lou Reed, who tested him by giving one-word answers for the first ten minutes of the interview, then started to open up. "I just keep pushing forward," Dye said.

It all started with Bob Dylan. While growing up in the 1960s in the Philadelphia suburb of Swarthmore, Dye listened to his older sister's Dylan records, which he calls "my whole entry to music." He tried the guitar himself, playing with a "really bad little band" named the Korvettes, after the discount store EJ Korvette. He snuck into the Woodstock-style rock and folk festivals at Swarthmore College by hiking through the wooded outskirts of campus. He heard Tim Buckley opening for Jefferson Airplane and caught the Allman Brothers, on their first tour north of the Mason-Dixon line, splashing in a forest stream after a show.

On his first day as an undergraduate at Swarthmore, he joined WSRM, the campus radio station. "I was so into it I used to go practice when I wasn't on the air," he said. His sophomore year, his roommate dared him to apply for a job opening at WMMR, a commercial progressive rock station in Philadelphia. He sent a demo tape in and, to his surprise, he was hired. He deejayed weekends and vacations throughout his college years. "It was pretty heady," he remembered.

"And it was a professor magnet, because they would come up to me and say, 'David, which Creedence record should I buy?'" What he remembers most fondly about getting his start at WMMR, though, was that there were no restrictions on what he could play, a practice almost completely unheard of today in commercial radio and increasingly rare in public radio.

Dye worked for WMMR for two more years after he graduated from Swarthmore, then began to have doubts about what he was doing. "I never got the feeling from my parents that this is what I should be doing with my life, so I always felt radio was a phase," Dye said. He quit to travel through the South and Southwest for three months with a group of friends, including fellow deejay and future *American Routes* host Nick Spitzer, only to find that he missed being on the air. "I went away to find myself, but all I did was find out that I wanted to do radio," he said.

He moved to the Maine woods to take a job at a radio station near Lewiston. After four years, the rural isolation got to him, and he went back to Philadelphia. He returned to WMMR for a couple of years. Then he worked for a few months running fund-raisers at public radio station WHYY, in the days when *Fresh Air* was a local, live two-hour interview show, run on a shoestring by the young Terry Gross and Danny Miller, still her executive producer. Dye became the program director at WIOQ, a commercial station in Philadelphia, but soured on the job after management forced him to turn the station from freeform to oldies overnight.

After WIOQ fired him, he hit an impasse. He was almost forty. His marriage was ending. It was the late 1980s. Radio station managers and consultants were exerting more control over what went over the air, formats were tighter and subjected to a battery of audience tests, and most announcers did little more than follow a predetermined playlist. He couldn't see any room for the kind of creative deejaying that drew him to radio in the first place. Except at one station: WXPN. For years, volunteer deejays had been playing wild mixes of anything from John Cage to Pharoah Sanders to Jimi Hendrix to space music. So after working professionally in radio for twenty years, Dye began at WXPN as an unpaid volunteer.

"They were very wary of me because I'd had a commercial radio background and I was not indie cool," he said. "But on the other hand there were things I knew about programming that nobody there knew, and the new management was interested in building more of an audience."

Dye was eventually hired full-time to administer a Corporation for Public Broadcasting grant to develop a national music program that would attract younger audiences to public radio. The show was named *World Cafe* because the format was originally intended to be world music, but audience testing showed that AAA would have a much wider appeal. The name stuck, though. "It's a name I've never been comfortable with because it sets up expectations in a certain way which we don't meet," he said.

As Dye prepared to launch the show, he went through stacks of audition tapes from deejays interested in hosting it. Few were any good, and he realized *he* wanted the job. He became the interim host. "And boy, I wasn't gonna let that go," he said.

The show began airing as a two-hour daily national program in 1991, with distribution by Public Radio International. *World Cafe* quickly attracting a number of illustrious guests. Joni Mitchell, Sting, and Elvis Costello appeared on the show in the early years, along with up-and-coming talent like Shawn Colvin, John Hiatt, Sarah McLachlan, David Gray, and others from the new wave of singer-songwriters gaining popularity in the 1990s. For the first thirteen years of the show, everyone endured the humble trappings and technical challenges of the record-library-turned-recording-studio, located on the third floor of a rickety Victorian house on the Penn campus. In September 2004, a few months after my interview with Dye, WXPN and *World Cafe* moved into a new building on the eastern edge of the campus. The state-of-the-art recording studio there, Dye told me in a follow-up telephone call, makes him feel like he's "moved out of the projects and into Beverly Hills." The station shares the building with *World Cafe Live*, a for-profit performance space, restaurant, and coffeehouse operated by Philadelphia entrepreneur Hal Real of Real Entertainment Group.

World Cafe and a companion program of artist interviews, *Conversations from the World Cafe*, have grown to attract more than 550,000 weekly listeners at 178 affiliate stations. In 2005, NPR made a successful bid to distribute the program, wresting it from Public Radio International. Dye said the show made the switch because NPR promised greater exposure through its web site and had the potential to get the show on more stations.

In the music industry, airtime on *World Cafe* is a much-sought-after commodity. That means Dye and his staff are besieged with music. Piles of CDs from new and established musicians trying to get on the show cover his desk and the floor of his car and surround his stereo at home. The job of finding new music to play comes on top of a day that ends at 7 p.m., after the daily work of putting together *World Cafe* and a three-hour live drive-time shift at WXPN. Dye's life has become proof that, yes, you *can* have too much of a good thing. "Right now I'm doing a lot of interview prep and music listening at home, at night, and with my kids . . . for my wife, it's just horrible," he said.

Dye's wife is Karen Heller, a features writer and columnist for the *Philadelphia Inquirer*. The couple has two children, Nicholas, eleven, and Cecilia, nine. The family lives in Mount Airy, a neighborhood in northwest Philadelphia that's gained national acclaim as a model of stable racial integration. On the weekends, he and Karen enjoy throwing what he describes as "salon-style" dinner parties. "I get to play deejay, and play the music I really love," he said.

The music he really loves. He's programming five hours of music a day and isn't playing what he really loves? So I had to ask: what do you love?

He loves jazz: old Blue Note classics and jazz fusion artists like Randy Weston. And, ironically, he loves the very stuff that didn't cut it with test listeners on *World Cafe:* world music. African and Brazilian in particular.

But Dye added that even though his off-hours tastes may change, he still gets excited about the music he plays on *World Cafe*. However grueling auditioning new discs day after day can be, the stacks of CDs still yields gems, artists like the Canadian singer Feist, or the Chip Taylor/Carrie Rodriguez duo, who give him the sense of emotional connection he's sought through a lifetime of listening to music. "I can go for a while and not find something, then right when I've given up the faith, decided I'm jaded and the old days were better, I find something that really grabs me," he said. "That's what keeps me going to the next record in the stack."

The Undefinable Aesthetic: Nic Harcourt

Host, *Morning Becomes Eclectic* and *Sounds Eclectic*

When **Nic Harcourt** got his start in radio in 1989, he was thirty-one, in recovery from years of alcohol abuse and, as he put it, had "never stuck with anything" before in his life. But he managed to persuade the powers that be at WDST, a progressive commercial station in Woodstock, New York, to train him and let him on the air.

His first shift was on a Monday night, following a jazz show that concluded with a Spyro Gyra tune. The first thing he had to do after the tune ended was open his microphone, give the station ID, say who he was, and press a button to get the first song on his show started.

"I did all that," he said. "The problem was, I forgot to turn down the Spyro Gyra album, so as I was making my first-ever opening, the next track came in behind me and unnerved me," he said.

But as alarming as that debut moment was, he didn't quit. "I found something I was going to stick to," he said. "I found something I really loved."

It is now difficult to imagine Harcourt, forty-seven, unnerved. He is the nonchalant, quick-talking, British- and Australian-accented voice of *Morning Becomes Eclectic*, a daily free-form show of music and live, in-studio interviews and performances on KCRW, a public radio station in Santa Monica, California. He also hosts a nationally syndicated spin-off, *Sounds Eclectic,* distributed by Public Radio International. Harcourt doesn't just sound cool on the air, he is one of the principal arbiters *of* cool. A 2005 *New York Times Magazine* article deemed Harcourt "The Star Maker of the Semipopular," a term that has come to refer to contemporary music that is artful, intelligent, complex, foreign, and/or ironically fun. Think Sigur Ros, The Like, Gillian Welch, Travis, and Meshell Ndegeocello, artists unlikely to have *People* magazine covers or a major presence on the playlists at Clear Channel Top 40 stations. But airtime or a live session on *Morning Becomes Eclectic* can catapult an unsigned or merely semipopular artist into no-holds-barred stardom, as happened with Norah Jones and Coldplay.

"Semipopular" is a vague and difficult to communicate term, though. The only thing that truly unifies the music Harcourt plays is that it all appeals to him. When I asked Harcourt if there was any way to describe his aesthetic, he said, "No. I look for something that grabs me, and I can't quantify that."

Harcourt grew up in Birmingham, England, listening to Radio Caroline, a pirate station operating from a ship on the North Sea in the days before the BBC broadcast pop. When the BBC did introduce the pop channel Radio One, Harcourt taped the chart shows and live Saturday night concerts on his reel-to-reel so he could listen to them again and again. Though his father (who left home when Harcourt was young after his parents divorced) was a television journalist, Harcourt didn't think he'd end up working in broadcasting himself. It was the music he was obsessed with. "It was a really important part of my life," he said. "I wasn't just a casual fan."

Harcourt began drinking heavily when he was a teenager. After he left high school, he worked factory jobs and did construction work.

He lived in Lichfield, a town outside Birmingham, and sang in a band called Red Cassette, at first doing covers of the Beatles and the Rolling Stones, then moving on to original music influenced by the Clash, the Buzzcocks, and other punk rock bands of the day. Red Cassette had a solid following in the Lichfield/Birmingham area, and a local newspaper one year named it the best live local band.

Harcourt moved to Australia in his midtwenties to follow his girl-friend, who would become his wife. When the marriage ended five years later, he went to America to visit an old bandmate in Woodstock. He'd planned to stay a couple of months but ended up living in the small Catskill Mountain town for nearly a decade.

Shortly after he arrived, he faced the alcohol addiction that had plagued him since high school. He told me that a friend "recognized I had a problem and gently suggested I might want to deal with it." He joined Alcoholics Anonymous, attended a meeting every day for the next year, and got sober. "Woodstock for me was a place where I began to heal from a lot of stuff," he said. "The time was right. I was sufficiently beaten up. I'd hit the bottom."

Sobriety left him seeking out new possibilities for his life. He'd col-lected lots of records during his time Down Under and approached the program director at WDST about doing an Australian music show, even though he had no radio experience. The show didn't come to pass, but Harcourt got work as part-time deejay. "It's small market radio," he said. "If it's got a pulse and will work for five bucks an hour, it's not that hard to break in." He worked his way up to a regular weekday morning shift. He said the station's free-form ethos at the time made the work "not dissimilar" to what he's doing now at KCRW. "There was a loose structure in place, a lot of opportunities to be cre-ative," he said.

In 1998, Harcourt was hired to be the host of *Morning Becomes Eclectic* and moved to Santa Monica. He is on the air from nine to noon every weekday morning. He told me he does not plan in ad-vance what he'll play. Before the show, he gathers about fifty CDs from the KCRW music library and his home and his car, both places where he gives new music a first listen. He'll plan out the first few tunes of the day. He said the rest of the show just "comes together" as the morning progresses.

The show is renowned around Los Angeles for its influence not only on run-of-the-mill music lovers, but also on the film and television industries. It's been a place for music supervisors to find tunes for soundtracks, and Harcourt himself has been hired to be the music supervisor for films, including *The Dukes of Hazzard* and *Igby Goes Down.* Harcourt has also been a key figure in one of the most powerful shifts in the broadcast landscape: Internet listening. There are no reliable ways to determine how many are listening to Harcourt online and through KCRW's music streams on AOL and Apple's iTunes software, but one indication is that KCRW has members from across the country, including about a thousand in New York City. "Those who are not satisfied with terrestrial radio now have a lot of different options," Harcourt said.

Harcourt and his girlfriend, Abba Roland, live in a cottage in Topanga Canyon with their two-year-old twins, Sam and Luna. "Being a parent is awesome, awe-inspiring, all the clichés," he said. "It makes me a lot less selfish." He tries to limit his nights out at concerts to once a week so he can be home with the twins. Roland, whom he met at an AA meeting in Woodstock, is a singer-songwriter with two CDs and a sound that has been described as "a collision between Ani DiFranco and Radiohead." Life with her, along with his own memories of trying to make it as a musician, has given him insight into the plight of struggling performers. "There's a certain empathy I have that comes from knowing it's tough," he said. "Tough to get people to play the music on the radio, tough to get anyone to give a shit." It's one of the reasons he plays so many unsigned artists, and in a number of cases the exposure has helped them get major label record deals.

The irony of this insight is that Harcourt feels limited in the extent that he can support Roland herself, who has played in the Woodstock twenty-fifth anniversary festival and Lillith Fair and tours regularly. She has gotten some airtime on *Morning Becomes Eclectic* and played at a few KCRW-sponsored concerts, but Harcourt feels ethically constrained from aggressively promoting her work. "I can't lead the charge for obvious reasons," he said. "It's tricky. Every relationship acquires baggage, and that for us is an ongoing wound."

KCRW receives about four hundred new CDs a week from record companies and artists self-releasing their work, all hopeful for airtime on *Morning Becomes Eclectic*. Harcourt, who is also the music director at the station, will listen to at least a couple of cuts from each one. Ninety-five percent of the artists never get airtime. The constant influx of music "can be daunting," he said, but he's spurred on by the prospect of the next great find. When we spoke, he was jazzed up about a self-titled self-released CD by the Brooklyn-based band Clap Your Hands Say Yeah and Neil Young's new record, *Prairie Fire*. "Neil Young is not considered a cutting-edge artist," Harcourt said. "But he's just delivered this fantastic new record, along the lines of the stuff he did back in the day, the more singer-songwriter stuff, and I love it."

Harcourt also keeps himself energized by being on the air every morning, letting himself move from one song to the next as he wishes, a rare process in a radio landscape of carefully calculated song rotations and program logs planned months in advance. "If I'm in the middle of a show and all of a sudden a trigger in my brain goes, wow, wouldn't it be good to follow this with that? I can go grab it and put it on," he said. "That's the spontaneity. I like the opportunity to change at any given moment."

On the Road: Nick Spitzer

Host, *American Routes*

When **Nick Spitzer** was a little boy, his mother would dress him and his brother in their pajamas in the evenings and take them for drives around New York City. The goal was to get them to sleep, but on their way to the Land of Nod she showed them the Savoy Ballroom and Duke Ellington's brownstone in Harlem, beatniks hanging out in Greenwich Village, the boats sailing on the Hudson River. It was the 1950s, so there were no traffic jams and his mother's 1953 Plymouth was wide and comfortable, with a split windshield and a soft teddy bear interior. By the time they got home, Spitzer and his brother would be fast asleep.

This "rolling dream state meets kiddy seminar on being open to cultures and neighborhoods," as Spitzer put it, was a harbinger of the radio show he would host as a grown-up, *American Routes*. He chooses music not by format or genre, but as elements in a journey— hence the show's "routes" metaphor, which is also a wordplay on the more familiar conceit of roots music. The show wanders through musical neighborhoods as diverse as the Cajun zydeco of Louisiana, Detroit Motown, Elvis Presley's Graceland, the Latin pop of postwar Los Angeles, and hip-hop from the New Jersey projects. He'll mix Janis Joplin, Miles Davis, Nirvana, Curtis Mayfield, Ella Fitzgerald, and the

Grateful Dead over the course of an hour, connecting the songs with themes that have included "Altered States: Music and Elixirs," "Streetbeats," "Harvest Time," and "Bad Luck/Good Luck."

There's a lot of thought behind all of this. Spitzer, fifty-five, is a University of New Orleans professor with a Ph.D. in folklore. He's extensively researched the music and cultures of the Gulf South and has gathered hundreds of hours of field interviews and recordings in the tradition of folk music collector Alan Lomax. Spitzer also has a dedicated staff of five to contribute ideas and develop shows, with an additional two contributing producers and an executive producer.

But Spitzer doesn't lecture on the air. His mike sets are surprisingly brief, his delivery relaxed. Though he grew up in the Northeast, his voice now has an easy swing he likely developed from all the years he's spent enthralled by the rhythms of the South (that's not to suggest he has one of those distressing adopted Southern accents—he doesn't). He may say a few words about the background of a song, but most of what he wants to express is contained in the music itself and the way it's arranged, with playlists developed from the show's twenty-thousand-plus album library. He'll also include excerpts from the more than fifteen hundred hours of interviews he's done, which range from Dolly Parton and Willie Nelson to the subjects of his field research, such as a Mississippi barber who can strop his straight razor in perfect time and play a mean blues guitar in between customers. One show may explore the influence of Tejano *ranchera* music with a segue between a Tejano tune and a rockabilly song. Another might juxtapose a Woody Guthrie song with the musings of a New Orleans plasterer.

The well-considered playlists, themes, and interviews all contribute to the big picture message of the show. *American Routes*, Spitzer told me, is meant to symbolize America. "It presents the unity Americans share in the culture and history as well as the diversity which continues between groups, classes, regions, different heritages, styles, different types of people," he said.

The more I thought about my conversation with Nick Spitzer, the more it became impossible to get away from the metaphor of routes in describing not only his show, but also his life. So I'll go all out. The experience of interviewing him, for one, was like being a passenger on a road trip, Spitzer the driver who opts out of the interstates, preferring the winding country byways, with plenty of fun little side excursions and stops that make you forget about where you're supposed to be headed in the first place. His answer to my question about how he came up with his music mixes, for example, included a short history of 1970s underground radio, a story about the first time he met Willie Nelson, and some self-analysis about how he always felt the need to justify his love for Fats Domino to his father, a devotee of European classical music.

His very biography is a journey, too, through contrasting geographical and cultural influences. His story starts in New York City, wanders into the woods of rural Connecticut, careens down the halls of the Ivy League in Philadelphia, and then descends into the Gulf South, the cultural epicenter of both *American Routes* and his scholarship and the place where he's made his home for much of his adult life. His father, Ernest Fritz Spitzer, emigrated from his native Germany to New York in the 1920s to attend Columbia University. Ernest Spitzer was raised Catholic, the religion of his father, but his mother was Jewish. His parents, who could see the Weimar Republic was tumbling toward fascism, pushed him to go to college in the United States. Inasmuch as Ernest Spitzer abhorred what Germany became after he left, he took great solace in German culture and throughout his life lauded classical music and literature from his native land. He met Virginia Randolph, the descendant of Virginia abolitionists and daughter of an artistic renegade single mother, at the St. Anthony, a social club on the East Side that's now a women's residence for Yeshiva University. They married, and she infused the Spitzer household with her loquaciousness, love for American history and culture, and liberal Republican politics.

Nick Spitzer was born in 1950, the second of three children. He told me he is both scholarly like his father and gregarious like his mother. As a boy, he was a "verbal entertainer" who could talk his way out of school yard tussles. He loved listening to rock 'n' roll, even though his parents didn't recognize it as important music. "I probably spent a fair amount of my life trying to be serious like them about it and deal with what it was in terms of music and where it came from and who made it and why they made it and for what community," he said.

The family lived in an apartment on Lexington Avenue and then in a house in Huntington, Long Island. When Spitzer was seven, his father, a chemist and translator for Pfizer, the pharmaceutical company, moved the family to rural Old Lyme, Connecticut, near the company's relocated research division in Groton. Radio, he said, was "the far away mystery that kept me in touch with the big civilization." In the summer, he would fill a jar with fireflies to light up his room and listen to rock 'n' roll broadcasting from New York, the Grand Ole Opry crackling out of Nashville, a deejay at WKBW in Buffalo who'd warn listeners not to be "dial twisters" or they'd get a "KB blister." In the winter, he'd pick up hockey games announced in French from Canada. "The radio was my secret companion," he said. "I knew there were thousands and thousands of souls out there listening, but I still felt the game, the host, the deejay, or the musician, it was all being played just for me."

He went to the University of Pennsylvania in 1968 with the practical plan of studying marketing at the prestigious Wharton School of Business. But he got caught up in the spirit of the times, and Jefferson Airplane's "Don't You Want Somebody to Love" had became his personal anthem: "When the truth is found / to be lies / you know the joy within you dies." He wasn't thinking about what the song had to say about love. He was thinking about the civics textbooks he'd read in high school about American democracy "and then seeing everything going up in flames and seeing the working kids from my town not go to college and going to Vietnam and some of them dying or coming back gravely wounded and thinking, what the fuck is this for?"

He transferred out of Wharton, switched his major to anthropology, and immersed himself in Penn's famous folklore department, much to the chagrin of his father. He admonished Nick that he was the one who was supposed to be making some money in the family (his brother, entranced by the woods of New England, was studying to become an ornithologist). His mother suggested he follow the path of Charles Ives, the classical music composer who kept a secure job in the insurance industry all his life and did his creative work on the side.

But Spitzer wasn't looking back. He studied under jazz anthropologist John Szwed and folk music recording documentarian Kenneth Goldstein. He took classes on jazz and Anglo-American ballads and did field research on a hippie commune in Philadelphia and on an old-time country singer in rural Maryland. The campus radio station, WXPN, then entirely student-run, also gave him a forum for his growing interest in diverse cultures. He deejayed a free-form program called Phase II, where he'd juxtapose Thelonious Monk with New Orleans piano players, country music with the Grateful Dead, and Ornette Coleman with Charles Ives. His fellow students played world music, bluegrass, classical, and jazz. The station was a vibrant incubator for talent then, Spitzer remembered. He rubbed shoulders with the future pop singer Bonnie Raitt, blues artist Buddy Guy, and Michael Cuscuna, who would go on to produce jazz albums and found Mosaic Records. His college sweetheart was fellow XPNer Carol Miller, who favored British invasion sounds and would go on to many years at WNEW-FM at the height of the rock era. John Diliberto, who was a freshman when Spitzer was a senior, started a space music program that would lay the foundation for his syndicated nightly public radio program, *Echoes*.

The station had such a strong following in Philadelphia that in 1971, well before the institutionalization of public radio on-air fund-raisers,

Spitzer and a group of student volunteers went on the air to ask listeners to donate enough money to keep WXPN on the air over the summer, when the station usually shut down. They raised $5,000 and turned the station into a year-round, seven-day-a-week operation. "It was the early seventies and a lot of music was busting out, and we all felt like, this is radio as a musical art gallery for the emerging progressive music scene," he said. "It was a committed audience and they paid money, and at the time that was a revolutionary thing."

After graduation, he got a job at WMMR, a commercial progressive rock radio station in Philadelphia. It was the height of the underground radio revolution on the FM radio band, newly embraced by a youth culture rebelling against the jingles and Top 40 music of AM stations and the banality of television. FM was "open territory," Spitzer remembered, and on WMMR he could develop the ideas about radio programming he'd began to incubate at WXPN. "I think if there was an overriding aesthetic of that rock underground radio era, it was that the radio shows could be journeys, music journeys, cultural journeys, personal journeys of the host," he said. "So you could put a lot of things together not only in cultural terms but in terms of what story it told, either explicitly or subliminally."

The creative freedom he had at WMMR was short-lived, though. After a couple of years, the music industry was exerting more of an influence on FM, courting deejays with heavy pitches and favors to get their albums played. His bosses didn't like Spitzer's fondness for Bessie Smith, Merle Haggard, and other "nostalgia music" and tried to hide him away on an overnight shift. So in late 1973 he left the station to take a "Woody Guthrie meets Jack Kerouac tour of America" with a bunch of friends, including fellow WMMR deejay David Dye, now the host of NPR's *World Cafe*. Spitzer ended up spending quite a bit of time in the southern mountains, Louisiana, and Texas and following up on interests in country music, Cajun and zydeco, and other musical forms of the South and Southwest. "I was sick of playing records on the radio and wanted to go to communities—to bars, dance halls, juke joints, churches, county fairs, pow-wows where music was played as part of local culture," he said.

He began graduate work in the folklore program at the University of Texas in Austin, studying blues and cowboy songs in Texas and the Creole African-French and Caribbean heritage of New Orleans and rural south Louisiana. He also worked a Saturday night shift at KOKE-FM, known as "goat roper radio," a station with an eclectic southern sound and a free-form aesthetic similar to WXPN's, but with an emphasis on country and roots rock 'n' roll. The sound called his attention to the "formative role of the Third Coast, as I would call it, the Gulf Coast, on American music and culture," he said. His sets mixed the Allman Brothers and the Rolling Stones with Etta James, Robert Johnson, and big-throated Texas singers like Ray Price. It was the kind of place where Commander Cody or Kris Kristofferson might show up unannounced to perform on the air. One night Willie Nelson stopped by to play "with a lot of elixirs in his bloodstream," Spitzer laughed.

In the late 1970s, he spent a year doing field recordings of zydeco music in Louisiana and produced two records. He became Louisiana's first official folklorist, a job he held until the mid-1980s, when he moved to Washington. As senior folklife specialist at the Smithsonian, he curated programs for the Festival of American Folklife and developed the Folk Masters concert series at Carnegie Hall and the Wolf Trap, broadcast on American Public Radio. He also returned to radio to work on a series of folklore documentaries for Radio Smithsonian and report features on traditional music and culture for National Public Radio. During the Clinton administration, he presented a live series of Fourth of July "American Roots" concert broadcasts on the Washington Mall.

In 1997, he and public radio producer Mary Beth Kirchner put together a Corporation for Public Broadcasting (CPB) grant application to launch *American Routes*. They asked for $90,000 in research and development money, but the CPB liked the demo tape so much that

they gave them three times the requested money to launch the show
nationally as soon as possible. Public Radio International agreed to
distribute the show, getting 39 stations to sign on to air it from the
start. By 2005, *American Routes* was airing on 191 stations, attracting
more than 350,000 weekly listeners and considerable critical acclaim.
Music writer Nat Hentoff wrote that he hadn't felt as exhilarated by a
mix of music since he spent an evening with a group of musicians at
Alan Lomax's apartment. Lomax himself said that, among those
who've followed in his footsteps, Spitzer is "one of the people I'm
proudest of."

Spitzer is married to Margaret Howze, a public radio producer who's
won two Peabody Awards for her work on the series *Wynton Marsalis:
Making the Music* and *Anthem,* a short-lived NPR program about
popular music. She is also a contributing producer for *American
Routes*. He told me that outside of working on the show and teaching,
they enjoying biking, rollerblading, and "swimming in cold water, especially me." Much of their time these days is taken up by their two
young sons, one-year-old Gardner and three-year-old Perry. Family
life and the demands of putting together a weekly radio show have
limited his traveling and fieldwork. Many of the interviews on *American Routes* are now done in the studio or remotely via a live-quality
telephone connection.

In the years since *American Routes* launched, he's also achieved a
recognition that's extended beyond public radio and the academic
world. In 2002, ABC's *Nightline* featured Spitzer and *American Routes*
in a program about American musical traditions. On a tense July 4th,
following the September 11 attacks, as news networks grappled with
the question of appropriate content, Peter Jennings asked Spitzer to
cohost a national tribute to American music and culture, featuring Los
Lobos, Hank Williams, Gillian Welch, and other artists often heard on
American Routes. The *New Orleans Times-Picayune* called him "a
quasi-official spokesperson for American musical tradition."

The attention is nice for Spitzer, and the work is fun, but underneath it all he's not much different from the college student who turned his back on the Wharton School in the sixties. He finds himself in the first years of the twenty-first century saddled with a similar sense of crisis he felt back then, when the war in Vietnam was raging and Jefferson Airplane told him the "true is found / to be lies." He is worried about the rise of religious orthodoxy, class hatred, environmental degradation, and unregulated capitalism, with a wariness that comes with being the son of a man with Jewish blood who slipped out of Germany just before the Third Reich. "I grew up with that sense of fatalism, of what happens when big civilization rolls out of control," he said.

Exploring the musical traditions of America on the radio, he told me, is his way to "participate in the process" of American democracy. "If I'm obsessed, I'm obsessed with getting a message out to Americans of all kinds that we can be a great country if we'd only look at what we are and what we have been, take some stock of our diversity and the freedom and tolerance that have built one of the most creative societies in the world, and not let ourselves fall victim to the simple passions," he said. "In the long haul, it's the big concerns that move me the most."

I was going to end the chapter here. But, just before this book went to press, Spitzer was swept up in the big concerns of the 2005 New Orleans flood in the aftermath of Hurricane Katrina, one of the most devastating natural disasters in U.S. history. He was able to evacuate his family safely. Then he went back to his beloved New Orleans to help ABC's *Nightline, This American Life,* the BBC, and other media outlets cover the disaster. He spent his nights huddled in a sleeping bag in the middle of Canal Street and served as an important voice for the cultural issues at stake in the recovery effort. "We have a public policy responsibility to preserve the culture and character of New Orleans," he told me. "We have to push to bring the musicians back. Without music the city will never be the same."

The *American Routes* offices were located on the second floor of a former bottling plant in the French Quarter in New Orleans. The historic building wasn't harmed, and he was able to rescue the show's equipment and most of its record library and sound archives. All that was damaged was a set of analogue masters of old field recordings, stored in a separate facility. The tapes received some water damage, but may be able to be repaired.

The show and Spitzer's family have temporarily relocated to Lafayette, Louisiana, about 140 miles west of New Orleans. *American Routes* has set up temporary headquarters at KRVS, an eclectic public radio station that features French language programming and Creole and Cajun music along with more traditional news and information offerings. Spitzer is looking for new permanent digs. Out of concern for his family, he doesn't think he'll move back to New Orleans, which he believes will take fifteen to twenty years to rebuild. "It's kind of a Wild West, not a great place to go back to from a kids' point of view," he said.

Spitzer, yes, is back on the road, but this time where he's going is "a complete unknown," he said. "With no direction home, like Dylan said."

Dream Job: John Diliberto

Host, *Echoes*

Listeners tell John Diliberto all the time how relaxing the music on *Echoes* is, how they love to tune into the program before bedtime to help them unwind.

Diliberto, fifty-one, the host and founder of the program, insists the music has a higher purpose. "I think we're doing an art show," he said. "The reaction we get is, 'Your music is so soothing.' Whereas I think, man, we're taking you to the edge of the abyss here!"

Echoes is a nightly show of "music of atmosphere and imagery," as he puts it. It's not an ideal pitch line, he admits, but he hasn't been able to come up with a more specific term to describe the program's blend of ambient music, new acoustic, contemporary classical, world, and jazz. He shuns the title "New Age," a category he sees as divided into meditation music and "schlocky" orchestral music such as that of Yanni. "We're much edgier," he said. Even worse is the term "wallpaper music"—thrown around by radio program directors who think that *Echoes* is only good as a background. "I don't know how many of them will say it to my face that that's what they think, but you can tell that's what they think," he said.

Whatever is the best word for the music Diliberto plays, he is the most significant figure promoting the stuff on American radio today.

He travels widely, recording live concerts in musicians' homes and doing interviews for artist profiles. He approaches these endeavors with the scholarship of the Ivy Leaguer he is, spending hours researching the show's guests and immersing himself in their music.

Yet for all Diliberto's efforts to resist *Echoes'* rap as a chill-out show, his on-air presence is pretty damn mellow. *Echoes* typically airs late at night, and his voice is pitched to fit, the sound deep, generously paced, and sensual (a female listener once called her public radio station to say that when she hears Diliberto, she wants to strip her clothes off). It's a late night voice, a voice you could half hear as you drift off to sleep and it would not yank you back to consciousness.

I met Diliberto in the *Echoes* studio in a converted chicken coop in Yellow Springs, Pennsylvania, a historic artists' enclave just up the road from the ruins of a Revolutionary War–era hospital where wounded soldiers from Valley Forge were treated. The studios had been shut down for several weeks, having been flooded when a frozen water pipe burst, and there was still drywall dust on the carpet and the smell of fresh paint in the air. Diliberto has dark hair, a white-gray goatee, and prominent, mischievously arched eyebrows. A former defensive tackle for the University of Pennsylvania, he still works out and has broad shoulders and a superhero bulge of a chest. I had read an article about him that expressed surprise at Diliberto's physical presence, as if a fellow with muscles would lack the sensitivity to do a show like *Echoes*. I had a different reaction: whoever guides us through the otherworldly landscape of the show *should* look mighty, able to take us to outer space and back.

Diliberto's physicality, in fact, plays an integral role in how he sounds on the air. I watched him tape one of the show's Living Room Concerts, so named because about half of them are actually taped in artists' living rooms. *Echoes*, once run out of Diliberto's own living room, hosts the rest. The guest was Ian Boddy, an electronic music artist from England. He was pale and thin, his wispy gray hair pulled back into a ponytail. Equipment surrounded him: a Macintosh iBook, two synthesizer keyboards, and a couple of digital mixers. Diliberto sat in the corner in front of a microphone stand, slouching a little, looking crowded by all the gear. Just before the session began, though, he took his space, breathing in, his trunk expanding. You could practically see his vocal chords relaxing for his well-modulated trademark sign-in: "I'm John Diliberto, and you're hearing *Echoes*."

Diliberto grew up in Tewksbury, Massachusetts, in the 1960s and 1970s, listening to Jefferson Airplane, Jimi Hendrix, Quicksilver Messenger Service, and the Beatles so obsessively on the living room stereo that his parents wired a set of speakers for him down in his basement bedroom. "The only time they would see me was when I would come up and turn the record over. Then I'd go back downstairs to listen," he said. Inspired by Jethro Tull, he took flute lessons in the ninth grade, but had to give it up because he couldn't juggle being in the marching band with his other passion—playing football. He was an all-conference defensive center, and his prowess on the field got him a scholarship to the University of Pennsylvania, where he majored in American civilization.

He went to the campus radio station, WXPN, then run entirely by students, during his first semester in 1973, hoping to get on the air. A staff member was dubbing a reel-to-reel tape of music at high speed. "The music's like, flying by, and he says, 'You know what that is?'" Diliberto remembered. "I said, 'No, I don't know what that is.' He said, 'Well, it's Gentle Giant, and if you don't know that, you can't work here.' And I said, 'What a fucking asshole,' and I walked out."

He came back the next year to take a free, student-run class called the Art of Radio, which exposed him to a new range of genres and musicians often played in the free-form format of the station: fusion, progressive rock, John McLaughlin's Mahavishnu Orchestra, Karlheinz Stockhausen, early Philip Glass, jazz saxophonist Anthony Braxton. He learned how to use segues to draw connections among diverse artists and genres, the key skill of free-form deejaying, and finally got

on the air as one of the evening free-form hosts. "Sometimes I listen
to those [old tapes] and I can't believe how many people listened, you
know?" he said. "Someone somewhere once said, 'Do I have to sit
through the John Cage piece to get to the Sex Pistols?'"

He came on the scene at WXPN in the last wild years of student
management, when avant-garde music aired during drive time and
one deejay did shows in the nude. The university administration
fielded several complaints about obscene broadcasts, including
readings from erotic literature and a fake advertisement for a "sexual enhancement" drug. Students at the university accused station
members of using alcohol and drugs on the air, and a suspicious
predawn fire scorched the inside of the Spruce Street building
where the station was housed. Diliberto remembers that one deejay
did an overnight show called the *XPN Acid Test*, going on the air
while on LSD. "Yeah, we tripped," Diliberto said. "We used to do
things, we had the Spontaneous Creation Space Ensemble, where
like ten or twelve of us would go up to the studio at night and wire
the whole place together, have all the studios cross-wired and jam
with the sound for like hours, hours. It was great." The jam session
evolved into *Star's End*, a space music program that still airs Satur-
days at midnight.

It was a completely different world from playing defensive tackle
for the Penn Quakers. His teammates were frat boys, while the XPN
crowd were "heads." "It was definitely a contrast," Diliberto laughed.
"A good contrast. I dug it." But radio gradually won out. Diliberto became WXPN's music director his senior year and quit the team. Two
years later, he hooked up with fellow deejay Kimberly Haas, now his
wife and the executive producer of *Echoes*; the two moved in together
in her off-campus housing collective. After the Federal Communications Commission refused to renew WXPN's license in 1975 for violating obscenity rules on its bawdy talk show, *Vegetable Report*, the
university reined in the station and Haas became its first paid pro-

gram director, helping usher in WXPN's gradual transformation to a largely professional staff.

After Diliberto graduated, he became a widely published music journalist and, to pay the bills, a producer for a group of political media consultants. He helped produce campaign advertising spots for former Cincinnati mayor Jerry Springer during his gubernatorial run in Ohio; back then, before his television fame, he was "a sharp guy, smart, genuine," Diliberto said. He also worked on Al Gore's first presidential campaign. At the time, he was collaborating with Haas on a public radio series called *Totally Wired*, weekly half-hour documentaries on new music. They interviewed Keith Jarrett, Tangerine Dream, John Cage, Kate Bush, Laurie Anderson, and Depeche Mode, among others, producing 140 segments in all. The contrast between his "day job" in political media and his radio work came to a head during the height of Tipper Gore's music censorship group, the Parents Music Resource Committee (PMRC), in the late 1980s. Diliberto felt conflicted interviewing PMRC nemesis Frank Zappa one day and then working on Al Gore's first presidential campaign the next. He chose Zappa.

Diliberto and Haas were also in the process of reevaluating *Totally Wired*. They were getting frustrated with the documentary form. They couldn't play any of the music in its entirety. So they thought up *Echoes*. The concept came together in a whirlwind twenty-four-hour grant writing and demo producing session to meet a Corporation for Public Broadcasting grant deadline. They got the grant and launched the show. Many of the stations that had broadcast *Totally Wired* picked up *Echoes*, distributed by Public Radio International, right away. Diliberto and Haas threw themselves into producing a nightly show with a devotion that bordered at times on the self-sacrificial. When Haas went into labor with their first child, a week before the show's debut, Diliberto had her in the sound booth reading voice tracks between contractions before they left for the hospital.

That child, Ariel, is now sixteen. Her younger sister, Grace, is twelve. *Echoes* has also grown, with 250,000 listeners on 126 radio stations across the country. Three thousand CDs pour into the *Echoes* offices every year from musicians hoping to score time on the show, with less than 10 percent actually making the cut after Diliberto and his staff take a listen. Critics call him a man with "a hip awareness of celestial harmonies" and *Echoes* a "dream of a radio show."

Though life is no longer full of madcap escapades like the Spontaneous Creation Space Ensemble, Diliberto is one of those rare guys who is still doing the thing he fell in love with in college: free-form deejaying.

But he is also a guy with a mortgage and two private school tuitions to pay, with college looming on the horizon. The bills can be daunting for a man who, as he put it, turned away from the path of more money to pursue the path of art. "Yes, I do feel like that guy, and I feel like maybe I should have abandoned it," he said.

It was a strange moment, like a fit of digital skipping on a CD track in the middle of a transcendental *Echoes* soundscape. I asked him a little later in our interview if he meant what he said enough to leave the career he'd built with *Echoes*. "No," he said. "People think I have the dream job, and in a way, I do. I spend every day of my life doing what I want to do."

At Home on the Air:
Fred Child

Host, *Performance Today*

When **Fred Child** was a small boy in Portland, Oregon, the piano in his family's living room was seldom used. Then one afternoon his father sat down and began to play Stephen Foster's "Jeanie with the Light Brown Hair." "It looked to me like he was moving his hands over a piece of furniture, and suddenly the room was filled with this beautiful sound," Child remembered.

Ever since, music has been as essential to him as breathing. "It feels like air," he said. "I can't live without it. I have to have music around me." And he does. He is the host of NPR's *Performance Today*, a daily program featuring classical music recorded in performance at NPR and at concert halls around the world.

But inasmuch as Child loves and knows music, he defies the stereotype of the old-school plump classical music announcer who reads off Köchel numbers and launches into tangential lectures on music theory in a basso profundo dripping with self-importance. Child is forty-two, a good fifteen years younger than the median age of his million and a half listeners, and sounds even more youthful on the air. He is balding and bearded, true, but he's also a trim runner and cyclist who favors the long sleeve T-shirts and flannels common to the casual lifestyle of his native Northwest. He talks about classical music in a distinctly unacademic manner, sounding more like the precocious student newly fired up by the sounds of Bach and Arvo Part than the professor who introduced the works to him. Child relishes the connections between classical music and other genres. He's just as likely to throw in a reference to Paul Simon as he is to Pietro Nardini, and he's extensively explored the influence of folk traditions and jazz on classical music.

Sitting behind a desk covered with compact discs, he told me that he prefers not to take a terribly formal approach to classical music. "What I bring to the show is more a kind of enthusiasm for music and the process of music making and the ideas and energy that are inspired by music, and I try to communicate that enthusiasm," he said.

After years of begging his parents, Child was allowed to start piano lessons at the age of six. Now he could make that piece of furniture in the living room come to life under his own fingers. He also studied guitar and percussion, and, after a trip to Scotland as a adult, he picked up the bagpipes.

There is a sorrowful side to Child's beginnings in music. His father, the man who opened up this new world to him, was a "deeply troubled man" who killed himself when Child was eight years old. "Despite the way he took himself out of my life, I'm grateful for the gifts he gave me while he was around," Child told me. "There was nothing in my life that was more important to me than music."

Though he continued to play while he was in college at Oregon State University in Corvallis from 1981–1985, he didn't know what he wanted to study. He took classes in everything from film to philosophy to physics to geology. He never declared a major or, consequently, got a degree. He did discover radio. He signed up to be an apprentice jazz deejay at the campus radio station, KBVR, named after the OSU

Beavers. "I could get on because everybody else wanted to be a rock deejay and nobody wanted to do jazz," he said.

At first, he was terrified of being on the air. "I remember spinning disc after disc—this was when it was LPs—you go back and forth between the turntables, and one would be ending and I'd have the next one cued up, be all set to say something, and then I'd chicken out and just go to the next song," he said. He'd put off going on the air for an entire hour before he had to squeak out the mandatory station ID. Then he'd launch into another hour-long set. He eventually got up enough nerve to spend more time talking and went on to become a newscaster. He also hosted a free-form show called *Confluence* and a women's music show. If you're curious, only one person, to his knowledge, openly objected to the fact that the host was male.

After he left Oregon State, he applied for a job at Oregon Public Broadcasting in Portland. He interviewed with Marv Ryum, an announcer who was "an absolute hero" of his growing up. The interview was at 11:30. When Child arrived, Ryum handed him a stack of paper and told him they'd be doing the news together at noon. "Which I was not ready for! You know? To go on the air with my hero?" Child said. But a half hour later, he found himself in the news booth with Ryum, reading from the script whenever Ryum pointed at him. After the newscast, Child was hired as what he calls "the anonymous voice in between shows telling you who paid for the show, and what time it is, and what the weather's going to be, and what's coming up next."

Child took on as much work as he could get at OPB. He was a classical music announcer on weekday afternoons, performed in a comedy show, read the news, and on weekend afternoons hosted a version of the free-form show he'd been doing in college, which evolved into a program featuring singer-songwriters. He juggled his radio schedule with his burgeoning, though maverick, musical career. He played in the Neal Gladstone Band, a folk rock group that did parodies of everything from country music to heavy metal, and in a percussion band called the Balafon Marimba Ensemble, which once opened for the Grateful Dead at the Oakland Coliseum.

When Child was thirty, he followed a girlfriend to New York and started at the bottom of the heap at WNYC as a fill-in overnight board operator. He worked his way up to become the weekend classical music host, then got his dream job hosting *Around New York*, a now-defunct daily two-hour program featuring live interviews and studio concerts with classical, jazz, and world music performers. At first, the old insecurity that stymied him when he was a rookie deejay too scared to go on the air threatened to return. "I still kind of felt like, I'm a guy from Corvallis, Oregon—what the hell am I doing here? I'm going to be discovered as a fraud!" he said. "I had this vision of at some point running out of things to say in the middle of the show, and I would take off the headphones and put them down on the table in a live show, and I'd get up and walk out and that would be the end of my radio career."

But he didn't run out of things to say. He stayed with the job and came to realize how deeply he was committed to radio. "It was a real turning point for me," he said. "I thought, okay, I've found my home, doing music on the radio. There was nothing I could imagine doing that would be more satisfying than sharing music in this way with musicians and sharing it with an audience that's curious."

As his radio career advanced, he spent less time performing his own music. He said though he missed the "incredible rush" of playing music onstage, he cherishes the different kind of connection to an audience that radio provides. "People don't listen to the radio in bunches, the way they go to concerts," he said. "You listen to the radio by yourself. You're in the car, the kitchen, the bathroom, the living room. So it's a very intimate connection, and I love that."

After WNYC canceled *Around New York*, Child left the station to host a morning drive-time program for Sony, which was trying to launch a nationwide classical music service. He returned to WNYC after a couple of years to become the station's music director and then got promoted to director of cultural programming.

He missed being on the air, though, and so when he found out in 2000 that NPR was looking for a host for *Performance Today*, he applied and was hired. The program at the time aired two in-depth features and interviews on classical music artists and issues every day, in addition to broadcasting recordings of classical music concerts at NPR's studios and venues around the world. In 2002, NPR cut the show's staff from fifteen people to five as part of a major reorganization of its cultural programming, a move critics said effectively "gutted" the show. Child said *Performance Today* remains strong as a showcase for classical music in concert, but he does miss the manpower of the old days. "I still find that frustrating sometimes, when I'd like to bring in an expert on an issue and have a discussion about it and have it edited and produced . . . and we just don't have the production staff to do that anymore," he said.

The show's ability to cover issues in the classical music world hasn't completely gone under, though. In 2005, Child and *Performance Today* scooped other news outlets by reporting the discovery in Germany of an unknown Bach aria. Child covered the finding for *Morning Edition*, and NPR quickly put together a group of musicians specializing in music from the era to play the piece on the air.

Child's main concern as host of *Performance Today* has been to treat classical music not as "high art" but as something relevant and appealing to listeners, no matter what their background. "We're NPR, and our audience tends to be educated, so on the one hand, it has to be intelligently done in the context of the history of classical music and we have to be smart about the music we play," he said. "But I think it's important, vitally important, that it be accessible to people who know nothing about classical music."

He also takes the time to explore issues in classical music off the air. Though he can't answer all his email, he has maintained correspondences with a number of listeners around the country. The exchanges sometimes start rather heatedly. "Sometimes people are upset about the choice of music," he said. "They'll write, Oh my God, how could you air *that* performance of Beethoven's Symphony Number 5, such a glorious piece and that one was too fast, and the balance between the strings and the winds wasn't right, and they just ruined it! How could you have ever let that on the air! One of the great monuments of human culture, how could you have destroyed it in that way!" Listeners are often surprised that he bothers to write back. "Almost inevitably, the angriest person is happy to hear an actual personal response, and even if we're in disagreement about something we can strike up a conversation about it," he said.

Recently, Child has started performing music publicly again. He has played piano duets—three Brahms waltzes—with Andre Michel Schub and played the castanet part of Luigi Boccherini's Fandango Quintet with guitarist Jason Vieaux and the Shanghai String Quartet on *Performance Today* in 2002 and then again with guitarist Sharon Isbin and a quartet she assembled for Summerfest La Jolla in 2003. Child said it was "oddly disconcerting" to play again, to step across that line from listener/interviewer to performer.

Yet there was no denying the thrill of it, either. "I felt like I was living the dream of every baseball fan," he said. "The team needs a new center fielder, and they ask the guy sitting in the bleachers to jump down and put on a pair of cleats!"

Kissing Walter Cronkite: Korva Coleman

Host, *Performance Today* and
SymphonyCast
Newscaster, NPR News

When **Korva Coleman** gets on the elevator at NPR in the morning, she often has to remind herself which floor to get off on. On Tuesdays and Wednesdays, she's the midday newscaster and works out of the NPR newsroom on the second floor. On Thursdays and Fridays, she goes up to the cultural division on the fourth floor to prepare the weekend broadcasts of *Performance Today*, a daily program of classical music in concert, and *SymphonyCast*, a weekly show featuring orchestral music performances.

So the first half of her week, she's writing news and clock watching; her newscasts start at exactly a minute past the hour from noon until 4 p.m. The second half of the week is spent in the less rigid world of Brahms, Mahler, and Telemann. Coleman's low voice, honey-smooth and reassuringly authoritative, crosses over easily from news to classical music announcing and back, and she enjoys the contrast. The real divide in her life, she told me, is not between news and classical music, it's between work and family.

Coleman, forty-two, and I spoke over coffee in NPR's brightly lit employee cafeteria on the seventh floor, one of the few places where staffers from the music and news divisions cross paths. It was a bitterly cold winter morning, and she got to work a little late because she didn't want her kids to wait outside for the school bus. She has short dark hair and wide shoulders, and she was dressed in a beige argyle sweater and running shoes. She kept a Polartec jacket and gloves beside her, as if she was worried the chill could still reach her. It was a Friday, and she was thinking about the *Performance Today* broadcast she had to finish taping that afternoon, and then what she'd have to do that weekend back home in Columbia, Maryland, a hefty thirty-five-mile commute from NPR (she often takes the train). There was the Valentine's Day party to plan, the laundry, the speed-skating carpools, and all the other myriad domestic details of life as the mother of two active daughters, Kaiia, twelve, and Alena, ten.

In the world of public radio, where workaholics and martyrs abound, Coleman limits her workweek to four days. She not only insists on having a life outside of work, she insists that life is more important than being a voice on NPR. "This may come as a shock to some people, but NPR is not my end all and be all," she said. "There are great swaths of time where I don't think about it. I don't listen to the news, I don't read the paper, because I've got responsibilities in other places in my life that I really need to deal with, and I will put work aside completely and deal with them."

Coleman speaks with a serious and warm intensity about her life. She is a woman who, though not traditionally religious, describes herself as spiritual and belongs to what she calls a "subversive" Southern Baptist church. She readily talks about what it means to be human and the ideals she has for herself: volunteering and being part of a community, sharing, recognizing opportunity, and cultivating "a sense of balance" amidst it all. She also has a keen concern for issues of justice and equality and easily muses about matters like due process in a way befitting to the former law school student she is. Spending a couple of hours with her left me in a reflective mood, the way I used to feel in college after reading Emerson or Audre Lorde.

A native of Arizona, Coleman was born in 1963, "a week after the March on Washington," she pointed out. Her mother is a white retired schoolteacher and accountant and her father was a black navy medic. Antimiscegenation laws, still widespread in the late 1950s, forced them to go to Massachusetts to be legally married. Her father served in Vietnam in the 1960s and came home ill. He died at thirty-four, when Coleman was four years old.

Coleman was drawn to world events from toddlerhood. Every night during the *CBS Evening News* she would go to the television set, kiss Walter Cronkite, and say, "Good night, Wa Wa."

As a teenager, she joined the theater club but lost interest because she wanted to do political dramas like *The Crucible* while everyone else was getting jazzed up about *Miracle on 54th Street*. She turned to journalism instead. Her idol was NBC newscaster Jessica Savage, who'd gotten her start in radio, so Coleman convinced a friend of a friend, who worked at a radio station, to let her in at midnight to record a two-minute tape of herself, reading copy of a television commercial. She sounded good enough to get a weekend announcing job at a tiny Christian AM station. She worked there on and off into her early twenties. Her first big scoop was discovering which shopping mall in Phoenix refused to let the Salvation Army ring bells during the Christmas season. The Salvation Army official she'd interviewed wouldn't identify the mall, but agreed to confirm it if Coleman found out. So she called every mall-based store she could think of until a Casual Corner employee spilled the beans. She filed a byline story with the Associated Press and then was deluged with calls from area television stations wanting to find out more.

Coleman attended Arizona State University for a year, then took some time off to work in commercial radio. She transferred to

Howard University in Washington, D.C., and got a degree in journalism, but decided to go to law school at Georgetown. She held down part-time newscaster jobs at NPR and WAMU, a public radio affiliate in Washington, to support herself while studying for what she hoped would be a career in a district attorney's office or a nonprofit, working on women's issues. "I was going to change the world," she said. After a year at Georgetown, she realized the public advocacy career she'd fantasized about wouldn't cover her law school bills and she'd be forced into corporate law. "I'd have to go be a schmuck, and I just couldn't," she said. "I'd rather eat glass."

So she quit. She told me that she went home that day in 1990 and cried her eyes out, lying on the living room floor, telling her husband, Alan Heck, a public health inspector she'd married just six months before, "I failed you!" Heck—whom she calls "a tremendous man, sometimes I don't feel like I'm worthy to tie his shoes"—assured her she had not. He gently encouraged her to see if she could find more work at NPR. She called her boss, who told her the midday newscaster had just been diagnosed with Carpal Tunnel Syndrome and was transferring to another department. Three days later, Coleman stepped into the job she's held ever since.

She began hosting *Performance Today* in 2000, a time when she needed a "new opportunity to be stretched in a way I hadn't been stretched," then took on *SymphonyCast* when it launched the following year. She is not a musician, and she describes herself as someone who "listens to classical music the way most people across the U.S. listen to it, not knowing much about it." She approaches hosting with a journalist's curiosity. She'll become fascinated, for example, by Debussy's influence on Duke Ellington, or the feminist ideas of Hildegard von Bingen, the Benedictine mystic and composer. "So when I look at classical music, I see the beauty of the music, but I'm not looking to see what I think a typical musician would see," she said. "I'm looking at Hildegard. What a woman. That's how I see classical music."

At NPR, Coleman has made it a point to mentor promising talent. Just that morning she spent a half-hour in a studio, coaching two reporters, Andrea Seabrook and Peter Overby, who'd told her they wanted to develop a more relaxed and conversational on-air presence. She is also one of the head shop stewards for the American Federation of Television and Radio Artists (AFTRA). She got involved with labor issues at NPR during her first pregnancy, when a switch in health care plans left her without coverage to see her midwife. She's carefully watched NPR's track record on minority hires over the years. In the mid-1990s, she filed an affidavit on behalf of foreign correspondent Sunni Khalid when he sued NPR for discrimination. She noticed the first glimmerings of a change in the complexion of public radio in 1996, when she showed up to speak on a panel in Philadelphia. She was astonished to realize that the two other panelists, both of them public radio colleagues, were also black, even though "we were not there to talk about a black issue," she said. "We were there to talk about public radio in general."

She told me she's seen more signs of progress lately, but she added that NPR still needs more minorities, in particular as senior editors. "It's really cool when you hear Claudio Sanchez on the air, or Mandalit del Barco, but what's really important is, who is Mandalit's editor? Who's calling the shots?" she said.

What concerns her the most, she said, is equal access to due process, at NPR and elsewhere. "So if you're an affluent white man who grew up and went to Harvard, you . . . are owed due process, same as everybody else, and I would fight for that," she said. "And I have, as a matter of fact."

Coleman has sensed over the years that some of her superiors at NPR look at her "with disdain" because she hasn't moved on to become an accomplished field reporter or the host of a news program. But she knows she's also won admiration, even from her more successful colleagues, for the way she's lived her life. She said journalism is full of broken marriages, kids so estranged from their high-powered parents they stop speaking to each other. A female colleague who came of age "at a time when you chose work or you chose family" confided to her tearfully one afternoon her regret at not having children. "She said, 'I don't know how you're balancing it, but I wish that I had that choice,'" Coleman said. "I know people look at this woman and say, 'Gosh, I wish I was so and so,' and my heart just breaks for her."

Coleman said there was a time when she was a contender for more visible news jobs. But she's stopped applying. What changed her mind was the day that, during a long guest hosting stint on weekend *All Things Considered*, she got a phone call that one of her daughters had fallen and been seriously cut. Her daughter turned out to be fine, but Coleman left as soon as she could to go to her. She sat holding her daughter in a rocking chair in the hospital room until midnight. "It totally puts things in perspective," she said. "I know I'm making the right choice for me."

Tangos, Radiohead,
and Teenagers:
Christopher O'Riley

Host, *From the Top*

T he music, Astor Piazzola's "Otoño porteño," starts slowly, with a feeling of great suspense. If it were the soundtrack to a movie, the main characters would be on their way to a heist or an illicit romantic tryst. Caleb Swaagh, the cellist, plays with a beatific expression on his face. With his rosy, full cheeks, he looks like an overgrown fairy tale character. Elly Suh, the violinist, slouches a bit, at first looking meek, but when the tempo picks up and the music becomes fiery, she gets bolder, holding her chin and her instrument higher, absorbed in the proud and sensual nature of the music. Jin Yi Zhang, the pianist, peers intently at the music from under her long bangs.

No one in the trio seems fazed that standing beside them turning pages is renowned pianist Christopher O'Riley, dressed in a dove-gray suit. He looks like he's taking the responsibility very seriously, as if, instead of being one of the most sought-after performers on the classical music concert scene, he was an ambitious music student glad for the proximity to accomplished professionals. Indeed, the musicians do sound like accomplished professionals. When the performance, taped in front of a live audience at Jordan Hall at the New England Conservatory of Music, airs on the radio, thousands will tune in in the middle and have no idea that none of the musicians is old enough to vote.

That is, until the applause dies down and O'Riley introduces the Astor Trio, giving each musician's age: Swaagh and Zhang are seventeen, and Suh is fifteen. They are all students in Juilliard's precollege program, selected by audition to appear on this broadcast of *From the Top*, a weekly radio show showcasing the nation's most outstanding young musicians with performances, interviews, and skits. O'Riley, whose thickset good looks are something of a cross between Martin Sheen and Lord Byron, ushers the trio members to a row of microphones on stage left. They stand shyly as he asks them about their lives. Zhang, who has recently moved to America from Beijing to study at Julliard, talks about her love of American food and working it off at the gym. Swaagh talks about how hard it is to find a room to practice in at home because he has five siblings, all of whom play an instrument. Suh, the daughter of Korean immigrants, confesses in a soft voice her love for the World Wide Wrestling program *WWW Smackdown*. The audience laughs.

"I guess they could hire you to make the sound effects at the WWW because you've got another amazing talent in addition to your violin playing," O'Riley says. "You can crack just about every joint in your body?"

"A lot of them," Suh says.

"It scares me," he says. "Would you maybe demonstrate your great gift?"

"I'll try."

"What's the loudest place?"

"Uh, my waist makes a big sound."

"Let's check that out."

Suh hands her violin to Zhang and sits down in a folding chair. Kim Rzemien, the show's production coordinator, holds a microphone to Suh's waist. She turns her torso. The cracks—a quick series of chiropractic pops—make the audience gasp, then clap like crazy. Suh cracks up.

"Gosh, that hurt just to hear it," O'Riley says.

"It's very refreshing," Suh says. After wowing audiences with her violin playing for half her life, suddenly she's able to wow them with her waist—and, to even her own surprise, her wit.

The first time I tuned in to *From the Top*, I thought I'd never last through the broadcast. The concept seemed a potentially saccharine celebration of teenage hyperachievement, showcasing the kind of kid who made me sick with self-doubt in high school. But as I listened, two things struck me: the music is very good—as I mentioned, for most ears virtually indistinguishable from other live performances on public radio. And, the talk in between performances is not a smug account of each prodigy's accomplishments. Rather, the interviews and skits highlight the kids' lives with a teasing humor. Sho Yano, a thirteen-year-old pianist who is in his second year of medical school at the University of Chicago, was given a "Medicine for Musicians" quiz, in which he had to diagnose the imagined throat and hand ailments of Dawn Upshaw and Joshua Bell. In a preproduced segment, tuba player Jens Petersen, sixteen, went for a spin in his dream car, a 360 Spider Ferrari, with the show's "Roving Reporter," Hayley Goldbach. In short, the show gives young musicians both the opportunity to perform seriously and to be something other than serious performers. The effect is charming.

O'Riley, forty-nine, establishes a strong rapport with the kids on both fronts. Musically, he works with them with the utmost respect. He is the accompanist for the solo musicians, and he treats them like colleagues, not students, following their musical judgment and taste. In rehearsal for the Jordan Hall show, Petersen whipped through the Mozart Horn Concerto with O'Riley, performing it flawlessly, though the tempo was faster than the piece is usually played. O'Riley asked for another run-through, but he didn't ask Peterson to slow down. "You're fine," O'Riley reassured him. "I just want to make sure I catch the tempo." On stage, in the interviews and skits between performances, he is quite funny and laid-back, cracking jokes about "the tragedy of piano butt" and playing along when a flirtatious young soprano tosses her white boa over his shoulders before singing.

"He is so freaking quick-witted," said Gerald Slavet, one of the executive producers and founders of *From the Top*, which is produced with WGBH Radio and the New England Conservatory of Music and distributed by PRI. "All the funny lines out of Chris are Chris's on the spot. He knows the kids' culture. He can relate to them."

Perhaps because he's been there himself. Growing up in Chicago in the 1960s, he began piano lessons in kindergarten. His mother had already taught him how to read by the time he started school. "I went to Catholic school, and they knew I would be bored and they didn't want a troublemaker," he said. "So they gave my mother an ultimatum. It was either piano lessons or French lessons. Piano was her choice."

He studied classical piano for years, and as he reached adolescence a curiosity about music outside the classical repertoire emerged. "I found out pretty quickly that I wasn't winning any popularity contests playing Hungarian rhapsodies," he said. "So I started a band in sixth grade because of course the overriding need to play the piano is basically to impress girls. Trace back the history of piano playing and you'll find that this is true."

The band didn't make him more popular, but he learned to play Doors and Iron Butterfly covers. Later he played with another band called Anomia, a word that describes a kind of amnesia which makes it difficult to remember certain everyday objects. The group played jazz fusion, "a sort of John McLaughlin Mahavishnu Orchestra kind of thing," he said. After his mother, Cecilia Sommers, got married and moved the family to Pittsburgh (where she became the station manager of WQED-FM, the city's classical music public radio station), O'Riley hooked up with Eric Kloss, a blind saxophone player who'd gigged with Chick Corea, Jack DeJohnette, and Jaki Byard. He and Kloss played a mix of modern jazz standards and original material at weekend gigs at a spot called Sonny Daye's Stage Door Club.

He attended the New England Conservatory of Music in Boston in the years when jazz scholar and composer Gunther Schuler was the school's president and "all music was created equal," O'Riley said. "There were things to be learned from all kinds of music, and Gunther was really very serious about that." But O'Riley eventually came to the conclusion that he would have to choose between genres.

"There was a whole history of jazz that even my most admired and cutting-edge pianists had under their belts and so if I was really going to be a jazz pianist I would really have to go back to the beginning and learn Jelly Roll Morton, Count Basie, and move my way up through Bill Evans, and I just thought, well, there's that whole history to be dealt with and I'm not really sure my heart is in it," he said. "At the same time, I also found it more compelling to reinvigorate pieces that were already written down, maybe two, three hundred years old, and that was for me maybe more of a challenge instead of giving my original point of view of 'Straight No Chaser.' So that's how I ended up playing more or less exclusively classical piano."

O'Riley has won top prizes at the Van Cliburn, Leeds, Busoni, and Montreal competitions; soloed with orchestras in Boston, Pittsburgh, New York, and Los Angeles; and collaborated with conductors Michael Tilson Thomas, Leonard Slatkin, Edo de Waart, and Neeme Jarvi. He has distinguished himself on the classical circuit as one of the new generation of musicians, including the Kronos Quartet, Matt Heimovitz, and Carter Brey, who are seeking out material outside the tried-and-true classical repertoire. He's released recordings of music by Stravinsky, Scriabin, Ferruccio Busoni, John Adams, and Robert Helps. He has developed an image as a musician with a distinctly non-stuffy public approach to classical music, As part of the Xerox/Affiliate Artists program, he played and spoke about classical music in "all sorts of odd places—car dealerships, hospices, managed care homes, schools, office buildings," he said. Eager to make connections among different musical genres, he could wax rhapsodic, as he did once on a segment on *CBS News Sunday Morning*, about the orchestral richness of the music of Public Enemy.

O'Riley is best known for his piano transcriptions of the English rock band Radiohead. He became curious about the group after their 1997 release, *OK Computer,* was hailed as the album of the decade and perhaps the most significant rock to come out since *The White Album.* He quickly became obsessed, listening to everything by Radiohead he could get his hands on, pulled in by the band's "sensual harmonic language" and unique textures. It wasn't enough for him to listen; he wanted to get inside the music. So he began to transcribe and play the songs.

"They're a very tight band, but they're also a very imaginative band, so that keeps you listening," he said. "Playing the songs as a pianist is very interesting because the texturization gives you lots of ways of making the song work." At first, he performed the arrangements as musical interludes on *From the Top* and in recitals. In 2003, he released *True Love Waits,* an entire CD of Radiohead songs. The CD won widespread critical attention in both the classical and rock music worlds, and his performances attracted teenagers and twenty-somethings to concert halls across the country.

O'Riley began hosting *From the Top* when the show debuted in 2000. *From the Top* cofounder Gerald Slavet said that O'Riley was chosen because he was passionate about how the show might help improve dwindling audiences for live classical music. "When we first hired him, I wasn't sure I would have believed that one of his greatest assets was the way he gives himself to the kids," Slavet said. "It's not about him, not about Chris the star or Chris the accompanist."

Interestingly, O'Riley describes himself as "a hermit," spending his time in between performing and working on *From the Top* (which, though based at the New England Conservatory of Music, tours nationwide) at home in Los Angeles, practicing and working on recordings. When I asked O'Riley whether there was anything he liked to do outside of music and the show, he answered simply, "No."

The irony here is that, for the kids who perform on *From the Top,* he is one of the rare adults who acknowledges their need to not be isolated by their art. "He understands what you're going through," said Elly Suh. "He seems to understand that we have a life outside of practicing all day."

Classical Music's Hotai
Buddha: Bill McGlaughlin

Host, *St. Paul Sunday*

The polished wood buddha in Bill McGlaughlin's Manhattan apartment is beaming, its arms in the air, as if in a joyous dance. It isn't like the other buddha figures I've seen, sitting in the lotus pose, their expressions serious and meditative.

The hotai buddha, as smiling buddhas are called, is perhaps the perfect talisman for McGlaughlin. He is the host of *St. Paul Sunday*, a weekly classical music program of performance and conversation with renowned musicians, from virtuoso violinist Joshua Bell to soprano Dawn Upshaw to the Albert McNeil Jubilee Singers, a gospel group. McGlaughlin has a hotai buddha–like approach in the often solemn and self-important world of classical music. He is cheerful and down to earth, a short man with a graying beard and merry blue eyes who wore, on the summer day of my visit, blue nylon shorts and a black short-sleeved shirt, his eyeglasses hooked over the collar. His posture was so straight I asked him if he himself meditated (he doesn't). On his show and in person, he laughs heartily and often and speaks in a peculiar accent that mingles the cadences of the working-class streets of north Philadelphia, where he grew up, and his grandfather's native Scotland.

A world-class conductor and composer, McGlaughlin is sophisticated in the language and theory of music and performance and knows many people in the classical music world. Yet he avoids overindulging in insider talk, and he's just as likely to exclaim "good stuff" or "cool" as he is "bravo." He'll let himself, as he puts it, be "the dumber Smothers Brother" in the room, asking questions meant to help listeners understand what's going on in the music and who the performers are. He'll have musicians repeat a theme or certain dramatic or interesting moment in the music they've just performed, then ask them to talk about it. His process takes listeners back into the music to help them develop a deeper sense of connection to it. He wants them to feel the wonder and enjoyment he feels. "The music is so bleeding beautiful," he said. "It can be so thrilling."

McGlaughlin was born in Philadelphia during World War II. He and his mother lived with his grandparents while his father served in the army air corps in India. He didn't get to meet his "pop," as he calls him, until he was two years old and his father was sent home to recover from malaria at the Fort Dix Naval Hospital in New Jersey. McGlaughlin kept begging his mother to take him to the hospital so he could finally meet his father. His earliest memory is walking into a room full of men in blue military-issue pajamas and robes. "He was something like forty beds down on the right, but I knew who he was," he said. "I went running down there, my little legs going boopboop-boopboopboop and jumped into his arms."

Once back home, his father, a draftsman, listened to opera in his workshop, playing recordings of *Carmen, Die Fledermaus, La Traviata,* and *Aida* until they were fixed in his young son's mind. When McGlaughlin was six, his father gave him a Hohner Marine Band C Major harmonica and showed him how to play a scale. McGlaughlin practiced the scale dutifully, then asked his father for the next lesson.

"No more lessons," his father said. "You know a lot of songs. Play them." Soon the two were playing opera melodies together on the harmonica. "What I learned that was really valuable was that music was a special kind of fun, something you did by ear with someone you loved," he said.

He didn't start to study music seriously until he was fourteen. His younger brother was taking music lessons and decided abruptly to quit. His mother had already paid for a month's worth of lessons, so she told McGlaughlin to go. He resisted at first, too preoccupied with refining his jump shot to be interested in playing the piano. Then he gave in. "By the second lesson, I thought, that's it. I'm going to be a musician," he said. "I had no idea what that meant. None."

It was a late start for a classical musician. He would have to catch up to the people who'd been playing Bach since they were barely out of diapers. He did, with the passion and willfulness of a precocious adolescent. "I was formed to a certain degree emotionally the way a six-year-old is not, and I had a great intellectual curiosity," he said. "I couldn't get enough of music."

When he was sixteen, his grandmother died, leaving his eighty-year-old grandfather, John Hogan, alone in the increasingly rough north Philadelphia neighborhood where he lived and still practiced dentistry. McGlaughlin, the oldest of six children, moved in with him for a measure of protection. His grandfather took him to see old black-and-white opera movies at Union Hall and tolerated what McGlaughlin described as his dreamy, solipsistic teenager "blathering" about history, civil rights, music, and everything else he was spending his days learning and thinking about. "I remember he said, 'You've got a sloppy mind,'" McGlaughlin mimicked in a mock Scottish accent. "I know he thought I could use a little more discipline."

The discipline was fast developing. He started playing the trombone later in high school. He mastered it so quickly that he was playing with the Philadelphia Orchestra by the time he was twenty. When I asked him how he became so accomplished so fast—did he spend

his entire day practicing?—he explained that brass players can't physically play that long because they'd wear out their lips. When he
couldn't play anymore, he'd keep learning by singing and tapping out
rhythms from the classic exercise book, *Elementary Training for Musicians* by Paul Hindemith. He still had the book and showed it to me,
his name scrawled inside the worn blue front cover. "That's a billion
years old," he laughed. "I would practice this because if you just
stopped playing and watched the ball game on television your head
goes in the wrong place and it's hard to get back to playing." He
opened the book up and began tapping and singing one of the
rhythms. "Almost like tongue twisters!" he said.

He went on to earn a master's degree in music at Temple University, where he studied conducting. In 1969, he began a six-year stint
with the Pittsburgh Symphony, then led by William Steinberg, who
encouraged his interest in conducting. In 1975, he became a conductor for the St. Paul Chamber Orchestra, eventually moving up to
principal conductor. In the 1980s and 1990s, he hopped around to
music director jobs in Eugene, Tucson, and San Francisco. His
longest gig was in Kansas City, where he was music director from
1986 to 1998.

While working in St. Paul, he began to dabble in radio, filling in
from time to time on Garrison Keillor's pre–*Prairie Home Companion*
morning radio program on Minnesota Public Radio (MPR). Tom
Voegeli, a second-generation public radio producer (his father, Don
Voegeli, composed the original theme to *All Things Considered*) with
a background in radio drama, came up with the idea for *St. Paul Sunday*, originally called *St. Paul Sunday Morning*, to be recorded in
MPR's new, state-of-the-art Studio M. He wanted a program with a
distinctly regional (meaning, not Washington, New York, or Los Angeles) origin that would present world-class musicians to a national
audience. When he asked McGlaughlin to host, McGlaughlin thought
he would need to take classes in broadcasting to learn how to act on
the air. But that was precisely what Voegeli, who went on to produce

Schickele Mix, *From the Top*, and other public radio programs, did not want. He wanted McGlaughlin to sound like a musician, to communicate to listeners what he saw and heard in the performances.

St. Paul Sunday piloted in 1980 and began to air nationally the following year. The show now has more than 380,000 listeners and is distributed by American Public Media, Minnesota Public Radio's national production arm. In 2003, McGlaughlin began hosting *Exploring Music with Bill McGlaughlin*, a series of discussions of various themes in classical music, on the Chicago-based WFMT Radio Network.

McGlaughlin has a deep sense of urgency about doing radio. He sees it as a way to reach out, to try to keep classical music from becoming an increasingly marginalized art form, with ever smaller and older audiences. He talked about how the average college-educated, somewhat affluent young couple will readily discuss an independent film or a challenging new painting, but they still feel tongue-tied after listening to Brahms or Stravinksy. They're embarrassed to be tongue-tied, he said, and this embarrassment might keep them from listening further, especially in an era when the average attention span for a pop song is about two and a half minutes. "So what do we do when even the first movement of a Haydn symphony takes the better part of ten minutes and Mahler, he's barely done clearing his throat?" he asked.

At this point, McGlaughlin got animated, going off on a tangent about Bruno Walter's last recording of Mahler's Ninth Symphony, just before Hitler annexed Austria. He went to the piano and played the symphony's hopeful opening theme and mused about the beauty of Austrian meadows and Mahler's memories of the death of his four-year-old daughter. A Mahler fan since high school, I listened, rapt, even though I wasn't quite sure where he was going with all of this. It was like listening to a completely unedited version of *St. Paul Sunday*, without any guest musicians, and enjoying every moment but feeling a bit of sympathy for the editor who'd have to make sense of it all.

"Man, this is cool," he said suddenly, as if talking to the ideas flooding into his own head, and sat back down on the couch. Then he told me a story about the afternoon he spent at the Minneapolis Institute of Art with his ninety-year-old friend Hans Archenaude, a Jewish refugee from Hitler's Germany. Archenaude sat him down in front of Rembrandt's *Lucretia*, a depiction of the moment after she stabs herself out of the shame of having been raped. Archenaude clasped McGlaughlin's hand and made him look at the painting for a full half hour. The only thing the old man said the whole time was, "Those eyes. Such sadness."

"That's why we're here," McGlaughlin said, his voice getting thick, his eyes shining. "We just need to get somebody to slow us down for a minute, because it doesn't take too many of those experiences before we can truly listen."

While McGlaughlin was the music director of the Kansas City Symphony, a young pianist who'd grown up locally, Kevin Oldham, sent him a piano concerto he'd written, a "snazzy" piece with hints of Gershwin and Broadway. McGlaughlin was so impressed he offered to debut the piece on a program he was planning for Kansas City composers, a year and a half away. Oldham agreed, but later a conductor friend told McGlaughlin not to wait that long because Oldham was dying of AIDS. McGlaughlin scheduled the piece as soon as he could. Oldham was just barely well enough to play it. After the performance, McGlaughlin held him up backstage and took him back out for an extra bow. The young man checked into the hospital after the concert and died shortly after.

The experience left McGlaughlin inspired to try composing himself. The result was *Three Dreams and a Question: Choral Songs on e.e. cummings*. Its lyrics were taken from the e.e. cummings poem that begins: "o purple finch / please tell me why / this summer world (and you and i who love so much to live) must die." The piece debuted with the Kansas City Orchestra in 1998. McGlaughlin had long been interested in new music, programming avant-garde composers Elliott Carter and Donald Erb for the Kansas City Symphony, with somewhat squeamish reactions from both the players and the audience. But he found himself seeking a more accessible sound in his own work. He played a bit of *Three Dreams* for me on the piano and gave me a recording to listen to later. His work is harmonic, tinged with jazz, an approach he called "old fashioned." "I think when composers turn completely away from tonality, they lose a big part of storytelling," he said.

McGlaughlin lives with acclaimed jazz singer Karrin Allyson, whom he met during his Kansas City years. He has two grown children from a marriage that ended in divorce. In 1998, McGlaughlin left full-time conducting to move to New York City and devote more of his time to composing. He and Allyson are on the road quite a bit, though. She tours frequently, and he's had a number of guest conducting gigs, in addition to regular trips to St. Paul to tape *St. Paul Sunday.*

After years of living in apartments where, as McGlaughlin put it, "all they could see out the window were people's ankles," the couple splurged on a two-bedroom apartment next to Riverside Park, overlooking the Hudson River. Inspired by the view, he is writing a piece about Icarus, under commission from radio station KRWG in Las Cruces, New Mexico, for its seventy-fifth anniversary. "I've been going goofy watching things fly, from jets to birds to scraps of leaves in the wind," he said.

The view also beckons him away from work. He said he was in the park every day, jogging or playing Frisbee. The afternoon I spent with McGlaughlin was the first mild day after a long heat wave, the cooler temperatures such a relief that, on my way to his apartment, passersby smiled at the sky and a man sighed to me, "Isn't this nice?" When the interview was over, I told McGlaughlin that I wanted to walk a bit and asked him for a good route to the subway stop. He said he'd walk with me. We strolled through the park along the Hudson, the view still hazy from the heat wave. He pointed out the boats on the Seventy-ninth Street Pier and the lighthouse beneath the George Washington Bridge, made famous, he told me, in the children's book *The Little Red Lighthouse and the Big Grey Bridge*. We discussed what books we were reading—he is fond of detective stories—and he showed me the garden where the last scene of *You've Got Mail* was set. We both sounded a bit embarrassed about admitting to having seen the movie.

At the subway stop, he advised me to try to grab an express train at Seventy-second Street on my way to Grand Central. Then he opened his arms to hug me goodbye. It was a sweet and genuine gesture, and I embraced him back. I felt in the presence of that rarest of beings: a person for whom each day was an opportunity for delight—in music, in people, in books, in ideas, and in a beautiful summer day in Riverside Park.

Bibliography

Adams, Noah. *Noah Adams on All Things Considered: A Radio Journal*. New York: W. W. Norton and Company, 1992.

Collins, Mary. *National Public Radio: The Cast of Characters*. Washington, D.C.: Seven Locks Press, 1993.

Douglas, Susan J. *Listening In: Radio and the American Imagination*. New York: Times Books, 1999.

Looker, Thomas. *The Sound and the Story: NPR and the Art of Radio*. New York: Houghton Mifflin Company, 1995.

McCauley, Michael P. *NPR: The Trials and Triumphs of National Public Radio*. New York: Columbia University Press, 2005.

Mitchell, Jack. *Listener Supported: The Culture and History of Public Radio*. Westport, CT: Praeger Publishers, 2005.

Wertheimer, Linda, ed. *Listening to America: Twenty-five Years in the Life of a Nation, as Heard on National Public Radio*. New York: Houghton Mifflin Company, 1995.

Witherspoon, John, and Roselle Kovitz. *A History of Public Broadcasting*. Washington, D.C.: The Current Publishing Committee, 2000.

The following web sites were frequently consulted, along with related links to individual programs and biographical information.

American Public Media: http://www.apmstations.org/apmstations/home/HomePage.do

Current, the newspaper about public TV and radio in the United States: http://www.current.org/

National Public Radio: http://www.npr.org/

Public Radio Fan: http://www.publicradiofan.com/

Public Radio International: http://www.pri.org/PublicSite/inside/index.html

Most audience figures cited are based on Arbitron ratings from Spring 2005. Figures for *A Prairie Home Companion* were taken from http://prairiehome.publicradio.org/about. Figures used for *St. Paul Sunday Morning* and *Marketplace* are an average of the Fall 2004 and Spring 2005 Arbitron audience estimates.

All figures used are based on "cume," or cumulative, statistics, which measure the number of individuals who tune in to a given radio program in a week. Additional audience information was taken from the report *Public Radio Today: How America Listens to Public Radio Stations*, 2005 edition, from Arbitron Inc.; and the Radio Research Consortium web site, at http://www.rrconline.org.

Chapters were mainly based on interviews conducted between January 2004 and September 2005. Additional references for selected chapters are as follows:

FOUNDING MOTHER: SUSAN STAMBERG

Feran, Tim. "Years of Radio Work Give Stamberg Plenty of Material for 'Talk.'" *Columbus (OH) Dispatch*, October 22, 1994, Features Accent and Entertainment section.

Hall, Steve. "Susan Stamberg on Monica Lewinsky, the Arts and Cranberries." *Buffalo News*, March 15, 1998, Lifestyles section.

Nelson Jones, Diana. "Her Names Is Synonymous with NPR News: The Stamberg Factor." *Pittsburgh Post Gazette*, September 18, 1995, Arts and Entertainment section.

Simon, Clea. "For Stamberg, Lots to Consider." *Boston Globe*, August 2, 2001, Living section.

Stamberg, Susan. *Every Night at Five: Susan Stamberg's All Things Considered Book.* New York: Pantheon, 1982.

———. *Talk: NPR's Susan Stamberg Considers All Things.* New York: Random House, 1993.

A SHY MAN FROM A SHY PLACE: NOAH ADAMS

Adams, Noah. *Far Appalachia: Following the New River North.* New York: Delacorte Press, 2001.

———. *The Flyers: In Search of Wilbur and Orville Wright.* New York: Crown Publishers, 2003.

———. *Piano Lessons: Music, Love and True Adventures.* New York: Delacorte Press, 1996.

Bunce, Alan. "Noah Adams Show Bows in Old Keillor Time Slot." *Christian Science Monitor*, January 13, 1988, Arts and Leisure section.

Eldredge, Richard L. "NPR's Adams Recalls Stint in Atlanta." *Atlanta Journal-Constitution*, February 21, 2002, Features section.

Nelson Jones, Diana. "His Message Carries an Accent on Appalachia, Not His Voice." *Pittsburgh Post-Gazette*, March 28, 1993, Lifestyle section.

Wilson, Craig. "Thirty Good Years of Radio Days: Hosts Delight in NPR's Quirky 'All Things Considered.'" *USA Today*, May 2, 2001, Life section.

WITNESS TO HISTORY: DANIEL SCHORR

Curie, Tyler. "Daniel Schorr—Commentator, National Public Radio, Washington. *Washington Post*, June 5, 2005, p. W05.

Schorr, Daniel. *Staying Tuned: A Life in Journalism.* New York: Pocket Books, 2001.

THE VOICE IN THE BOX: BOB EDWARDS

Adelman, Ken. "Voice in the Box." *Washingtonian*, March 2000, p. 31.

Barbash, Fred. "NPR Replaces 'Morning Edition' Host." *Washington Post*, March 23, 2004, p. 1.

Dorsey, Tom. "NPR Pulls Edwards from Job as Anchor." *Louisville Courier-Journal,* March 24, 2004. http://www.courier-journal.com.

Edwards, Bob. *Edward R. Murrow and the Birth of Broadcast Journalism.* Hoboken, N.J.: John Wiley and Sons, 2004.

———. *Fridays with Red: A Radio Friendship.* New York: Simon and Schuster, 1993.

Frey, Jennifer. "Former NPR Host Bob Edwards to Be XM's New Morning Star." *Washington Post,* July 29, 2004, p. A01.

Hinkley, David. "Ratings: NPR's 'Edition' Is Top of the 'Morning.'" *(New York) Daily News,* March 30, 2005, p. 84.

Johnson, Peter. "Edwards Ousted as 'Morning Edition' Host: NPR Yet to Name Replacement." *USA Today,* March 25, 2004, p. 1.

Marshall, Alexandra. "What about Bob?" *Salon,* March 25, 2004. http://www.salon.com/mwt/feature/2004/03/25/bob_edwards/index_np.html.

Ostrow, Joanne. "NPR Was Right: With Edwards Out, the Morning Show Is Better." *Denver Post,* May 1, 2005, p. F01.

Pugh, Clifford. "NPR Anchor Is Tuned In to His Listeners." *Houston Chronicle,* June 18, 2003, p. 1.

Shin, Annys. "Satellite Radio Is a Hit: Ask Howard Stern and Mel Karmazin." *Washington Post,* November 29, 2004, Financial section.

Tavernise, Sabrina. "The Broad Reach of Satellite Radio." *New York Times,* October 4, 2004, Business section.

Thompson, Bob. "NPR Yanks Top-Rated Show Host." March 24, 2004, p. A01.

Vuijst, Freke. "My View from Satellite Radio." *Boston Globe,* May 22, 2005, p. A12.

THE FALLOPIAN JUNGLE: COKIE ROBERTS, NINA TOTENBERG, AND LINDA WERTHEIMER

Adelman, Ken. "Strom Thurmond Kissed Me." *Washingtonian,* January 2004, pp. 27–30.

Alterman, Eric. "Farewell, My Cokie." *The Nation,* August 5, 2002. http://www.thenation.com/doc.mhtml?i=20020805&s=alterman.

Borsuk, Alan J. "How Sept. 11 Helped Save the U.S. Supreme Court." *Milwaukee Journal Sentinel,* October 6, 2003, News section.

Carlin, Peter Ames. "NPR's Wertheimer Reflects on News, Radio and Her New Reporting Gig." *Oregonian,* February 16, 2002, Television section.

"Cokie Roberts: Intimate Portrait." *Lifetime: Television for Women.* http://www.lifetimetv.com/shows/ip/portraits/9945/9945_index.html.

Conconi, Chuck. "Once upon a Time." *Washingtonian,* August 1998, p. 65.

Dreifus, Claudia. "Cokie Roberts, Nina Totenberg and Linda Wertheimer." *New York Times,* January 2, 1994, Magazine section.

Feder, Don. "Liberal Hatred a Loser's Response." *Boston Herald,* January 15, 1996, Editorial section.

———. "Monitoring Bias in Fourth Estate." *Boston Herald,* December 14, 1995, Editorial section.

Holtz, Patricia. "One Link along a Chain of Women; Roberts Finds Joy in Connections." *San Francisco Chronicle,* May 8, 1998, Daily Datebook section.

Kettman, Steve. "NPR Ace Survives U.S. 'Harassment': Nina Totenberg Broke Anita Hill Story." *San Francisco Chronicle,* June 7, 1992, Sunday Datebook section.

Kuczynski, Alex. "They Conquered, They Left." *New York Times,* March 24, 2002, Style section.

Kurtz, Howard. "Where's the Indictment? CNN's Scoop Gone Awry." *Washington Post,* May 16, 1992, Style section.

Lenhart, Jennifer. "Conspiracy, Speech Issues May Shadow Abortion Debate." *Houston Chronicle,* January 27, 1995, p. A23.

Marchan, Linda. "Father-Daughter Bond Is His Biggest Reward." *Boston Globe,* March 17, 1999, Living section.

Ostrow, Joanne. "Colorado Familiar to Totenberg: NPR Correspondent Visited Often as Child." *Denver Post,* October 29, 2002, p. F01.

Rahner, Mark. "NPR Host Considers Some Things She Hadn't." *Seattle Times,* May 18, 2001, Scene section.

Real Audio clip excerpt of *Inside Washington,* ABC News broadcast, July 8, 1995. http://www.mediaresearch.org/notablequotables/dishonor1999/welcomeaward6.asp.

Rieder, Rem. "Both Sides of the Street." *American Journalism Review,* March 2003, p. 6.

Rizzo Young, Kathleen. "From Public Radio, the Sound of People Thinking." *Buffalo News,* January 29, 1995, Book Review section.

Roberts, Cokie. *We're Our Mothers' Daughters.* New York: William Morrow and Company, 1998.

Roberts, Cokie, and Steve Roberts. *From This Day Forward.* New York: William Morrow and Company, 2000.

Schorow, Stephanie. "Capital Observer: Nina Totenberg Brings Insight from Reporting on Sexual Harassment to BU Address." *Boston Herald,* September 27, 1995, Features section.

Stainer, Harry. "Reporter Says Anita Hill Charges Ignored at First." *(Cleveland, OH) Plain Dealer,* November 15, 1992, Metro section.

Violanti, Anthony. "Nina Totenberg's High-Level Insider's View." *Buffalo News,* May 14, 2002, Entertainment section.

Wiltz, Teresa. "NPR's Wertheimer Leaves Anchor Post." *Washington Post,* December 11, 2001, Style section.

TROUBADOUR: SCOTT SIMON

Austin, April. "Listening to What Simon Says." *Christian Science Monitor,* February 2, 1989, People section.

Cuprisin, Tim. "Larry King to Quiz Clinton: NPR's Simon Puts Hopes in Listeners' Loyalty, Wallets: The 'Weekend Edition' Host Stops in for a WUWM Fund-raiser." *Milwaukee Journal Sentinel,* September 21, 1995, Cue section.

Dickinson, Amy. "After His Big Break on NBC, Scott Simon Is Back Being a Star on NPR." *Washingtonian,* June 1994, p. 39.

Drew, Mike. "NBC's Homicide Is Down, but Not Out." *Milwaukee Journal Sentinel,* October 2, 1995, Cue and Health section.

Feder, Robert. "Radio Gangs Up to Battle Dailies." *Chicago Sun-Times,* August 11, 1992, Features section.

Hoyt, Mike. "Fixing the World." *Columbia Journalism Review,* November 1977, p. 71.

Julian, Sheryl. "One of Radio's Most Familiar Voices Discusses His Early Years and Passion for Chicago Sports." *Boston Globe*, June 6, 2000, Living section.

Kaufman, Joanne. "Rituals: One Boy's Golden Age of Radio." *New York Times*, January 10, 2003, Section F.

"Public Radio Heartthrob Sells Out the Hall." *Boston Herald*, January 17, 1995, Features section.

Sandstrom, Karen. "Slam-Dunks of Life; Sports Timeline Gives Personal Sketch of National Public Radio's Scott Simon." *(Cleveland, OH) Plain Dealer*, May 30, 2000, Entertainment section.

"Scott Simon Releases First Novel: Pretty Birds." WKAR News. http://wkar.org/enews/story.php?fill=050830/prettybirds.

Simon, Scott. "Bringing Home an Adopted Daughter." *Weekend Edition Saturday*, National Public Radio broadcast, April 17, 2004.

———. *Home and Away: Memoir of a Fan*. New York: Hyperion, 2000.

Vancheri, Barbara. "Sports Form the Backdrop for Scott Simon's Paean to Family and Fandom." *Pittsburgh Post-Gazette*, April 30, 2000, Arts and Entertainment section.

"Young Irena Millic Endures War-Torn Sarajevo." *All Things Considered*, National Public Radio broadcast, August 26, 1993.

RENAISSANCE MAN: ROBERT SIEGEL

Hinkley, David. "Siegel Loves Role as NPR 'All' Star." *(New York) Daily News*, May 3, 2001, Television section.

BEYOND THE BRIGHT LIGHTS: MICHELE NORRIS

Trescott, Jacqueline. "NPR Taps Two New Hosts to Consider 'All Things.'" *Washington Post*, October 10, 2002, p. C04.

A CLOSE SECOND TO WATERSKIING: KAI RYSSDAL

Parvin, Paige P. "Dream Job." *Emory Magazine*, Winter 2004. http://www.emory.edu/EMORY_MAGAZINE/winter2004/kai.html.

THE OUTSIDER INSIDE: JUAN WILLIAMS

de Leon, Ferdinand M. "Juan Williams Is the New Voice of NPR's 'Talk of the Nation.'" *Seattle Times*, February 10, 2000, Scene section.

Jaffa, Eric. "Ideal for Journalists: Be Adversarial to Any Administration, 'Comfort the Afflicted, Afflict the Comfortable.'" *MoveLeft Media*. http://www.moveleft.com/moveleft_essay_2004_06_03_ideal_for_journalists_be_adversarial.asp.

Kee, Lorraine. "The Changing Face of Juan Williams." *St. Louis Post-Dispatch*, July 30, 2001, *Everyday Magazine* section.

Ranta, John. "NPR Lite." *Boston Globe*, May 31, 2005, Letters section.

Williams, Juan. "Bush Shouldn't Write Off the Black Vote." *New York Times*, June 16, 2004, Editorial Desk section.

FOLLOWING THE ORIGAMI CHAIN: JACKI LYDEN

"Daughter of the Queen of Sheba." *Weekend Saturday*, National Public Radio broadcast interview, September 27, 1997.

Drew, Polly. "Correspondent Offers Her Views from the Front Lines of Our World Crisis." *Milwaukee Journal Sentinel*, October 7, 2001, Lifestyle section.

Eichenberger, Bill. "'Royal Daughter Celebrates Life She Wouldn't Reorder.'" *Columbus (OH) Dispatch*, October 11, 2000, p. 10H.

Feder, Robert. "Infertility Gives Birth to Morning Radio Stunt." *Chicago Sun-Times*, September 29, 2004, Media Mix section.

Kalson, Sally. "From Memoir to Movie." *Pittsburgh Post-Gazette,* June 19, 1999, Arts and Entertainment section.

Kurson, Bob. "A Queen's Daughter: Memoir Details Mom's Mental Illness." *Chicago Sun-Times*, November 17, 1997, Features section.

Lyden, Jacki. *Daughter of the Queen of Sheba: A Memoir*. New York: Houghton Mifflin Company, 1997.

Thomas-Lynn, Felicia. "Reporting from the World's Danger Spots." *Milwaukee Journal Sentinel*, April 11, 2001, News section.

THE NICEST MAN IN PUBLIC RADIO: CARL KASELL

Dart, Bob. "Trace of South Lingers in Voice of NPR News." *Atlanta Journal and Constitution*, August 6, 2000, Dixie Living section.

Wilson, Mike. "Love Found Him When He Wasn't Looking." *St. Petersburg (FL) Times*, May 26, 2003, Floridian section.

MASTER LISTENER: IRA GLASS

Barrera, Sandra. "Listen Up! He's Got a Way with Words." *Los Angeles Daily News*, April 12, 2004, Arts section.

Barton, Julia. "The Thief Who Wiped His Butt on Fudge-Colored Towels, and Other Tales from 'This American Life.'" *Salon*. http://www.salon.com/july97/media/media2970723.html.

Cox, Ana Marie, and Joanna Dionis. "MoJo Interviews Ira Glass, Host of Public Radio's Hippest Show." *Mother Jones,* August 11, 1998. http://www.motherjones.com/news/feature/1998/08/glass.html.

Edgers, Geoff. "He's Finding Ways to Keep 'This American Life' Vital." *Boston Globe*, April 15, 2005, Arts section.

Francesca, Zoe. "A Conversation with Ira Glass." *On the Page*, Summer 2001. http://www.onthepage.org/adolescence/interview_with_ira_glass.htm.

Gilson, David, and Lyssa Mudd. "The World According to Glass." *Brown Alumni Magazine*, January–February 2000. http://www.brown.edu/Administration/Brown_Alumni_Magazine/00/1–00/.

Graves, Jen. "A Window on Glass." *(Tacoma, WA) News Tribune,* July 12, 2005. http://www.thenewstribune.com/.

Greenberg, Paul. "The Semio-Grads: How an Obscure Brown Concentration Trained Graduates to Crack the Code of American Culture—And Infiltrated the Mainstream." *Boston Globe*, May 16, 2004, Ideas section.

"Ira Glass." *Transom Review.* July 2004. http://talk.transom.org/guests/review/200406.review.glass1.html.

Mamet, David. "Radio Host: Ira Glass." *Time Online Edition,* June 2001. http://www.cnn.com/SPECIALS/2001/americasbest/pro.iglass.html.

Martin, Douglas. "Shirley Glass, 67, Expert on Infidelity, Is Dead." *New York Times,* October 14, 2003, Section C.

Montopoli, Brian. "Ira Glass on Working in Television, Public Radio's Struggle for Innovation, and Hanging Up on People." *Columbia Journalism Review Daily,* August 12, 2005. http://www.cjrdaily.org/archives/001738.asp.

Pruzan, Todd. "Glass's Menagerie." http://www.stim.com/Stim-x/8.3/IraGlass/iraglass.html.

Pugh, Clifford. "His American Life: Is Ira Glass as Charming as He Sounds?" *Houston Chronicle,* May 2, 2004, Lifestyle and Features section.

Rabin, Nathan. *Onion,* Volume 39, Issue 43, November 5, 2003.

Salamon, Julie. "Now on Video, Briefly Back from the Dead to Give Mourners Some Advice." *New York Times,* December 29, 2000, Performing Arts section.

Sella, Marshall. "Ira Glass Is, Um (Pause, Delete) . . . Listening." *New York Times,* April 11, 1999. http://www.nytimes.com/library/magazine/home/041199sella.html.

Sigesmund, B. J. "All about Ira." *Newsweek* (web exclusive), November 29, 2001. http://www.msnbc.msn.com/id/3032542/site/newsweek/.

Simmons, David Lee. "The Glass Menagerie." *Gambit Weekly,* February 22, 2005. http://www.bestofneworleans.com/dispatch/2005–02–22/cover_story.html.

Snyder, Rachel Louise. "My Lunch with Ira Glass." *Salon,* July 16, 1999. http://www.salon.com/people/lunch/1999/07/16/glass.

Upski Winsatt, William. "Ira Glass: A Cure for the Common Radio." *Horizon Magazine,* September 1, 1999. http://www.horizonmag.com/2/ira-glass.asp.

Zuckerman, Lawrence. "Close Your Eyes and It's Almost Like Radio." *New York Times,* July 24, 2005, Arts and Leisure section.

VOICE OF A SAGE: DIANE REHM

Frey, Jennifer. "At WAMU, Deficits of Money and Morale." *Washington Post,* October 20, 2003, p. A01.

Levins, Harry. "Raking and Muckraking: Yard Work, Talk Radio Go Hand and Hand." *St. Louis Post-Dispatch,* September 23, 2002.

Rehm, Diane. *Finding My Voice.* New York: Alfred A. Knopf, 1999.

Rehm, Diane, and John B. Rehm. *Toward Commitment: A Dialogue about Marriage.* New York: Alfred A. Knopf, 2002.

Roberts, Roxanne. "Staying Power: To Diane and John Rehm, Marriage Isn't Bliss. It's Hard Work." *Washington Post,* September 13, 2002, p. C01.

Simon, Clea. "NPR Host Likes to Communicate." *Boston Globe,* October 3, 2002, Metro/Region section.

RADIO OF THE RESTLESS: NEAL CONAN

Conan, Neal. *Play by Play: Baseball, Radio and Life in the Last Chance League.* New York: Crown Publishers, 2002.

Fisher, Marc. "Playing in a New Field: NPR Newsman Takes a Swing at Baseball Announcing." *Washington Post,* May 17, 1997, Style section.

Hedges, Chris. "Captured: Kindness Lit Newsman's 5 Days of Terror." *St. Louis Post-Dispatch*, March 13, 1991, War Page section.

Interview with Neal Conan. WFYI Radio web site. http://www.wfyi.org/wfyi2003/totn.asp.

Karl, Jonathan. "Interview with Neal Conan of National Public Radio." *CNN Saturday Morning* broadcast transcript, February 22, 2003. http://edition.cnn.com/TRAN-SCRIPTS/0302/22/smn.09.html.

Proven, Patricia. "Neal Conan: What's Fair and Foul in War Reporting." December 3, 2004. http://www.gotoemerson.com/jsp/news/index.jsp.

Siedel, Jeff. "For Conan, a Voice of Reason; NPR Host Feels at Home in Baseball Broadcast Booth." *Washington Post*, July 27, 2000, Extra section.

WALKING AROUND THE WORLD: IRA FLATOW

Allen, William. "NPR's Real Dr. Science." *St. Louis Post-Dispatch*, May 22, 1995, *Everyday Magazine* section.

Dreifus, Claudia. "A Conversation with Ira Flatow." *New York Times*, April 4, 2000, Section F.

Musante, Fred. "Talking Entertainingly about Science." *New York Times*, September 14, 1997, Connecticut Weekly section.

TEACHER: TERRY GROSS

Bergstrom, Bill. "After 25 Years, Terry Gross Still Sounds 'Fresh.'" *Detroit News*, December 11, 2000. http://www.detnews.com/2000/entertainment/0012/11/f05–160514.htm.

Dotinga. "Keeping Things Fresh with Terry Gross." *North County Times*, November 6, 1998. http://www.nctimes.com/articles/2005/09/20/entertainment/radio/91405112749.txt.

Freedman, Samuel G. "Arts in America; A Prospector Panning for Cultural Nuggets." *New York Times*, March 8, 2000, p. E1.

Gross, Terry. *All I Did Was Ask: Conversations with Writers, Actors, Musicians, and Artists*. New York: Hyperion, 2004.

Habich, John. "Hers for the Asking: On Public Radio's 'Fresh Air,' Terry Gross Boldly Goes Where No Interview Has Gone Before." *(Minneapolis, MN) Star Tribune*, October 24, 2002, Variety section.

Hinckley, David. "NPR 'Ref' Sides with O'Reilly in 'Air' Battle." *(New York) Daily News*, October 21, 2003, Television section.

Kunkel, Thomas. "The Woman behind the Microphone." *American Journalism Review*, July–August 2001, p. 4.

Leibovich, Lori. "Turning the Tables on Terry Gross." *Salon*, June 1998. http://www.salon.com/mwt/feature/1998/06/cov_22feature.html.

McCoy, Adrian. "Terry Gross Bringing a Breath of 'Fresh Air' to the Byham." *Pittsburgh Post-Gazette*, April 22, 2003, Arts and Entertainment section.

Mechanic, Michael. "Question Authority." *Metro Santa Cruz*, November 7–13, 1996. http://www.metroactive.com/papers/cruz/11.07.96/terry-gross–9645.html

The O'Reilly Factor. Fox News, partial transcript, September 21, 2004. http://www.foxnews.com/story/0,2933,133177,00.html.

Ryan, Laura. "NPR Host Still Rides Wave of Success." *(New Orleans) Times-Picayune*, November 28, 2002, p. C1.

Rys, Richard. "Gene Simmons vs. Terry Gross." *Philadelphia Magazine*, April 2002, p. 35.

Schell, Orville. "Proving the Singular Value of a Voice in the Dark." *New York Times*, December 30, 2001, Arts and Leisure section.

Shaw, Julie. "A Breath of Fresh Air." *Delaware News Journal*, February 23, 2005. http://www.delawareonline.com/spark/2005/02/23abreathoffresha.html.

Simon, Scott. "Terry Gross Discusses Her New Book, 'All I Did Was Ask.'" *Weekend Edition Saturday*, National Public Radio broadcast, September 18, 2004. http://www.npr.org/templates/story/story.php?storyId=3925277.

Sommer, Mark. "Talking with Terry Gross Is a Breath of Fresh Air." *Buffalo News*, November 13, 2002, Entertainment section.

Starr, Michael. "NPR Jock Shock." *New York Post*, February 6, 2002, p. 30.

Tiger, Caroline. "No One Sells Books Like Oprah, Terry." *Philadelphia Magazine*, July 2002, p. 14.

Violanti, Anthony. "NPR's Gross Masters Art of Thoughtful Conversation." *Buffalo News*, May 9, 2004, Arts section.

WAMC Northeast Public Radio. "A Conversation with Terry Gross." Audio compact disc.

Weed, William Speed. "Terry Gross: Twenty-five Years Fresh." *Mother Jones*, July/August 2000. http://www.motherjones.com/arts/qa/2000/07/gross.html.

Wieder, Tamara. "For Two Decades, Radio Host Terry Gross Has Charmed Guests and Listeners on National Public Radio's *Fresh Air.* Now She's Taking Her Interviews to the Page." *Boston Phoenix*, October 15–21, 2004, p. 19.

KING OF QUIPS: MICHAEL FELDMAN

Conciatore. Jacqueline. "Born Bent: Michael Feldman: Public Radio's Original Saturday Wisecracker." *Current*, December 1, 1997, p. 1.

Drew, Mike. "Feldman Knows Humor: Unsinkable Host of 'Whad'Ya Know' Outquips 'Em All as He Brings His Radio Show and a Titanic Gag Home." *Milwaukee Journal Sentinel*, April 12, 1998, News section.

Durchholz, Daniel. "Wouldn't Ya Know It? Michael Feldman Puts a Local Spin on His Visit to St. Louis." *St. Louis Post-Dispatch*, October 9, 2003, Get Out section.

Feder, Robert. "Michael Feldman Scouts Out Skokie.' *Chicago Sun-Times*, November 29, 1993, Features section.

Fischer, Joan. "Fans in the Know Tune in the Show." *Chicago Sun-Times*, July 7, 1992, Features section.

Graham, Brad L. "Well, St. Louis; Whad'Ya Know?" *St. Louis Post-Dispatch*, June 11, 1999, *Everyday Magazine* section.

Hoekstra, Dave. "Durable Blend: Feldman's Words, Sieger's Music." *Chicago Sun-Times*, October 31, 2003, Weekend Plus section.

Justin, Neal. "Outsmarting the Idiot Box." *(Minneapolis, MN) Star Tribune*, August 9, 1995, Variety section.

Kolbert, Elizabeth. "A Quiz Show That Disdains the Right Answer." *New York Times*, December 13, 1993, p. C11.

McCoy, Adrian. "'Whad'Ya Know Show Brings Its Quirky Format to Soldiers and Sailors Hall." *Pittsburgh Post-Gazette*, March 21, 1996.

Miksch, Joe. "Wait, Wait . . . Tell Us!" *Fairfield County Weekly*, September 9, 2004. http://westchesterweekly.com/gbase/News/content.html?oid=oid:80646.

Shuger, Scott. "Mike's On: Radio's Obscure Comic Genius, Michael Feldman." *Slate*. http://slate.msn.com/id/3273/.

Springen, Karen. "Dairy Home Companion." *Newsweek*, April 23, 1990, p. 65.

Turegano, Preston. "Good Morning; Best Bet." *San Diego Union-Tribune*, May 18, 2004, Lifestyle section.

Weintraub, Joanne. "Tuning in Public Radio's Resident Wit with Michael Feldman." *Milwaukee Journal Sentinel*, July 6, 1997, Lifestyle section.

Weiss, Richard. "Radio Show Serves Up a Staple of Silliness." *St. Louis Post-Dispatch*, August 16, 1992. Everyday Magazine section.

A FUNNY PERSON WHO READS A LOT OF NEWSPAPERS: PETER SAGAL

Brantley, Ben. "Theater Review: A Right to Free Speech When Hate Is the Subject." *New York Times*, December 28, 1995.

Leiby, Richard. "The Reliable Source." *Washington Post*, March 3, 2004, Style section.

Medrek, T. J. "There's No Denying That Writer Enjoys NPR Stint." *Boston Herald*, November 14, 1998, Arts and Life section.

Rahner, Mark. "NPR's 'Wait, Wait' Goes Live in Seattle." *Seattle Times*, May 16, 2001, p. E3.

Yeado, Brian. "Radio Stars: An NPR Game Show's Crazy Cast of Characters Blow Alex Trebek out of the Water." *Daily Northwestern*, February 13, 2003.

PUBLIC RADIO'S GREASE MONKEYS: TOM AND RAY MAGLIOZZI

Ahrens, Frank. "Boyz under the Hood; 'Car Talk' Hosts Mix Advice and Idle Chatter." *Washington Post*, August 21, 1999, Style section.

Barol, Bill. "Tuning In, Tuning Up." *Newsweek*, June 1, 1987, p. 68.

Brown, Elizabeth. "'Car Talk' Fans Bop to a Greasy Beat." *Christian Science Monitor*, June 28, 1989, People section.

Collins, Monica. "Radio: Lydon Makes the BUR-Car Talk Connection." *Boston Herald*, February 27, 2001.

Danzinger, Jeff. "If Your Car's a Joke, They'll Tell It." *Christian Science Monitor*, April 27, 1988, National section.

Diesenhouse, Susan. "Out in Car Country, Banter Is Their Language." *New York Times*, February 28, 1999, Arts and Leisure section.

Hart, Melissa. "A Guest on NPR's 'Car Talk' Gets an Unexpected Answer." *Christian Science Monitor*, April 9, 2003, Home Forum section.

Homeyer, Henry. "At Home with Ray Magliozzi." *Boston Globe*, Life at Home section.

Mansnerus, Laura. "On 'Car Talk,' Sound Repair Tips, No Charge for the Humor." *New York Times*, May 25, 1988, Living Desk section.

Martin, Keith. "For Worst Performances by a Car: The Envelope, Please . . . " *New York Times*, April 2, 2000, Automobiles section.

McCrummen, Stephanie. "Since We're on Public Radio, We Might as Well Have Fun." *Current*, June 19, 1995, p. 4.

A PRAIRIE HOME WHIRLWIND: GARRISON KEILLOR

Barol, Bill. "What Now, Wobegon?" *Newsweek*, October 5, 1987, p. 42.

Bolick, Katie. "Atlantic Unbound Interview." *Atlantic Unbound,* October 8, 1997. http://www.theatlantic.com/unbound/factfict/gkint.htma.

Carr, David. "Lake Wobegon? It's Where Men Are Persistent." *New York Times*, December 21, 2004, Arts and Leisure section.

Cohen, Richard. "The Courage to Quit." *Washington Post*, July 12, 1987, Magazine section.

Cooperman, Jeannette Batz. "Keillor Is Turning from Restless Life to Contentment." *St. Louis Post-Dispatch,* Get Out section.

Cowen, Matthew. "Cowen on . . . Honda." *Campaign*, June 14, 2002, Opinion section, p. 19.

Cryer, Dan. "America's Hottest New Storyteller." *Newsday Magazine*, October 13, 1985, p. 45.

Fedo, Michael. *The Man from Lake Wobegon.* New York: St. Martin's Press, 1987.

Fisher, Marc. "Constant Companion; Winging It with Garrison Keillor and His Radio Road Show." *Washington Post*, June 14, 1998, Style section.

Gross, Terry. "Interview with Garrison Keillor." *Fresh Air* broadcast, September 4, 2003. http://www.npr.org/templates/story/story.php?storyId=1419921.

Haga, Chuck. "Lake Wobegon Comes to Life." *(Minneapolis, MN) Star Tribune*, November 21, 2000, News section.

Hemingson, Peter. "Plowboy Interview." *Mother Earth News*, May–June 1985, p. 23.

Holston, Noel. "Longtime 'Companion.'" *(Minneapolis, MN) Star Tribune*, July 4, 1999, Entertainment section.

Inskeep, Steve. "Interview with Garrison Keillor." *Morning Edition* on NPR News, December 22, 2004. http://www.npr.org/templates/story/story.php?storyId=4240302.

Jacobs, Tom. "Wobegone in New York." *St. Petersburg (FL) Times*, June 13, 1989, Floridian section.

Jones, Meg. "Novelist Finds Humor in Politics." *Milwaukee Journal Sentinel*, September 5, 2003, News section.

Karlan, Neal. "A Prodigal Son Makes His Way Home." *New York Times*, March 27, 1994, Art and Leisure section.

Kaufman, Peter. "Radio for the Eyes: Robert Altman and Garrison Keillor, Unlikely 'Prairie' Film Companions." *Washington Post*, July 24, 2005, p. E1.

Keillor, Garrison. "In Search of Wobegon." *(London) Sunday Telegraph*, January 28, 2001, p. 1.

———. *WLT: A Radio Romance.* New York: Penguin Books, 1991.

Kettle, Martin. "A Kinder, Gentler, Better America." *(London) Guardian,* February 22, 2000, Features section.

Klose, Kevin. "Sad News from Lake Wobegon: Garrison Keillor Ending 'Prairie Home Companion.'" *Washington Post*, February 16, 1987, Style section.

Langway, Lynn, and Sylvester Monroe. "Meeting the Gang at Lake Wobegon." *Newsweek*, December 7, 1981, p. 108.

Laurence, Robert P. "A One-Man Garrison." *San Diego Union-Tribune*, November 18, 2003, Lifestyle section.

Reiter, Amy. "Garrison Keillor Feels Your Pain." *Salon*, September 2, 2003. http://www.salon.com/books/int/2003/09/02/keillor/index_np.html.

Rosengren, John. "Garrison Keillor." *Northwest Airlines World Traveler*, January 2000, p. 45.

Ryback, Deborah Caulfield. "Garrison Keillor Keeps Busy with Radio Show, New Column." *Minneapolis Star Tribune*, July 3, 2005, p. E1.

Simon, Clea. "Radio Losing Its Sense of Humor, Keillor Says." *Boston Globe*, June 2, 2005, p. E1.

Skow, John. "Wild Seed in the Big Apple: Garrison Keillor Returns with a New York–based Radio Show." *Time*, December 11, 1989, p. 109.

Weintraub, Joanne. "A Famous, Well, Wisconsinite Dishes Out Delights, Diatribes." *Milwaukee Journal Sentinel*, December 14, 1997, Lifestyle section.

THE LAST TOY IN THE CEREAL BOX: BROOKE GLADSTONE AND BOB GARFIELD

Bunn, Dina. "Advertising Age Critic Is a Supporter, Too." *(Denver) Rocky Mountain News*, April 21, 1997, Business section.

Garfield, Bob. *And Now a Few Words from Me: Advertising's Leading Critic Lays Down the Law, Once and for All*. New York: McGraw-Hill, 2003.

———. "Garfield's AdReview: Always Spot Celebrates That Time of the Month." *Advertising Age*, August 15, 2005, p. 25.

———. *Waking Up Screaming from the American Dream*. New York: Scribner, 1997.

Kissinger, Meg. "Keeping Watch on Government Watchdogs." *Milwaukee Journal Sentinel*, May 2, 2003, News section.

Moore, Frazier. "'On the Media' Analyzes Press Landscape." *Detroit News*, July 29, 2005. http://www.detnews.com/2005/screens/0507/29/E02–262514.htm.

COLORING THE INVISIBLE: TAVIS SMILEY

Kurtz, Howard. "Broadcast All Over: Tavis Smiley's NPR Show Is History." *Washington Post*, January 17, 2005, p. C01.

Martin, Roland S. "Smiley Is an Activist, Not a Journalist." September 14, 2004. http://poynteronline.org/forum/view_post.asp?id=7970.

Meisler, Andy. "A Different Voice Comes to Public Radio." *New York Times*, April 21, 2002, Arts and Leisure section.

Smiley, Tavis. *Keeping the Faith: Stories of Love, Courage, Healing, and Hope from Black America*. New York: Doubleday, 2002.

———. "Left? Right? Wrong! The Misguided CPB Debate." *Washington Post*, July 31, 2005, p. N05.

A VIEW FROM THE TOWER: KURT ANDERSEN

Andersen, Kurt. *Turn of the Century*. New York: Random House, 1999.

Eisenbeis, Hans. "Kurt Andersen: The Rakish Interview." http://www.rakemag.com/printable.asp?catID=58&itemID=2679&pg=all.

Reynolds, Jonathan. "Kitchen Voyeur: Kitchen Sage." *New York Times*, July 17, 2005, Magazine section.

GRAND DAME OF JAZZ: MARIAN MCPARTLAND

Gross, Terry. "Interview with Marian McPartland." *Fresh Air* broadcast, December 28, 2000. http://www.npr.org/templates/story/story.php?storyId=1116180.

Gourse, Leslie. *Madame Jazz: Contemporary Women Instrumentalists*. New York, Oxford: Oxford University Press, 1995.

Hendrickson, Paul. "The McPartlands: Love Song to a Jazz Beat: 46 Years Together, Married or Not." *Washington Post*, April 29, 1991, p. C01.

Jung, Fred. "My Conversation with Marian McPartland." November 1999. http://www.allaboutjazz.com/iviews/mmcpartland.htm.

Kane, Ted. "Marian McPartland: Lady Legend." *Jazz Review*. http://www.jazzreview.com/articleprint.cfm?ID=1045.

McPartland, Marian. *Marian McPartland's Jazz World: All in Good Time*. Urbana and Chicago: University of Illinois Press, 2003.

———.*Willow Creek*. New York: Warner Brothers Publications, 1985.

"McPartland, Marian." *The New Encyclopedia of Jazz*. Leonard Feather, editor. New York: Bonanza Books, 1960.

"Marian McPartland: Concord Records Biography." http://www.concordrecords.com/bios/mcpartlandbio2.html.

"Marian McPartland." *Jazz: The Rough Guide: The Essential Companion to Artists and Albums*. Ian Carr et al., eds. London: The Rough Guides, Ltd., 1995.

Staudter, Thomas. "At Work, at Ease, McPartland, 84, Remains a Perfect Foil." *New York Times*, October 13, 2002, p. 14 LI.

NOT INDIE COOL: DAVID DYE

Guensburg, Carol. "Reserved Seating Just for Us at 'The World Cafe': Public Radio's Eclectic Mix of Music and Talk Dishes Up Something Special Just for Milwaukee Listeners." *Milwaukee Journal Sentinel*, November 14, 1999, Cue section.

Margolis, Lynne. "Fresh Radio Music Frees Listeners from Teen Pop and Shock Talk." *Christian Science Monitor*, October 27, 2000, Features section.

Mervis, Scott. "Café Society." *Pittsburgh Post-Gazette*, August 13, 1999, Arts and Entertainment section.

THE UNDEFINABLE AESTHETIC: NIC HARCOURT

Interview with Nic Harcourt on *Frontline*, May 27, 2004.

Morris, Chris. "Whatever Is on the Show Reflects the Eclectic Nature of My Taste." *Billboard*, August 21, 2004.

Walker, Rob. "Consumed: Easy Listening." *New York Times*, January 23, 2005, Magazine section.

Wolf, Jaime. "The Star Maker of the Semipopular." *New York Times*, June 26, 2005, Magazine section.

ON THE ROAD: NICK SPITZER

Bambarger, Bradley. "'American Routes' Gets to the Roots." *Billboard*, June 3, 2000.

Davis, Heather A. "Spitzer Puts America in Touch with Its Routes." *University of Pennsylvania Current,* April 15, 2004.

de Barros, Paul. "'Routes' Roots Are on the Road: Radio Host Doing a Rare Seattle Talk." *Seattle Times*, April 21, 2002, Entertainment and the Arts section.

Kunlan, David. "American Routes: Nick Spitzer's Highway of Sounds." *Offbeat Magazine*, May 2003, p. 49.

Simon, Clea. "The Cultural Voyage of 'American Routes.'" *Boston Globe*, May 10, 2001, Living section.

Swoboda, Ron. "Eclectic Chair: American Music and Nick Spitzer." *New Orleans Magazine*, August 2002, p. 27.

Walker, Dave. "America's Bandstand." *(New Orleans) Times-Picayune*, May 14, 2003, Living section, p. 1.

DREAM JOB: JOHN DILIBERTO

Lidz, Franz. "The Stir of Echoes." *Philadelphia Magazine*, October 13, 2002, p. 32.

TANGOS, RADIOHEAD, AND TEENAGERS: CHRISTOPHER O'RILEY

Simon, Clea. "Serious Music but Classically Kids." *New York Times*, April 28, 2002, Television/Radio section.